P9-AOT-654

TOWARD BLACK
UNDERGRADUATE STUDENT
EQUALITY IN AMERICAN
HIGHER EDUCATION_____

Recent Titles in
Contributions to the Study of Education

TOWARD BLACK UNDERGRADUATE STUDENT EQUALITY IN AMERICAN HIGHER EDUCATION

Edited by Michael T. Nettles

With the Assistance of A. Robert Thoeny

Contributions to the Study of Education, Number 25

No Longer Property of
Phillips Memorial Library

Greenwood Press
New York • Westport, Connecticut • London

Phillips Memorial
Library
Providence College

*LC
2781
T69
1988*

Library of Congress Cataloging-in-Publication Data

Toward Black undergraduate student equality in American higher
education / edited by Michael T. Nettles, with the assistance of A.
Robert Thoeny.
    p. cm. — (Contributions to the study of education, ISSN
0196-707X ; no. 25)
  Bibliography: p.
  Includes index.
  ISBN 0-313-25616-0 (lib. bdg. : alk. paper)
  1. Afro-American college students — History. 2. Educational
equalization — United States — History. I. Nettles, Michael T.,
1955- . II. Thoeny, A. Robert. III. Series.
LC2781.T69 1988
378'.1982 — dc19   87-24956

British Library Cataloguing in Publication Data is available.

Copyright © 1988 by Michael T. Nettles

All rights reserved. No portion of this book may be
reproduced, by any process or technique, without the
express written consent of the publisher.

Library of Congress Catalog Card Number: 87-24956
ISBN: 0-313-25616-0
ISSN: 0196-707X

First published in 1988

Greenwood Press, Inc.
88 Post Road West, Westport, Connecticut 06881

Printed in the United States of America

The paper used in this book complies with the
Permanent Paper Standard issued by the National
Information Standards Organization (Z39.48-1984).

10 9 8 7 6 5 4 3 2

Contents

Figures

Tables

Acknowledgments

This book addresses some of the most important issues of equity and equality for Black undergraduate students in higher education during the late twentieth century. Although the contents of the book are the principal responsibility of the authors, the sphere of influence, motivation, participation, and cooperation is much broader. Much of the empirical research that is reported in this book was made possible by grants from the Ford Foundation and the Southern Education Foundation. Without the support of these foundations a great many of the challenges as well as the solutions to achieving equality in higher education would be undiscovered. Certainly the research presented herein would not have been possible. We are most appreciative to Alison Bernstein, program officer for education and culture at the Ford Foundation, who first suggested that Michael Nettles develop this book. Her initial support and continuous encouragement throughout are largely responsible for its completion. We are grateful to Elridge McMillan, president of the Southern Education Foundation, who has provided enduring support and urging to produce the book. Much of the research in this book was supported by the Southern Education Foundation.

We owe special appreciation to Joan Baratz-Snowden who, in her role as director of the Educational Policy Research and Services Division of the Educational Testing Service, provided continuous support and encouragement for the completion of the book.

We are also appreciative for the encouragement provided by Laura Bornholdt, special assistant to the president, University of Chicago, formerly program officer with the Lilly Endowment, Inc. Laura Bornholdt realized the need for research to address the important qualitative issues and urged us to address some of the topics included in this book.

Beyond the initial and continuous encouragement and support, the process of producing the research and writing the book in its final form has evolved over three years, involving several people in a variety of capacities. We greatly appreciate various critical reviews of the book by

Joan Baratz-Snowden, Eileen Freeman, and Arie L. Nettles.
Their attention to detail, their concern for consistency,
style, and content, and their reactions to substantive
issues were invaluable contributions. The responsibility
for the final product, however, rests solely with the editor
and authors and not with these reviewers.

We are also grateful for the many hours of effort by
Gail Morris of the Tennessee Higher Education Commission for
her efforts in organizing and transcribing early drafts of
the manuscript and Rebecca Gougis for preparation of the
final draft. We also appreciate the work of Joyce Gant,
senior research assistant at the Educational Testing
Service, for her review of the document and for her library
research. To Richard Martz and Sheila Sutterland for their
assistance with the graphic illustrations which help to
convey statistical analyses. Finally, we are grateful to
Karen McQuillen, librarian at Educational Testing Service,
for searching for needed source documents and for securing
important documentation needed to support the research.

Preface

Higher education is viewed as the essence of upward social mobility and equality for Blacks in the United States. It is the vehicle through which they achieve occupational status and income as well as lifestyles that are analogous to those of many majority citizens. Although access to educational opportunity has improved over the past three decades, barriers to equality continue to be pervasive in the nation's colleges and universities and the downward trends in the current decade are cause for alarm. The purpose of this book is to identify and explain the reasons for many of the vestiges of inequality between Black and white undergraduate students and to suggest strategies for colleges and universities to eliminate these inequalities.

The book consists of ten chapters that analyze Black undergraduate students backgrounds, performance, attitudes, and experiences at various types of colleges and universities and assesses the roles played by various types of organizations toward improving the trends, performance and experiences of Black undergraduate students. The topics addressed are:

- academic performance and experiences;

- improving preparation for post collegiate occupational and educational experiences;

- improving preparation for careers in the sciences;

- expanding the role of the federal government;

- expanding the role of state governments; and

- developing an agenda for private-interest group involvement in achieving equality for Blacks in higher education.

By focusing primarily on undergraduate student processes and outcomes, this book concentrates upon the lower tier of the postsecondary education hierarchy. The future achievements of Black Americans are greatly dependent upon the achievements of today's Black undergraduates. Undergraduate education is the cornerstone of advanced educational and professional opportunities.

Chapters 1 through 9 are divided into two parts. Chapters 1 through 6, Part 1, focus upon enrollment trends, educational processes and outcomes of undergraduate students. Chapters 6 through 9, Part 2, focus upon the functions of the organizational structural components of society that are essential vehicles for achieving qualitative equality. Chapter 10, the concluding chapter, presents strategies for improving Black student processes and outcomes in higher education based upon the results and findings presented in Parts 1 and 2.

In the introductory chapter, Michael Nettles presents the fluctuating trends of Black student participation in higher education and presents several explanations including student motivation, societal changes, and legal actions that have produced the enrollment changes as well as changes in student performance.

In Chapter 2, Michael Nettles compares and contrasts the undergraduate performance and experiences of Black and white students, demonstrating some of the important challenges to Black student equality. The academic performance criteria analyzed are students' progression rates through college and their grades. In addition to comparing academic performance, Nettles makes comparisons of students' educational and personal backgrounds by race. Students attitudes and behaviors in college are examined to illustrate their relationship to students' college performance. The relationships of faculty characteristics to student performance are also examined. Finally, Nettles makes recommendations for improving the performance of Black collegians.

In Chapter 3, Nettles presents comparative and predictive analyses of the academic performance and experiences of Black and white college students at different types of universities. Students' grades and progression rates as well as their background, attitudinal, and behavioral characteristics are analyzed at each of five different types of universities. The five types of institutions are (1) predominantly white public research universities, (2) historically Black public universities, (3) predominantly white regional public universities, (4) predominantly white private prestigious universities, and (5) historically Black private universities. Significant racial differences in students' performance, backgrounds, and experiences are discovered at each type of university where comparisons are made. Some important variables associated with students' performance at all types of universities are identified as well as variables unique to each type. Although there are some strategies that are appropriate for use by all universities, Nettles concludes that universities should capitalize on their unique opportunities to achieve equality in their students' college performance based upon their unique environment and constituents.

     In Chapter 4, Walter Allen presents a sociological
perspective on the issue of qualitative equality by
comparing the status of Blacks' participation and
performance in American higher education today with their
status prior to the Brown v. Board of Education of Topeka,
Kansas court case. College attrition rates, grades,
graduation rates, and student perceptions about their
college environment (peers, faculty, and administrators) are
analyzed in the context of equality. Allen compares Black
students with Asians, Hispanics, and white students on
several performance indicators. His recommendations are
predicated upon his arguments throughout the chapter that
Black students are educationally disadvantaged in America
because of the ineffectiveness of the American educational
systems to address the unique educational needs of Black
students.
     In Chapter 5, Jomills Braddock and James McPartland
examine some important qualitative outcomes for Black
college students entering the labor market upon receiving a
baccalaureate degree. This chapter focuses on the
advantages and disadvantages that Black students have in
terms of occupational attainment and degree completion by
choosing to attend a historically Black university as
opposed to a predominantly white university. Braddock and
McPartland examine the effects of the predominant race of
the university on Black students on their; likelihood of
completing a degree; and on their occupational attainment.
They also make observations regarding Black students'
adjustment in the labor market in relation to the
predominant race of the institution they attended. The data
presented in this chapter are taken from the National
Longitudinal Survey (NLS) of the High School Graduating
Class of 1972, which at the time of this study had tracked
high school graduates for seven successive years.
     In Chapter 6, Willie Pearson analyzes Black students'
performance in scientific fields. Admission into and
successful completion of degrees in the scientific
disciplines present the greatest challenge to equality for
Black students in higher education and in American society.
Pearson describes the severe shortage of Blacks in American
scientific professions and suggests possible ways colleges
and universities can eliminate the shortages. Pearson
illustrates the demographic characteristics of America's
scientists, noting stark racial differences in geographic
origin, parental occupations, size of families, and economic
status of families. He compares the educational experiences
of Black and white scientists from high school through
graduate school, showing differences in the length of time
it takes to complete studies and differences in grades.
Pearson explains why whites require less time to complete
their studies and why a higher percentage of whites have
higher grades in undergraduate school. Additionally,
Pearson explains why white scientists are likely to train in
more prestigious graduate schools and are more likely to
receive academic appointments in the most prestigious
universities.
     Part 2 focuses upon three types of institutions in

America that have a critical role to play in achieving
qualitative equality for Blacks in higher education: the
federal government, state governments, and private-interest
groups.

In Chapter 7, Cynthia Brown presents the federal
government's role more specifically, she describes major
federal judicial activities, and the resulting
administrative activities by the United States government
over the past thirty years. Brown points out that much of
the federal government's involvement regarding Blacks in
higher education has been through the judicial branch. She
attributes much of the progress made by Black Americans in
higher education during the past two decades to the efforts
made by federal agencies at the urging of the courts. Brown
compares the qualitative progress made at the elementary and
secondary levels with that of higher education, concluding
that the progress in higher education has been much less
than at the lower levels. Brown describes the federal
government's approach to achieving higher education equality
in southern states and points out the recent resistance by
some southern states to actively pursue change. Finally,
Brown presents recommendations regarding the role that the
federal government should play in the future.

In Chapter 8, John Williams examines the magnitude of
the role state governments play in achieving equality of
higher education. Williams explains how the provisions of
Title VI of the Civil Rights Act provide the mechanism by
which many states have pursued racial equality in higher
education. Through his analyses of state desegregation,
Williams reports changes in state roles that suggest both
optimism about the future and a need for more activity than
currently planned. He observes variations in the statutory
or judicial authority of state higher education offices
responsible for planning and implementing Title VI.
Williams also discusses the state and federal relationships
as being an obstacle to achieving equality for Blacks in
higher education. He cites examples of disagreements
between the states and federal government and among the
various agencies within the federal government.

In Chapter 9, Reginald Wilson examines the important
role that private-interest groups play in achieving racial
equality in higher education. A survey conducted in 1984
serves as his source of data to illustrate the various types
of activities of private-interest groups. Wilson contrasts
the role of government and that of private-interest groups
in pursuing equality in higher education. He distinguishes
the two by pointing out that the government is obligated to
enforce laws, while the private-interest groups are
obligated to advocate the views and goals of their
constituents who are most frequently dues paying members.
Wilson asserts that although private-interest groups are not
forced by law, they have an equal obligation to achieve
equality. He recommends types of activities such groups may
engage in in order to have a positive impact on qualitative
equality.

In the concluding chapter, A. Robert Thoeny summarizes
the findings of the research presented in preceding

chapters.   Thoeny notes the importance of acknowledging
progress made toward equality and identifying the reasons
for success as a way to plan and to encourage future
success.   Thoeny points out that higher education today is
in a critical period in terms of pursuing equality for
Blacks.   He proposes some strategies for improving the
status of Black students in American higher education.
Among the strategies, Thoeny suggests increasing attention
to qualitative dimensions of Black college students'
experience and targeting energy and resources toward the key
levers of change, such as providing more positive role
models, increasing Black student attendance in prestigious
undergraduate and graduate schools, and placing more Black
college graduates in well-remunerated business employment.
Thoeny concludes that while all of society must play a
supporting role, the primary lever of change lies with the
Black community.
     We hope that the research presented in this book will
be a valuable source of information for identifying and
eliminating barriers to equality for Black students in
American higher education.

TOWARD BLACK UNDERGRADUATE STUDENT EQUALITY IN AMERICAN HIGHER EDUCATION_____

1

Introduction: Contemporary Barriers to Black Student Equality in Higher Education

MICHAEL T. NETTLES

THE EMERGENCE OF BLACK STUDENT PARTICIPATION IN HIGHER EDUCATION

Education has always been the most measured yet most elusive earthly commodity for Blacks in the United States. Throughout Black American history, education has been tantamount to freedom and equality in American society. Indeed, education for Blacks has been the typical route to upward social, cultural, and economic mobility. The history of education for Black Americans is remarkable for its transitions through lengthy period of legal prohibition up to the Emancipation Proclamation, then nearly one hundred years of de jure separation and subordination up through the mid-fifties, and now more recently three decades toward assimilation and equality. For the past three decades progress of Black Americans in higher education has been in the area of gaining greater access and opportunity to attend a broader range of colleges and universities. Although the challenges to equality continue to include greater access and opportunity, equally important challenges to equality pertain to achieving qualitative performance, progress, and achievement.

In 1981 Gail Thomas and her colleagues documented the enormous increase in Black Americans attending college during the sixties and seventies. Thomas (1981) observed that in 1975, 21 percent of Black Americans between the ages of 18-24 were enrolled in college, compared to only 13 percent in 1960. In 1960, 134,000 Black students between the ages of 18-24 were attending college. By 1975, the college enrollment of Black 18-24 year-olds had increased nearly fivefold to 665,000 students. Blacks represented 6 percent of college and university enrollment in 1960 and 9.6 percent in 1975 (U.S. Bureau of the Census, 1986).

This extraordinary growth coincided with the unprecedented growth in overall higher education enrollments. It took over 320 years, from the founding of Harvard University in 1636 until 1957, for America's colleges and universities to enroll the first 3 million students in a single year, but only ten more years to more than double that number - 7 million students - enrolled in 1967 (U.S. Bureau of the Census, 1975). By 1975, college enrollments in the United States had reached 10 million (Grant & Snyder, 1984). But, as reflected by the proportional increase from 6 percent to 9.6 percent between 1960 and 1975, Black enrollment increased at a rate more than three and a half times that of total enrollment growth.

The overall growth in higher education is generally attributed to three political and social phenomena: (1) the GI Bill, which provided educational opportunities to veterans of the U.S. military, (2) the Great Society programs initiated by President Lyndon B. Johnson, which encouraged and supported all American citizens who desired to pursue higher education, and (3) the post-World War II baby boom, which provided the greatest population increase of any period in the history of the United States. Thomas (1981), however, attributes Black enrollment growth to five different political and social phenomena: (1) the successful civil rights movement, which culminated in the Civil Rights Act of 1964, which abolished segregation; (2) the Supreme Court decision in the case of Brown v. Board of Education of Topeka, Kansas, which ended de jure racial segregation in education; (3) the federal government's report entitled Equality of Education Opportunity Report (Coleman et al., 1966), which pointed out numerous racial inequalities in American educational institutions; (4) the 1965 U. S. Higher Education Act, which included numerous financial aid programs for economically disadvantaged citizens; and (5) the Federal Court decision of 1973 in the case of Adams v. Richardson, which compelled institutions of higher education to develop desegregation plans.

In addition to these political and social events, student financial aid, primarily from state and federal governments, has provided greater access and opportunity for Blacks to attend college. Alexander Astin (1982) pointed out that in the seventies, although many financial aid programs were not statutorily directed toward minorities, a disproportionately high number of minorities were beneficiaries. These included programs such as Pell Grants, College Work Study, Guaranteed Student Loans, and National Direct Student Loans. At the graduate and professional school levels, however, such financial aid programs as the Graduate and Professional Opportunities Program and the Health Professions Opportunity Programs, were, by statute, designated for minority and economically disadvantaged students and therefore contributed to greater access by design. These financial aid programs coupled with the progressive and innovative admission and recruitment efforts of colleges and universities during the sixties and seventies have represented the greatest initiatives ever enacted to achieve racial equality in higher education.

Despite the financial assistance programs and other political and social movements, Blacks have always been underrepresented at all levels of higher education, and lately Black enrollment has been declining in tandem with declining grants aid and increasing admission standards of higher education institutions. In 1985 the Black population

in the United States was about 12 percent of the total
population; yet Blacks represented only 8.8 percent of
undergraduate enrollment (down from 9.6 percent in 1975),
only 4.7 percent of the graduate enrollment, and 5.1 percent
of the first professional school (law, medicine, pharmacy,
veterinary medicine) enrollment (HEGIS, 1985). The
percentage of Black high school graduates enrolling in
college declined from 32 percent in 1975 to 27 percent in
1985, while the proportion of white high school graduates
entering college increased from 32 to 35 percent and the
Hispanic college entrance rate remained constant at 31
percent (U.S. Department of Commerce, 1986 and 1987).
America's colleges and universities enrolled 76,554 fewer
Black undergraduates in 1985 than in 1976, a decline of 8.9
percent and 69,059 fewer Black undergraduates in 1985 than
in 1981, a decline of 8.1 percent. Both predominately white
and minority universities figure into the enrollment
decline; 30 percent of this decline is accounted for by
predominately white universities and 70 percent by
predominantly minority universities. The number of Black
baccalaureate degree recipients has also declined sharply-
6 percent - over the last decade from 58,515 in 1976 to
54,920 in 1985 (NCES, 1977, 1986).

Many of the efforts that brought about greater access
over the past two decades have been thwarted, and recent
changes in financial aid policies, in particular, appear to
reduce minority students attendance in college. According
to Janet Hansen (1987) of the College Board, federal
financial aid policies in recent years have shifted emphasis
away from grants in favor of loans. In 1976, federal grants
represented 80 percent and loan guarantees, 20 percent of
federal financial assistance to college students. By 1984,
federal grants and loan guarantees represented 50 percent
each of federal financial aid, reflecting a reduction in
grants, an increase in loan guarantees, and an increase in
the debt ceiling for college students (Hansen, 1986). This
is particularly significant for Black students, because they
are less willing and less able to accumulate debt to pay for
their college education than white students (Halloran, 1986;
Newman, 1985), and because of the inequitable opportunities
after college graduation, the debt burden of Blacks is
greater than it is for whites (Nettles, 1987).

Given Thomas's (1981) explanations for Black enrollment
growth in the sixties and seventies, it appears that higher
education is in need of new initiatives and different policy
directions in order to increase the numerical representation
of Blacks in higher education. A closer examination of
recent enrollment conditions reveals that the problem is
even more severe than the aggregate enrollment statistics
suggest.

An inordinate number of Black undergraduates are
enrolled in two-year colleges and receive their
baccalaureate degrees in fields in which Blacks are
overrepresented rather than underrepresented. For instance,
they are more likely to be enrolled in lower-level and
lower-quality higher education institutions than whites.
Table 1.1 illustrates that in 1985, 42.8 percent of Black
undergraduate students were enrolled in two-year colleges,

compared to 37.7 percent of white students (National Center
for Education Statistics [NCES], 1985).   Table 1.1 also
illustrates that whites are much more likely than Blacks to
be enrolled in universities, where the financial and
academic resources are superior, rather than in four-year
colleges where resources are more limited.

Table 1.1

Enrollment Distribution of Black and White Undergraduate
Students in U.S. Colleges and Universities in 1985

Type of Institution	Ethnicity		
Universities	Black	White	Total
Number	102,501	1,685,068	2,025,761
Percent	12.4%	21.9%	20.9%
Four-Year Colleges			
Number	367,442	3,269,906	4,124,854
Percent	44.5%	42.5%	42.7%
Two-Year Colleges			
Number	355,827	2,730,158	3,519,744
Percent	43.1	35.5	36.4%
Total Number	825,770	7,685,132	9,670,359

Note: Unpublished Tabulations from Higher Education General
        Information Survey by the National Center for
        Education Statistics, 1986.

        Moreover, even though among four-year institutions in
1985, predominantly Black universities enrolled 3.2 percent
of total (all races) undergraduates and produced 2.5 percent
of the total baccalaureate degrees, 32.8 percent of the
Black undergraduates attending four-year institutions were
enrolled in Black universities and 31.9 percent of the Black
baccalaureate degree recipients received their degrees from
Black universities (NCES, 1986). Of all two-year and four-
year Black undergraduates in 1985, 27 percent were enrolled
in predominantly Black institutions. In southern states, in
1985, 36.8 percent of all Black students were enrolled in
predominantly Black colleges and universities, and 50.4
percent of all four year Black college students were
enrolled in Black universities.   Interestingly, in the

South, the proportion of Blacks attending community colleges
is only 3/10ths of 1 percent higher than the proportion of
all students attending community colleges - 38.3 percent
compared to 38.0 percent. Outside the South, 47 percent of
Black undergraduates attend community colleges compared to
38.8 percent of all other college students (NCES, 1986).
Blacks only constitute 6.6 percent of all undergraduate
enrollment outside the South - 2 percent below the national
Black representation. These data suggest that community
colleges outside the South and historically Black colleges
in the South are shouldering extraordinary responsibility
for providing access for Black undergraduate students, while
predominantly white universities throughout the nation
account for the lions share of the underrepresentation of
minority undergraduate students. As illustrated earlier,
this underrepresentation of Black students is most profound
at the institutions with the greatest resources.

Regardless of the predominate race, quality, or type of
university, Black recipients of baccalaureate degrees are
more likely to receive their degrees in the fields of
education, business administration, and social sciences,
than in the arts and humanities, engineering, and the
natural and physical sciences. Table 1.2 shows that, in
1985, although a higher percentage of Blacks received their
degrees in business administration than whites, the highest
percentage of both Blacks and whites received baccalaureate
degrees in the field of business - 27.1 percent and 24.3
percent, respectively. However, the second largest
percentage of Blacks received degrees in the social sciences
(11.2 percent), followed by education (10.1 percent), and
public affairs and services (3.8 percent), all of which are
fields that already have a relatively high concentration of
Black professionals. Only 2.8 percent of Black
baccalaureate degrees were awarded in the field of fine
arts, 3 percent in letters, and 3.8 percent in engineering.
By contrast, whites are much more evenly distributed among
the most popular major fields, with 9.8 percent in
education, 9.7 percent in the social sciences, and 7.8
percent in engineering. (The contemporary problems
associated with low Black participation in scientific
professions are examined in Chapter 6.)

The enrollment distribution among different levels and
among major fields notwithstanding, the steady growth in
Black enrollment during the sixties and early seventies from
6 percent to 9.6 percent offered hope that Blacks would
achieve a level in higher education that reflects their
representation in the U.S. population well before the
twenty-first century. This 9.6 percent was just 2.5 percent
short of overall parity. But recent Black enrollment trends
present a rather bleak outlook at least for the near future.
The recent downward trends in Black enrollment and degree
production suggest that numerical growth to the point of
equality is highly unlikely in the twentieth century unless
new initiatives are undertaken by colleges and universities,
federal and state governments, and private-interest groups
to reverse the recent decline in Black enrollment and degree

Table 1.2

Bachelor Degrees Conferred by Institutions of Higher Education and by Major Field of Study in the United States, 1984-1985

		Total	Total %	White	% of White Grads.	Black	% of Black Grads.
1.	Agriculture	17,866	2.0	16,305	2.1	367	0.7
2.	Architecture	9,038	1.0	7,528	1.0	324	0.6
3.	Area studies	2,770	0.3	2,187	0.3	212	0.4
4.	Business	218,548	24.4	186,131	24.3	13,951	27.1
5.	Communications	40,264	4.5	35,113	4.6	3,030	5.9
6.	Computer science	37,644	4.2	30,592	4.0	2,087	4.0
7.	Education	85,279	9.5	74,918	9.8	5,221	10.1
8.	Engineering	74,114	8.3	59,894	7.8	1,980	3.8
9.	Fine arts	35,745	4.0	31,562	4.1	1,469	2.8
10.	Foreign language	9,466	1.1	7,940	1.0	290	0.6
11.	Health science	61,566	6.9	53,894	7.1	3,704	7.2
12.	Home economics	15,128	1.7	13,349	1.7	930	1.8
13.	Law	1,112	0.1	945	0.1	83	0.2
14.	Letters	32,563	3.6	29,366	3.8	1,539	3.0
15.	Library	194	0.0	173	0.0	16	0.0
16.	Mathematics	14,544	1.6	11,891	1.6	757	1.5
17.	Military sciences	298	0.0	284	0.0	4	0.0
18.	Physical sciences	22,737	2.5	19,938	2.6	801	1.6
19.	Psychology	37,879	4.2	32,610	4.3	2,515	4.9
20.	Public affairs	11,272	1.3	8,655	1.1	1,811	3.5
21.	Social science	87,594	9.8	74,511	9.7	5,799	11.2
22.	Theology	11,250	1.3	10,090	1.3	405	0.8
23.	Interdis. studies	31,138	3.5	26,320	3.4	2,282	4.4

Note: Unpublished Tabulations from Higher Education General Information Survey by the National Center for Education Statistics, 1986.

6

production and to address the problems of enrollment distribution.

THE NEED FOR QUALITATIVE FOCI

In addition to the quantitative concerns of declining enrollment and distribution among levels and major fields, policymakers and educators must be equally concerned with qualitative inequality. In contrast to the sixties and seventies, when concerns for expansion and access were paramount, higher education in the eighties has made quality assurance its highest priority. The previous two decades were periods of expanded opportunity in which open or more flexible admissions policies prevailed and many new colleges and universities were built to accommodate the seemingly endless rise in student demand. The college curriculum became more diversified, although many believe less rigorous, and universities offered new and often nontraditional academic degree programs with more flexible degree requirements (Association of American Colleges, 1985). During the eighties, higher education has launched a reform of a different type. Expansion and diversity have been replaced by a new emphasis on raising admissions standards, improving educational processes, and assessing student achievement, all for the sake of accountability and quality assurance.

This shift in emphasis appears to be contributing to the decline in Black enrollment; despite being far short of equal representation, and with no immediate prospect for improvement. Failure to recognize and address the Black equality issues in the context of quality in higher education threatens to erode the accomplishments of the past two decades.

Although most education policymakers are now busy raising admissions standards and designing plans for assessing student outcomes, the federal courts and other advocates of racial equality unfortunately continue to focus primarily, if not exclusively, upon the quantitative dimensions of equality. The guidelines for racial equality set forth by the federal courts in the cases of Adams v. Califano and Geier v. Blanton (1977) help to illustrate this point. In these two cases the federal courts have charged the executive branches of the federal government and the twenty states that operated de jure segregated systems of higher education prior to 1964 with developing plans for achieving racial equality in public higher education. The criteria established by the federal courts in each of these two cases covering these twenty states are summarized in Table 1.3. With regard to college students, the criteria require colleges and universities to develop and execute plans to increase the number of minority students enrolled at all levels of colleges and universities.

Enrollment goals are most frequently based purely upon the number and racial composition of high school graduating classes without regard to differences between the quality of preparation of minority and majority high school graduates.

Table 1.3

Summary of the Adams and Geier Case Criteria for Achieving
Equality for Blacks in Higher Education

1. The evolution of Adams Criteria and the Tennessee Plan

Adams Criteria were developed in a suit filed by Kenneth Adams against the Secretary of the United States, Department of Health, Education, and Welfare, 1969-1970.

Tennessee Plan was developed out of a suit filed by Rita Saunders Geier against the State of Tennessee in 1968 in the Middle District Court of Tennessee.

2. Dismantling the dual system of higher education

Adams Criteria focused upon (1) role and mission distinctions, (2) strengthening traditionally Black institutions, and (3) the elimination of unnecessary program duplication.

Tennessee Plan stressed cooperation and sharing between Tennessee State University (TSU) and the University of Tennessee in Nashville (UTN), but a subsequent merger order by the court replaced that portion of the Tennessee Plan. The court also ordered expansion of degree offerings at TSU, but there was no mention of strengthening traditionally Black institutions, nor the elimination of unnecessary program duplication in the Plan.

3. Desegregating faculty, administrative staffs, and nonacademic
    personnel and governing boards.

Adams Criteria specified, (1) that the Black faculty and staff with masters degrees should be equal to the proportion of such persons graduating with such degrees in appropriate disciplines in the state, (2) proportion of faculty and administrators requiring doctoral degrees shall be equal to such in the national labor market, (3) same for governing board personnel, and (4) plan shall specify goals and timetables.

Tennessee Plan specified (1) goals for doctoral level faculties and administrators are based on national labor market availability of such individuals, (2) professional staff goals are set to reflect the percentage of Blacks in the state with the required credentials. Although the goals for each institution may vary, the goals for all institutions combined must reflect the percentage of Blacks in the state's population.

Table 1.3 (Continued)

4. **Desegregating student enrollment.**

Adams Criteria recommended (1) equal proportion of Black high school graduates shall enter college (two-year and four-year institutions), (2) there shall be an annual increase in the proportion of Black students in traditionally white institutions, (3) equal proportion of white and Black baccalaureate recipients to enter graduate schools, and (4) increase the proportion of students attending Black institutions.

The Tennessee Plan set the statewide goal of 16% Black enrollment which is the proportion of Blacks in the general population (not based on proportion of high school graduates). Each institutional goal is based upon the number and percent of Blacks in the institutions' service area. For professional schools the goals are 16% which is the Black representation of the state population. Professional schools have a statewide mission and therefore mush reflect the statewide population distribution. Graduate programs have the statewide goal of 16% if the program is the only one of its type in the state. If the graduate program is offered by more than one institution, then the goal is based upon the racial distribution in the institution's service area.

5. **Planning and monitoring desegretation progress.**

States under the Adams Criteria report annually to the Office of Civil Rights (OCR) in the United States Department of Education, and must show progress. If institutions fail to meet interim goals, OCR may impose more stringent requirements, or initiate enforcement proceedings under Title VI of the 1965 Civil Rights Act. Adams Criteria recommends a bi-racial advisory committee to advise institutions.

The Tennessee Plan requests that a progress report be submitted annually to the Middle District Court. The Plan also established a bi-racial monitoring committee to evaluate the progress, and to advise institutions on meeting their goals. The monitoring committee has twelve members. The twelve members include the chief executive officer and three lay members of each of the three governing boards for higher education in the state. These three governing boards are also the three defendants in the court case.

Source: The Federal Register (1978).
Source: <u>Geier v. Blanton</u> (1977).

All the courts' criteria focus on the quantitative components of racial equality.

But, in order to eliminate the barriers to Black equality in higher education, the federal courts and other advocates of Black student equality in higher education will need to place greater emphasis upon addressing the qualitative issues that are at the forefront of contemporary higher education. College and university officials, for example, frequently argue that there are too few "qualified" minority applicants for admission to their universities and too few available minorities with "requisite training" to assume faculty and administrative positions. As a result they feel they cannot meet the criteria established by the federal courts. Yet, there remains little evidence of judicial or educational activity to eradicate the qualitative barriers to equality.

DEFINING QUALITATIVE EQUALITY IN HIGHER EDUCATION

The qualitative indicators of equality are less frequently examined than the quantitative ones, suggesting a lack of awareness and understanding among researchers, educators, and policymakers about what these qualitative indicators are. They include:

- performance on college admissions examinations;

- type and quality of college attended;

- major field selected;

- retention and persistence toward completing degree programs;

- academic performance as measured by grades earned and rate of progress through the curriculum;

- performance on college outcome assessments;

- academic, social, and extracurricular experiences during college;

- involvement with faculty and peers in the college environment; and

- academic and career success after completing college.

In recent years, educators and policymakers have become more aware of the problems of Black Americans in some of these critical areas, but have barely scratched the surface in explaining the origin of and the reasons why the problems persist. There is even less experience in using information to formulate successful strategies to eliminate the inequalities.

Data compiled by the College Board are frequently cited to describe the qualitative performance and experiences of

Black Americans in higher education, but there is seldom a
search for explanations and strategies for improving these
conditions.   In fact some policymakers and educational
leaders appear to desire the more expedient route of
temporarily suspending or eliminating completely the use of
these indicators in order to achieve greater access rather
than determining how to improve Black student performance.
In other words they tend sometimes to attack the messenger
for short term gains instead of heeding the message and
attacking the problems for permanent solution.   In terms of
preparation for college, for example, Table 1.4 illustrates
that, in 1985, only 65.1 percent of Blacks who took the
Scholastic Aptitude Test (SAT) were enrolled in an academic
or college preparatory curriculum in their high school
compared to 81.2 percent of whites.   On the other hand, a
larger percentage of Blacks than whites were enrolled in a
general high school curriculum (19.2 percent versus 12.5
percent) or a vocational curriculum (14.5 percent versus 5.9
percent) (Ramist & Arbeiter, 1984).   These important
statistics reflecting radical differences in the preparation
of Black and white college-bound seniors are frequently
reported by policy analysts and researchers.   But
explanations for why Black students are more concentrated in
the non-college-preparatory tracks are seldom presented;
analyses of the impact that differential tracking has upon
the SAT performance and subsequent postsecondary educational
and vocational pursuits of Black students are rarely
conducted; therefore acceptable solutions based upon
empirical analyses to these inequalities are seldom
advanced.   Without these policy analyses, policymakers will

Table 1.4

Type of High School Program Completed by Black and White
Scholastic Aptitude Test Takers in 1985

	Total	White	Black
Academic or College Preparatory Track	78.5	81.2	65.1
General Curriculum	14.0	12.5	19.2
Career Oriented/Vocational	6.9	5.9	14.5
Other	.06	.4	1.2

Note: From Profiles, College-Bound Seniors by L. Ramist and
        S. Arbeiter, 1986.   New York: Admissions Testing
        Program of the College Board.   Copyright 1986 by
        College Entrance Examination Board.

remain unknowing about important racial differences and will therefore be unable to develop adequate policies and strategies to eliminate racial inequalities in student preparation for college.

Performance on college admissions tests is another area of frequently documented differences between racial groups in the United States. These comparisons, for example, are exhibited annually in the American Council on Education's annual report on Minorities in Higher Education (ACE, 1985). Table 1.5 illustrates recent trends in the verbal and quantitative components of the (SAT) comparing the scores of Blacks and whites and showing substantial racial differences that have remained constant for several years. On the 1985 SAT, for example, the average verbal score of 346 for Blacks was 103 points below the average score of 449 for whites. (The maximum possible score for each component is 800.) The average quantitative score of 376 for Blacks was 114 points below the average of 490 for whites (Ramist & Arbeiter, 1986). Very little, however, is known about the racial differences in the distribution of these scores, such as the proportion of minorities in the higher levels of performance, very little is known about the effects of these scores on minority student access to various types and

Table 1.5

Average Verbal and Quantitative SAT Scores of Blacks and Whites for Selected Years Between 1976 and 1985

	Verbal			Math		
	Total	White	Black	Total	White	Black
1976	431	451	332	472	493	354
1978	429	446	332	468	485	354
1980	424	442	330	466	482	360
1982	426	444	341	467	483	366
1984	426	445	342	471	487	373
1985	431	449	346	475	490	376

Note: From Profiles, College-Bound Seniors by L. Ramist and S. Arbeiter, reports 1977 through 1986. New York: Admissions Testing Program of the College Board. Copyright 1977 through 1986 by College Entrance Examination Board.

quality of undergraduate institutions and little is known about their success in various types of colleges. Greater examination of the personal, experiential, and educational factors that contribute to students' performance is needed in order to develop strategies to improve Black students' performance. Analyses of these factors are likely to yield answers to such important questions as the following: Does differential quality of elementary and secondary schooling result in differential test performance for Black and white examinees? If so, what are the appropriate policies for eliminating the differential schooling and inferior educational opportunities of Black youngsters? Does the fact that Black students tend to be in the vocational curriculum in high school contribute to their overall lower average admission test performance? If so, how much does it contribute to explaining racial difference compared to other personal and educational background experiences and characteristics? Only by examining these critical questions will appropriate policies be developed for eliminating the racial differences and for increasing Black students' test performance. Such research, is not the most expedient route and certainly should not be the exclusive route to achieving equality; but research is likely to uncover some critical information leading to a more permanent solution to the problems of Black student underrepresentation and underachievement in higher education.

Students' college performance, experiences, and outcomes are very important qualitative equality indicators for which sufficient explanatory evidence is unavailable. On the average, Black college students in the early eighties have higher college attrition rates, progress through college at a slower pace, receive lower college course grades, have less satisfying college experiences, and have fewer career opportunities after graduation than their white counterparts. These educational processes and outcomes are important to the morale and educational improvement of Black students, and are critically important to the efficiency and effectiveness of colleges and universities. These outcomes are also important for achieving equal racial representation in the labor force and in all of American society.

This book addresses many of these qualitative equality issues in higher education and examines the role of the federal government, state governments, and private-interest groups toward improving the quality of higher education for Blacks.

REFERENCES

Adams v. Richardson, 356 F. Supp. 92, 94 (D.D.C. 1973).

Adams v. Califano, 356 F. Supp. 92 (D.D.C. 1977).

Adams v. Califano, 430 F. Supp. 118 (D.D.C. 1977).

American Council on Education. (1985). <u>Minorities in higher education</u> (Fourth Annual Status Report, 1985). ACE Annual Meeting, Miami, FL.

Association of American Colleges. (1985, February). <u>Integrity in the college curriculum: A report to the academic community</u> (project on redefining the meaning and purpose of baccalaureate degrees). Washington, DC: Author.

Astin, A. W. (1982). <u>Minorities in American higher education: Recent trends, current prospects, and recommendations</u>. San Francisco: Jossey-Bass.

Coleman, J. S., Campbell, E. Q., Hobson, C. J., McPartland, J. M., Mood, A. M., Weinfeld, F. D., & York, R. L. (1966). <u>Equality of educational opportunity</u>. Washington, DC: U.S. Government Printing Office.

The College Board. (1985). <u>Equality and excellence: The educational status of Black Americans</u> (Educational Equality Project). New York: College Entrance Examination Board.

<u>Federal Register</u>. (1978). <u>43</u>(32), 6663-64.

<u>Geier v. Blanton</u>, 427 F. Supp. 646 (M.D. Tenn. 1977).

Grant, W. V., & Snyder, T. D. (1984). <u>Digest of education statistics 1983-84</u> (National Center for Education Statistics 0-417-806). Washington, DC: Superintendent of Documents, U.S. Government Printing Office.

Halloran, M. H. (1986). Commentary. <u>College Scholarship Service Proceedings: College scholarship service colloquium on student loan counseling & debt management</u>. New York: College Entrance Examination Board.

Hansen, J. S. (1987). <u>Student loans: Are they overburdening a generation?</u> New York: College Entrance Examination Board.

National Center for Education Statistics. (1985). <u>The condition of education: 1985</u>. Washington, DC: U.S. Department of Education.

National Center for Education Statistics. (1986). <u>Higher education general information survey</u> [machine-readable data file]. Washington, DC: U.S. Department of Education.

Nettles, M. T. (1987). <u>Financial aid and minority participation in graduate education</u>. Princeton, NJ: Minority Graduate Education Committee of the Graduate Record Examination Board.

Newman, F. (1985). Higher education and the American resurgence. Carnegie Foundation for the Advancement of Teaching.

Ramist, L. & Arbeiter, S. (1986). Profiles, college-bound seniors, 1985 (Admissions Testing Program of the College Board). New York: College Entrance Examination Board.

Thomas, G. E. (Ed.). (1981). Black students in higher education: conditions and experiences in the 1970s. Westport, CT: Greenwood Press.

U.S. Department of Commerce, Bureau of the Census. (1986). Statistical abstract of the U.S.: 1986 (106th edition). Washington, DC: Author.

U.S. Department of Commerce, Bureau of the Census. (1987). Statistical abstract of the U.S.: 1986 (107th edition). Washington, DC: Author.

U.S. Department of Commerce, Bureau of the Census. (1975). Historical statistics of the U.S., colonial times to 1970 (Bicentennial Education, Part 1). Washington, DC: Author.

2
Factors Related to Black and White Students' College Performance

MICHAEL T. NETTLES

Are there significant differences on account of race in the academic performance and experiences of Black and white college students? If so, what are they? What causes them? What can be done to eliminate them? This chapter addresses these questions by exploring the performance, experiences, and personal background characteristics of Black and white college students. It also examines faculty attitudes and behaviors and their relationship to student performance.

For many years Black Americans in higher education have been the victims of both <u>de jure</u> and <u>de facto</u> discrimination. Efforts to address problems of past discrimination typically focus upon increasing access and have been, over the past several years, only partially successful in achieving genuine equality. Equality of student performance is equally important, but it is a frequently neglected goal. Equality of performance is very important for achieving equality in the college environment and for occupational and professional equality in the work force after college graduation. In order to achieve social equality in professional occupations, Black college graduates must be concerned not only with attending college, but also with the quality of their academic performance and achievement. Employers of recent college graduates report that grades are among their most important criteria when hiring (Nettles et al., 1985). Graduate and professional school admissions officers also apply the same criteria in making admissions decisions. Therefore, merely having the opportunity to enter a university does not represent total equality of education or postcollegiate opportunities. Beyond access, the barriers to societal and educational equality are caused by the differences in learning and achievement exhibited in student college performance. Unfortunately, for the past three decades major legal and political attempts to achieve Black racial equality in higher education have devoted too little attention to performance and outcomes.

To address the four questions raised at the outset, the college performance of students attending 30 colleges and universities of five different types is presented in this

chapter. These data are taken from a 1985 study directed by
the author, in which a stratified random sample of Black and
white students and faculty were surveyed to compare their
performance and the causes of any significant differences by
race. Participating in the study were 4,094 students and
700 faculty members. The students completed a 109-item
instrument called the Student Opinion Survey. It contained
information about students' academic and personal
backgrounds prior to entering college, their college
academic performance, and their attitudes and behaviors
while attending college. The faculty of the 30 colleges
completed a 77-item instrument called the Faculty Opinion
Survey, which was concerned with their personal and academic
backgrounds, their professional experience and teaching
styles, and their perception about the institution in which
they work.

DIFFERENCES IN BLACK AND WHITE STUDENTS' COLLEGE PERFORMANCE

     Are there differences in the college performance of
Black and white students? Students' college cumulative
grade-point average and their progression rate are the two
most important indicators of college performance.
Cumulative grade-point average, of course, describes the
average grade students receive in all college courses. It
is the best available measure of student learning
performance in a college curriculum. Progression rate is
the average number of credit hours successfully completed
per term of enrollment and is the best available measure of
efficiency in the pursuit of a college degree. Figure 2.1
illustrates that Black students and white students differ
significantly on each of these two performance measures.
The average college grade-point average for white students
is equivalent to a B, compared to grades between B- and C+
for Black students. The progression rate of white students
overall is 15.3 credit hours per term, compared to 14.4
credit hours per term for Black students. These differences
by race are not surprising, because it is common to find
Black and other minority students on the lower end of most
indicators of educational achievement (Astin, 1971, 1982;
Peterson et al., 1978; Thomas, 1981).
     These are, however, undesirable and important findings
in light of efforts made legally, politically, and
educationally in the sixties, seventies, and the eighties to
close the performance gap. Numerous legal proceedings have
been undertaken in order to provide greater access; public
policies have been adopted to assure greater opportunity;
colleges and universities have poured enormous resources
into recruiting minority students, and institutional
policies have been adopted in an effort to facilitate
student adjustment and success; yet the performance gap
remains. It is very likely that numerical progress will be
stalled until the performance issues are adequately
addressed. The factors related to racial group differences
in performance must be examined as a starting point for

Figure 2.1

Comparison of Black and White Students' College Grade Point
Averages and Progression Rates

Student Performance
Mean College GPA

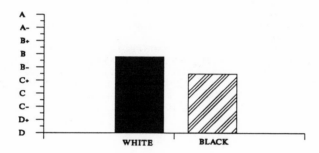

Mean Progression Rate

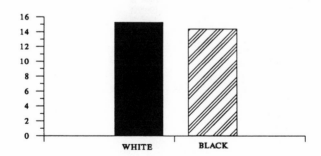

eliminating the performance gap and ultimately eliminating
racial inequality in higher education.

       Factors   Related   to   Racial   Differences   in   Student
Performance

       What   factors   enable   students   to   perform   well   in
college?   Several   personal,   academic,   attitudinal,   and
behavioral characteristics of students, as well as faculty
attitudinal   and   behavioral   characteristics,   are
significantly related to student college performance.   By
identifying the significant factors related to students
cummulative GPA and progression rates and then by presenting
the differences on these factors by race, educators and
policy makers may begin developing strategies aimed at
eliminating the gaps.
       A multiple regression analysis was conducted with
college grade-point averages and progression rates as the
dependent   variables   and   the   student   and   faculty
characteristics   as   predictor   variables.   Figure   2.2
illustrates the results of regression analysis of college
grade-point average showing 20 significant predictors;

Figure 2.2

Summary of Results of Regression
College Grade Point Average

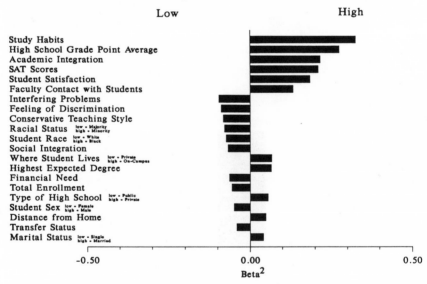

Figure 2.3 illustrates 16 significant predictors of students' college progression rates. The variables are listed in order of importance, with the most important variables appearing at the top and the least important predictors at the bottom. Figure 2.2 shows that the college students with the highest grades are those who have: (1) relatively good study habits, (2) high, high school grade-point averages, (3) high academic integration, (4) high SAT scores, (5) high satisfaction with their university, (6) high contact with faculty, (7) low number of interfering problems, (8) relatively low feelings that their university is racially discriminatory, (9) faculty with nontraditional teaching styles, (10) a student body with a racial majority, (11) white students, (12) those with low social integration, (13) those who live in on-campus housing, (14) those with low financial need, (15) those who attend colleges with low enrollments, (16) those who attended private high schools, (17) female students, (18) those who attend college a relatively great distance from home, (19) those who are nontransfer students, and (20) married students.

Figure 2.3 shows that most predictors of college progression rates differ from those for high grade-point averages. Students with the faster progression rates: (1) attend larger universities, (2) are younger students,

Figure 2.3

Summary of Results of Regression
Progression Rates

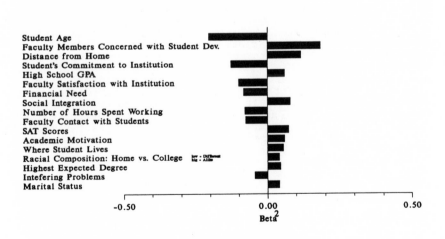

(3) have faculty with a high concern for student development, (4) attend college relatively distant from home, (5) have relatively low satisfaction with their university, (6) have low financial need, (7) have high social integration, (8) work a low number of hours on a job while in college, (9) have a low level of faculty contact, (10) have high SAT scores, (11) have relatively good study habits, (12) live in on-campus housing, (13) attend a college with a similar racial composition to their home neighborhood, (14) have higher degree aspirations beyond the bachelor's degree, (15) have a low number of interfering problems, and (16) are married.

The significant predictors of college grade-point average and progression rates are different, but within each of these performance measures, the significant predictors for Blacks are the same as for whites with only three exceptions. First, feelings that a university is racially discriminatory has a negative effect upon Black students' progression rates but has no effect upon white students' progression, even when they are in the minority group on campus (white students are generally in the minority racial group only at historically Black institutions). Second, lack of social integration has a negative effect upon both Black and white students' college grade-point averages, but the effect is not as great for Black students as it is for white students. Third, interfering problems (which have a negative influence upon the grades of both groups) have a less negative effect upon Black students' college grades than they have upon the grades of white students. Other than these three variables, the factors related to white students' performance are identical to those for Blacks. Therefore, differences in performance by race may be partially explained by the three variables that predict differently for the two groups, but also by the differences on the other significant predictor variables.

How do Black students and white students differ on the significant predictor variables? Now that the significant predictors of students' college performance have been presented, the racial differences within these key variables are examined to search for strategies for eliminating racial inequality for purposes of conceptualizing the many significant variables. It is useful to discuss them under the following general headings: (1) students' precollegiate characteristics; (2) students' in-college characteristics, attitudes, and behaviors; and (3) faculty attitudes and behaviors.

STUDENTS' PRECOLLEGIATE CHARACTERISTICS

Admissions Tests and High School Grades

Colleges and universities typically make admission decisions on the basis of a student's prior performance. While personal characteristics and recommendations from teachers and counselors have some bearing upon admissions, students' high school grades and their scores on college admission tests - most commonly the Scholastic Aptitude Test (SAT) and the American College Test (ACT) - weigh most prominently in most admission decisions. It is not surprising, therefore, that high school grades and college entrance test scores are the second and fourth most significant predictors of both cumulative college grade-point average and progression rates. Breland (1983) documents numerous studies in which these two variables are consistently related to a student's college performance in the freshman year and a few that illustrate somewhat less but consistent strength beyond the freshman year. These are expected to be correlates, because the skills and knowledge requirements to obtain good high school grades and to perform well on the admissions tests are the same skills required to perform in college. These skills are reading comprehension, analytical abilities displayed in the form of quantitative problem solving, and verbal ability displayed in the use of grammar and syntax.

In one sense, the findings presented in this chapter on admissions tests and high school grades only replicate many prior validity studies. On the other hand, they serve to substantiate the less frequently studied subject of the validity of these measures for minority students. On the basis of the data presented earlier, both high school grades and entrance test scores provide stable predictors of Black college student performance. High school grades are the stronger of the two for both groups.

The fact that Black students have lower mean high school grades and college entrance examination scores may explain to some extent their lower college grades. At the same time, it may substantiate the claims made in Chapter 1 that Black students in America are not receiving adequate precollege education to prepare them to perform as well as white students in college. Manning and Jackson (1984) analyzed the impact of these two variables upon minority students' college success. They suggest that the lower performances of many minority students may be attributed to lower socioeconomic status, which exposes them to less adequate educational preparation at the precollege level. Some researchers in the sixties and seventies concluded that, because of the unfairness of test scores for minority students, colleges and universities should rely more heavily upon non-cognitive criteria such as student biographical characteristics, student motivation, goals, and aspirations (Clark & Plotkin, 1964; Sedlecek, Brooks, & Mindus, 1973).

Three additional precollege student characteristics are significantly related to student college grade-point averages, and two different precollege variables are predictors of progression rate. For college grade-point average, the three significant variables are race, type of high school attended, and gender. For progression rate, age and the fit between the racial composition of a student's high school and college are significant.

Race

Although it is not a significant predictor of college progression rates, race is a significant predictor of college grade-point averages. This is one of the most important and unique discoveries of this research in terms of its implication about the status of desegregation. Specifically, white students are predicted to receive higher college grades even if their Black counterparts have equal SAT scores, high school grade-point averages, and social and personal characteristics. Although several studies have concluded that there are some differences in the predictors of Black and white students' college grades (Borgen, 1972; Farver, Sedlacek & Brooks, 1975; Astin, 1982), none has found that a student's race is a significant factor. This finding suggests that either there are some differences between Black and white students' aspirations for grades or that there is widespread discrimination in grading practices in higher education. Gurin and Epps (1975) offered one possible explanation when they found that Black students who felt that fate was responsible for their disadvantageous status were outperformed by Blacks who believed barriers to their achievement were sociological and could be overcome. This supports the theory that the aspirations of Black students are to some extent dependent upon how much positive reinforcement they receive for their high goals.

For whatever reason, race is significantly related to college grades; it represents a major challenge for college and university administrators in their quest to achieve qualitative racial equality. As long as race itself is a factor, addressing all the remaining significant factors will not eliminate the performance differences of Black and white college students.

Type of High School Attended

Consistent with other studies on college performance, attending a private high school contributes to students' college grades. This study confirms that the same is true for Black students. This is not surprising, because many private schools are college preparatory in nature, and all are free to enforce high academic expectations and discipline that often exceeds the expectations in public schools. A greater portion of both Black and white private school students are enrolled in an academic track compared to their public school counterparts (Coleman, 1981). The recent High School and Beyond survey conducted by the National Center for Education Statistics indicates that 74.4 percent of the 1982 Black private high school students were in an academic track compared to 30.7 percent of their public school counterparts (National Longitudinal Survey of High School and Beyond, 1982).

Gender

Both Black and white women are predicted to receive
higher grades than men of their same race. Being female,
however, has no effect upon college progression rates. The
relationship of gender to grades is consistent with
practically every study on the subject. A significant
finding in this research is that, whereas the gender ratio
for white students is 50:50, 63 percent of Black students
are female and 37 percent are male. The lower
representation and performance of Black males in college is
a major challenge to efforts to equalize higher education
access and opportunities.

Age

Younger students of both races are predicted to
progress faster than older students, but age has no effect
upon college grades. The faster progression rates of
younger students is partially explained by the fact that
older students are more likely to attend college part-time
and may be a little more focused and more patient in their
pursuit of a baccalaureate degree.

Fit Between Racial Composition of Student's High School
and College

Students who attend a college or university with a
racial composition similar to that of their high school are
more likely to progress faster than students who attend
institutions with different racial compositions.
Desegregating high schools simultaneously with colleges and
universities is likely to lead to faster progression of
Black students. But the relationship of school racial
composition has no effect upon college grade-point averages.

STUDENTS' COLLEGE CHARACTERISTICS, ATTITUDES, AND BEHAVIORS

The majority of variables illustrated in Figures 2.2
and 2.3 predicting college progression rates and grade-point
averages are students' attitudinal and behavioral
characteristics. Thus, students' college attitudes and
behaviors, collectively, are more significant predictors of
their college performance than are their precollege
characteristics. The attitudinal and behavioral variables
that are significantly related to both college grade-point
averages and progression rates are academic motivation,
academic integration, commitment to the university,
interfering problems, feelings of racial discrimination,
social integration, where students live while attending
college, students' transfer status, their employment status
while attending college, and their degree aspirations. Each
of these variables is defined and discussed below. Table
2.1 illustrates the racial differences of students on these

variables. In general there is no significant racial difference in terms of academic motivation, but white students have significantly greater academic integration and commitment to their institutions, while Black students have significantly greater interfering problems, greater social integration, and more feelings of racial discrimination.

Table 2.1

Summary Comparison of White Students' and Black Students' Attitudinal/Behavioral and Academic Characteristics

Attitudinal/Behavioral Characteristics	Overall Significantly Greater
Academic integration	White students
Financial need	Black students
Commitment to the institution	White students
Academic motivation	No differences
Feelings of discrimination	Black students
Social integration	Black students
Intefering problems	Black students
High school grade point average	White students

Study Habits

Study habits represent the strongest of all predictors. Study habits reveal student's conscientiousness and determination to perform well, even under difficult conditions. Students with good study habits are conscientious about completing homework on time and study for class even when they don't like the course; therefore, it is not surprising that this is the strongest predictor of college grade-point averages, even above high school grades, standardized test scores, and environment of the institution. Table 2.1 illustrates that there are no significant racial differences in study habits.

Academic Integration

Academic integration is a factor that describes students' relationships with faculty and overall satisfaction with the college environment. Academic integration is a predictor of college grade-point averages but not of progression rates. Students with high academic integration are likely to have higher grade-point averages. White students as a group have higher academic integration than Black students, as shown in Table 2.1. Thus, efforts to improve Black students' college grade-point averages should focus upon improving their relationships with faculty and should also address their relative dissatisfaction with their academic environments.

Satisfaction with the Institution

Student satisfaction with the institution refers to overall satisfaction with various aspects of college life, such as the courses offered, student organizations on campus, and the college/university administrators. Table 2.1 illustrates that white students are significantly more satisfied with their universities than Black students. While a high degree of satisfaction is not related to faster progression, it is related to higher college grades. In light of this and the results of other studies that have demonstrated the importance of student satisfaction as a contributor to student performance (Tinto, 1975; Astin, 1982), college and university officials should give greater attention to reversing the relatively low satisfaction rates of Black students.

Interfering Problems

Interfering problems include physical illnesses, emotional problems, and other problems that interfere with student academic performance such as relationships with others on campus. Black students, as shown in Table 2.1, have significantly more interfering problems than white students, and their interfering problems have a negative impact upon both their progression rates and their college grade-point averages. It is no surprise that students with fewer interfering problems have higher grades and progress faster. Thus, colleges and universities should also consider methods for reducing interfering problems of students when addressing racial differences in performance.

Social Integration

Social integration is a factor that describes student participation in campus clubs or organizations, their discussions of personal problems with faculty and peers, and their career planning. Social integration has a negative effect upon college grade-point averages, but a positive effect upon progression rates. In other words, students with high social integration have lower grades but graduate in a shorter time period. Table 2.1 shows that Black students have relatively high social integration, which contributes somewhat to their lower college grade-point

averages.   Like satisfaction, social integration is
generally encouraged and is viewed as a positive aspect of
the college experience.   It appears that a proper balance of
social integration and academic integration is necessary to
improve the college grade-point averages of Black students.
A common prescription for all colleges is not likely to be
effective, since the needs are likely to vary for different
students and campuses.

Feelings of Racial Discrimination

Feelings   of   racial   discrimination   indicate   that
students   feel   that   members   of   their   own   race   are
discriminated against by faculty members, administrators,
and students on campus.   These feelings have a negative
effect upon both the progression rates and college grade-
point averages of Black students but virtually no effect
upon white student performance.   Table 2.1 shows that Black
students also have significantly greater feelings of racial
discrimination than white students.   Thus, it is clear that
colleges and universities need to work to eliminate the
problem of high feelings of racial discrimination among
Black students.   Recently publicized incidents in which
Black college students have been assaulted and harassed by
white college students give rise to Black students' feelings
of racial discrimination.   When college faculty and
administrators respond to white student offenders with mild
reprimands, they convey the impression of tolerance or
acceptance of racially discriminatory behavior.

Where a Student Lives While Enrolled

Students generally have a choice of living off campus
or in on-campus residence halls.   Living in on-campus
residence halls contributes to higher grades and faster
progression rates of college students.   A higher percentage
of Black students than white students live in on-campus
residence hall, which should contribute to the overall
performance of Black students.

FACULTY ATTITUDES AND BEHAVIORS

Five factors that characterize faculty attitudes and
behaviors are now examined to discover their relationship to
student performance.   These factors are:

1.   Amount of contact with students outside the classroom

2.   Satisfaction with the institution

3.   Teaching style

4. Feelings about whether their institution is racially discriminatory

5. Concern for student development

     Two of these factors are significant predictors of students' grade-point averages, and two are significant predictors of their progression rates. The amount of contact faculty members have with students is related to both college grade-point averages and progression rates, but in opposite directions. High faculty contact leads to higher college grade-point averages, but slower progression rates. Faculty satisfaction is a significant predictor of progression rates but not of grade-point averages.
     The two faculty factors related to grade-point averages are faculty contact with students outside the classroom and faculty teaching style. Faculty contact is a factor that represents the number of students a faculty member meets with to discuss course work, personal problems, academic plans, and careers. Generally, students who have frequent contact with faculty outside the classroom receive higher grades. Black students have significantly less contact with faculty outside the classroom than white students, and this contributes to the lower grades for Black students.
     Teaching style is a factor that represents faculty use of: class participation; instructional aides such as computer-assisted instruction; slides, tapes, and video discs; and the inclusion of multiethnic points of view in the educational process. Faculty who use these methods are viewed as having a nontraditional teaching style. Nontraditional teaching styles contribute to higher grade-point averages overall and for Black students. In this study, Black students are found to be more likely to experience faculty with more traditional teaching styles than are white students. Faculty members in predominantly Black institutions have more traditional styles than faculty at predominatly white institutions, a matter that will be discussed further in Chapter 3. It may also be the case that faculty in the major fields frequently chosen by Black students have more traditional teaching styles. This has been substantially supported in research on college teaching (Sheffield, 1974; Dressel & Marcus, 1982). Furthermore, if college grades are indeed a reflection of learning, as this writer believes, then this relationship between teaching styles suggests that nontraditional teaching styles should be considered by faculty seeking to influence the learning and grade performance of Black students.
     In terms of progression rates, high faculty satisfaction and low faculty contact with students are related to faster progression rates. Faculty satisfaction refers to faculty members' satisfaction with their university's research program, opportunities for personal growth, overall confidence in other faculty on their campus, and the academic reputation of their university. Black students are found to attend colleges disproportionately with relatively dissatisfied faculty. A change to an institution with more satisfied faculty may contribute to

Black student progression rates. Alternatively, efforts made by colleges and universities to improve faculty morale may have a positive effect upon student performance.

Faculty Contact with Students

Finally, unlike grade-point averages, where high faculty contact with students contributes to higher grade-point averages, low faculty contact contributes to faster progression rates. In spite of this finding, it is not constructive to recommend lower contact, because this connotes negative human behavior. However, it does appear, as in the case of academic and social integration, that an appropriate balance should be sought between faculty and student contact that contributes to students' learning and performance rather than interferes with student productivity. This is especially important, because Black students today attend colleges where they are in the racial minority and because most of their instructors are white.

CONCLUSION

The data presented in this chapter indicate a variety of student characteristics, attitudes, and behavior as well as faculty attitudes and behaviors that are associated with student performance in college. The primary actions that should be taken by policymakers and educators in order to improve the overall college performance of Black students are the following:

1. Improve the quality of education provided for Black citizens prior to entering college. This, of course, is directed at the elementary and secondary school levels where the quality of education provided for Black students is inferior to the educational preparation provided for white students. This challenge is nonetheless indirectly applicable to colleges and universities, since they bear the responsibility for training the teachers of elementary and secondary schools. Colleges with teacher education programs must do a better job of addressing the effectiveness of their graduates in educating minorities.

2. Improve the level of academic integration of Black students in college. It has been pointed out in this chapter that Black students have a lower level of academic integration than white students. Academic integration is no doubt a combined responsibility of students and faculty that colleges and universities must address more vigorously as they determine how to improve Black student performance. Improving student relationships with faculty regarding schoolwork is essential to improved academic performance for Black students.

3. <u>Reduce the disproportionately high level of interfering
    problems Black students experience while attending
    college</u>. Interfering problems refer to students'
    physical and emotional health as well as other personal
    problems and their ability to establish strong
    relationships with others on their college campus. The
    fact that Black students experience significantly more
    interfering problems than white students suggests that
    they have a more stressful experience in college than
    white students do. Colleges and universities generally
    address these types of difficulties through their
    student affairs programs. Colleges and universities may
    not be able to address all the personal problems of
    students, but greater effort should be made to assure
    that the college environment and its programs do not
    contribute prejudicially to the interfering problems
    Black students face.

4. <u>Eliminate the feelings of racial discrimination among
    Black college students</u>. Since the majority of Black
    college students attend institutions where they are in
    the minority racial group, it is not surprising that
    they feel a greater degree of racial discrimination than
    white students do. This, however, does not justify the
    existence of these feelings among Black students, and
    colleges and universities should have ongoing programs
    and activities that are aimed at eliminating the
    feelings of discrimination among Black students.
    Students' feelings of discrimination refer to their
    beliefs that the policies and practices of their
    university are racially biased; that they are not
    effective in establishing relationships with peers of
    different races on their campus; that their university
    does not make enough effort to attract students of
    diverse ethnic groups; and that faculty members
    discriminate against students of their racial group.
    Colleges and universities should focus their attention
    upon these matters when addressing Black students'
    feelings of discrimination.

5. <u>Advise Black students of appropriate levels of social
    integration</u>. Social integration, like academic
    integration, is a positive factor. However, students
    with too much social integration are likely to find that
    it has a negative effect upon their performance. The
    problem of social integration on some campuses is that
    colleges and universities, in an effort to have minority
    representation on committees and in campus
    organizations, often find themselves calling upon the
    same minority students to serve in various capacities to
    the point of interfering with student academic progress.
    College administrators and students must be aware of
    these effects when making decisions about students'
    extracurricular activities.

6. <u>Improve the level and quality of faculty contact with Black students</u>. Very little is known about the frequency and quality of faculty contact with college students. However, this study has observed that faculty contact with students contributes to student grades. It is further observed that Black students are less likely to have contact with faculty than are white students, and this has a negative effect upon their college grades. Further study needs to be conducted to determine the nature and origin of faculty/student relations in order to resolve the racial differences. Colleges and universities, however, in view of the racial differences in faculty/student relations should undertake such analyses and then take actions that will ensure equality in the level and quality of faculty contact with Black students.

7. <u>Encourage college faculty to adopt nontraditional teaching styles</u>. Inasmuch as nontraditional teaching styles contribute to student learning and performance, they should be encouraged. Additionally, in recognition of greater attendance of Black students in college, and especially in predominantly white colleges, faculty members should attempt to include minority perspectives in the course content and experiences whenever possible and appropriate.

8. <u>Advise Black students to attend colleges and universities with a highly satisfied faculty</u>. Faculty satisfaction contributes to student performance, and Black students are less likely than are white students to attend institutions with a high degree of faculty satisfaction. Perhaps the recommendation should be for colleges and universities to give greater attention to faculty satisfaction. The goal for Black students is to be exposed to faculty who are satisfied with their university, its resources, and their own work as a means of achieving higher student performance.

REFERENCES

Astin, A. W. (1982). <u>Minorities in American higher education</u>. San Francisco: Jossey-Bass.

Astin, A. W. (1971). <u>Predicting academic performance in college</u>. New York: Free Press.

Clark, K. B., & Plotkin, L. (1964). <u>The Negro student at integrated colleges</u>. New York: National Scholarship Service Fund for Negro Students.

Borgen, F. N. (1972). Differential expectations? Predicting grades for Black students in five types of colleges. <u>Measurement and Evaluation in Guidance</u>, <u>4</u>(4), 206-12.

Breland, H. M. (1978). <u>Population validity and college
    entrance measures</u>. Princeton, NJ: Educational Testing
    Service.

Clark, K. B., & Plotkin, L. (1964). <u>The Negro student at
    integrated colleges</u>. New York: National Scholarship
    Service Fund for Negro Students.

Coleman, J., Hofer, T., Kilgore, S., & NORC. <u>Public and
    private schools</u>. Washington, DC: Educational
    Resources Information Center. (ERIC Document
    Reproduction Service No. ED 197 503)

Coleman, J., Hofer, T., & Kilgore, S. (1982). <u>High school
    achievement: Public, Catholic and private schools
    compared</u>. New York: Basic Books, Inc.

Dressel, P., & Marcus, D. (1982). <u>On teaching and learning
    in college</u>. San Francisco: Jossey-Bass.

Farver, A. S., Sedlacek, W. E., & Brooks, G. C. (1975).
    Longitudinal predictions of university grades for
    Blacks and whites. <u>Measurement and Evaluation in
    Guidance</u>, <u>7</u>(4), 243-50.

Gurin, P., & Epps, E. G. <u>Black consciousness, identity and
    achievement</u>. New York: Wiley.

Lee, V. E. (1985). <u>The effects of curriculum tracking on
    the social distribution of achievement in Catholic and
    public secondary schools</u>. Princeton, NJ: Educational
    Testing Service.

Manning, W., & Jackson, R. (1984). <u>College entrance
    examinations: Objective selection or gatekeeping for
    the economically privileged in perspectives on bias in
    mental testing</u>. New York: Plenum Publishing
    Corporation.

Nettles, M. T. (1985). <u>The causes and consequences of
    college students' performance: A focus on Black and
    white students attrition rates, progression rates and
    grade-point averages</u>. Nashville, TN: Tennessee Higher
    Education Commission.

Peterson, M., et al. <u>Black students on white campuses: The
    impacts of increased Black enrollments</u>. Ann Arbor, MI:
    University of Michigan.

Sedlacek, W. E., Brooks, G. C., & Mindus, L. A. Black and
    other minority admissions to large universities: Three
    year national trends. <u>Journal of College Student
    Personnel</u>, <u>9</u>, 177-179, 968.

Sheffield, E. F. (Ed.). (1974). <u>Teaching in the
    universities: No one way</u>. Montreal: McGill-Queen's
    University Press.

Thomas, G. E. (1981). The effects of standardized
    achievement test performance and family status on
    Black-white college access. In G. E. Thomas (Ed.),
    <u>Black students in higher education: Conditions and
    experiences in the 1970s</u>. Westport, CT: Greenwood
    Press.

Tinto, V. (1975). Dropout from higher education: A
    theoretical systhesis of recent research. <u>Review of
    Educational Research</u>, <u>45</u>, 89-125.

3

Black and White Students' Performance and Experiences at Various Types of Universities

MICHAEL T. NETTLES

Among the many virtues of American higher education, diversity is perhaps its most alluring feature. Nowhere else in the world is there such an array of colleges and universities, differing in size, governance, and tradition. The more than 3,200 higher education institutions in the United States vary in admissions requirements and practices, in the types and levels of academic and vocational degree programs, in courses required for degree completion, in instructional approaches, and in student evaluation practices. Despite this long tradition of diversity, however, prior to the sixties most universities in the United States had the common practice of prohibiting Blacks from attending. In the South, for example, in 1952, 100 percent of Black college students attended historically Black colleges and universities (Mingle, 1981) and were prohibited by law from attending white colleges and universities[1]. In the long and illustrious history of American higher education, only during the last two decades have the majority of colleges and universities amended their admissions policies to admit and actively recruit Black undergraduate students.

Over these past two decades, Black Americans have gained access to the full range of America's colleges and universities. However, they continue to be underrepresented at most predominantly white universities, particularly at the most selective and most prestigious institutions. Table 1.1 in Chapter 1 illustrates the enrollment distribution of Black undergraduate students at several types of colleges and universities. In general, the largest percentage of Black students are enrolled in two-year colleges, followed by four-year colleges, and the smallest proportion attend

---

[1]In this chapter, the terms Black university and white university are used rather than "predominantly" or "traditionally" Black or white universities. While these terms reflect the predominant race of the institutions they are not intended to infer that these institutions are racially exclusionary.

the universities with the greatest resources. Prior to and even during the sixties, analyses of Black enrollment distribution were much simpler because the vast majority of Black students attended historically Black institutions (Arce, 1976; Mingle, 1981). The decades of the sixties and seventies brought about gradual redistribution to the point that today the vast majority of Black students (72.9 percent) are enrolled in predominantly white institutions.

Over the last decade, however, access has proven to be an uncertain achievement. Researchers and college faculty and administrators have discovered that, despite the fact that more Black students now enter four-year predominantly white universities, their attrition rates are so high that far too few ever receive a baccalaureate degree. Recent estimates suggest that Black students represent anywhere from 5 to 20 percent more of their entering freshmen classes than they represent in their graduating classes (Astin, 1977 and 1982; Allen, 1986; Lenning et al., 1980; Cross & H. Astin, 1981; Thomas & McPartland, 1984; Nettles et al., 1985). Recent evidence also indicates that college persistence through graduation for Black undergraduate students is - surprisingly - a much greater problem at historically Black institutions than at predominantly white universities. Based upon a national survey of college students, for example, Astin (1981) found that, over a nine-year period, 67 percent of Black students who initially enroll in predominantly white universities received baccalaureate degrees compared to 65 percent at historically Black institutions. He also reported that 73 percent of white students completed their baccalaureate degrees within nine years of first entering college. Nettles and his colleagues (1985) found that 49 percent of Black students attending predominantly white universities graduated after five years compared to 29 percent at historically Black institutions. However, Gosman (1983) and Nettles (1985) and their colleagues discovered that, after controlling for students' entering abilities and financial aid awards, Black students at historically Black institutions actually had higher retention rates and faster progression rates than Black students attending predominantly white universities. Thus, the differences in retention are apparently due in part to the differences in the types of students who attend the two types of universities rather than a particular type of university's programs and faculty. Historically Black institutions in the seventies and eighties have educated a larger proportion of economically disadvantaged Black students than predominantly white universities.

There can be little doubt that the enrollment redistribution of Black students during the past two decades has been costly to historically Black institutions. Hill (1983) reported that in 1980, historically Black institutions enrolled 38 percent of all Black undergraduates in states where they are located and 29 percent of all Black undergraduates in the United States. More recent statistics collected by the U.S. Department of Education (1984) indicate an even lower proportion (fewer than 25 percent) of Black students enrolled in historically Black institutions.

In addition to the concern over the decline in the number of Black students enrolled in historically Black institutions and universities is the concern over the shift in the best-qualified students away from historically Black institutions to predominantly white universities. For two decades researchers have documented the higher academic ability, the superior precollegiate education, and higher socioeconomic status among Black students attending predominantly white universities compared to those attending historically Black institutions (Blumenfeld, 1968; Bayer & Boruch, 1969; Davis & Borders-Patterson, 1973; Gosman et al., 1983; Nettles et al., 1985). An important question that has not been adequately addressed is: What effect does the Black enrollment redistribution have upon Black students' performance and the quality of their college experiences? This chapter employs the same data base used in Chapter 2 to compare and contrast the performance and experiences of Black and white students within and among various types of colleges and universities in an effort to explain why the differences in performance and quality of experience exist.

CHARACTERISTICS OF THE SAMPLE UNIVERSITIES

The five types of universities for which students' performance and experiences are examined in this chapter are: (1) white public research universities, (2) Black public universities, (3) white regional public universities, (4) white private prestigious universities, and (5) Black private universities. Six universities in each of the five categories (totaling 30 universities) constitute the sample of universities for this research. These five categories of institutions have distinctly different historical and present missions, but in recent years the predominantly white universities have become increasingly more popular among Black students. This makes it very important to assess how well Black students are performing at these different types of universities.

To illustrate some of the differences in the five types of universities, Table 3.1 presents the enrollments, racial composition of the student bodies, composite SAT scores, average family income of the student body, and the racial composition of the faculty for each of the 30 universities. As expected, the two types of universities with the greatest resources have the least representation of Black students. These are the white public universities and the white private prestigious universities. The white public research universities are the largest of the universities in the sample, with enrollments ranging from 14,000 to 52,000; but they have the lowest overall representation of Black students (4.2 percent). The white private prestigious universities are the most selective, with overall average composite SAT scores of 1,126, and are only slightly better than white public research universities in terms of Black student representation (4.6 percent). These two types of universities also have very low representation of Black

Table 3.1

Student and Faculty Characteristics of Sample Institutions

Type of Institution	Undergraduate Student Enrollment, Fall 1981			Average Composite SAT Score for Student Body, Fall 1982	Average Annual Family Income for student Body, Fall 1982	Faculty Composition, Fall 1981		
	Total	% Black	% White			Total	% Black	% White
Predominantly white large public university								
1	51,800	2.6%	95.6%	1,044	$32,500	2,095	.9	94.6
2	25,389	5.3	86.2	967	27,500	2,646	2.9	95.7
3	17,873	5.0	92.0	937	27,500	1,917	1.2	96.6
4	14,618	9.2	89.0	994	27,500	2,013	3.3	93.5
5	18,410	5.5	90.8	966	27,500	1,167	2.4	93.8
6	38,111	2.5	85.2	1,020	37,500	2,015	1.6	93.1
Predominantly black public university								
1	2,260	83.6	11.5	753	17,500	179	54.2	38.0
2	5,193	89.1	8.5	809	22,500	265	63.4	32.8
3	2,143	84.1	15.5	779	22,500	120	59.2	29.2
4	7,730	63.9	30.3	835	17,500	390	56.2	34.6
5	9,173	55.1	.6	840	17,500	369	74.5	13.8
6	1,069	71.6	20.6	874	22,500	90	47.5	37.8
Predominantly white regional public university								
1	4,148	19.4	76.8	921	22,500	280	2.5	94.3
2	5,148	15.2	77.6	902	27,500	380	2.3	95.0
3	5,729	9.1	90.1	848	22,500	395	2.3	96.5
4	7,861	2.8	96.4	979	32,500	528	.6	97.5
5	4,964	3.8	94.7	868	22,500	364	2.5	94.8
6	5,246	5.5	91.9	833	27,500	318	.3	97.2
Predominantly white private university								
1	3,049	3.9	96.1	1,134	37,500	192	2.6	92.2
2	2,257	3.6	84.7	1,261	37,500	305	1.3	93.4
3	8,318	7.3	65.0	966	27,500	1,375	2.6	85.3
4	9,103	5.2	76.2	1,224	37,500	2,110	1.6	92.2
5	6,117	3.1	92.1	1,031	37,500	514	1.6	94.9
6	5,318	2.9	95.8	1,144	37,500	483	1.2	93.2
Predominantly black private university								
1	1,281	99.9	.1	671	12,500	112	67.9	21.4
2	757	100.0	0.0	866	27,500	67	53.7	41.8
3	3,235	96.8	1.2	866	27,500	324	57.7	40.1
4	1,065	98.7	0.0	772	12,500	75	52.0	25.3
5	1,447	100.0	0.0	851	27,500	122	70.5	28.7
6	2,221	91.0	6.6	870	22,500	171	36.8	56.1

Note: Undergraduate enrollment and faculty composition figures were obtained directly from the participating institutions. Average SAT and income figures were obtained from the student responses to the Student Opinion Survey.

faculty (only 2 percent each). They also have the wealthiest students, with average family incomes of $37,500 at white private universities and $30,000 at white public universities.

STUDENT AND FACULTY CHARACTERISTICS OF SAMPLE INSTITUTIONS

The white regional universities have an average enrollment of 5,500 students, with an average of 8.4 percent Black enrollment. Although the Black enrollment at white regional universities is higher than that at the other two types of predominantly white universities, the Black faculty representation is lower (1.7 percent). These regional universities can be characterized as having open admissions policies, with average composite SAT scores of 892. The student bodies of the white regional universities are predominantly middle-class, with average family incomes of $26,000.

The two types of historically Black institutions, while having some similar characteristics, are clearly not monolithic. Their average student is from a lower-middle income family ($20,000 annual family income). Both have open admissions policies, with average composite SAT scores of 815 at Black public universities, and 816 at Black private universities. Both types of historically Black institutions have racially mixed faculties, with an average Black-to-white faculty ratio of 55:45 at the Black private universities and 62:38 at Black public universities. They are different in size and in terms of the racial composition of their student bodies. The Black private universities have an average enrollment of 1,668 students, compared to an average enrollment of 4,595 at Black public universities. Overall, white students represent 31 percent of the enrollment of Black public universities, but only 3 percent at the Black private universities. The comparatively large white enrollment at Black public universities is to a great extent the result of federal court orders requiring desegregation of public universities in the South, which is discussed in great detail by Cynthia Brown in Chapter 7 and by John Williams in Chapter 8.

Overall, with the exception of the Black private universities, the four other types of universities have made great attempts over the past two decades to diversify their enrollments. Although the percentage of Black students enrolled in the three types of predominantly white universities is low, there are nearly three times as many Black students enrolled as there were in the sixties and early seventies. This is also true of Black public universities and their progress in enrolling white students. Because of the recent increases in minority enrollment at these four types of universities, they provide very good case study institutions for assessing the impact of increased minority enrollment upon students' college performance, attitudes, and behaviors.

STUDENTS' COLLEGE PERFORMANCE, ATTITUDES, AND BEHAVIORS BY
TYPE OF UNIVERSITY

Consistent with Chapter 2, student performance is
measured by cumulative college grade-point averages and
progression rates.   Racial and institutional comparisons of
college grade-point averages and progression rates are
presented in Figure 3.1.   Black and white student
performance is significantly different at each of the four
types of universities where comparisons are possible.
Because the white enrollment at Black private universities
is so small, racial comparisons are not feasible.   However,
it is important to point out that compared to all types of
universities Black students perform best at Black private
universities in terms of both progression rates and grade-
point averages.   White students have higher grades than
Black students at each of the other four types of
universities, and they progress faster at all except the
Black public universities.
Comparing different types of universities, students of
the same race have different grade-point averages and
progression rates at different types of universities.

Figure 3.1

Student Performance by Type of University

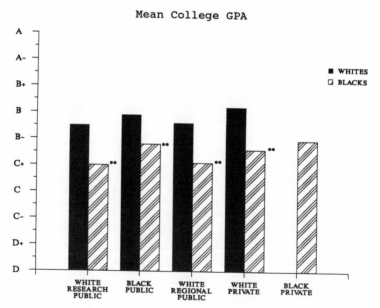

Mean College GPA

●●Significant at .001 level

Mean Progression Rate

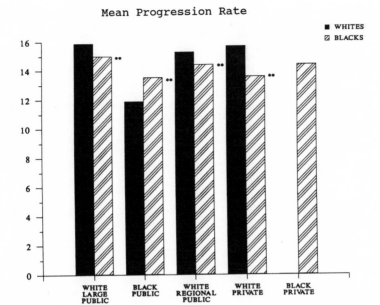

••Significant at .001 level

Beyond the Black private universities, where grades and progression rates are the highest for Black students, the rank order of both Black and white students' grade-point averages is different from the rank order of their progression rates. In terms of grade-point averages, Figure 3.1 illustrates that the second highest grades earned by Black students are at Black public universities (B-) and white private universities (B-), followed by white regional universities (C+) and white public research universities (C+). Contrary to the ranking of grade-point averages, Figure 3.1 illustrates that the second-fastest progression rates for Black students are at white public research universities (15.03), followed by white regional universities (14.39), white private universities (13.65), and Black public universities (13.52).

As with Black students, the rank ordering of grade-point averages of white students by type of university differs from the rank ordering of progression rates. Figure 3.1 shows that white students attending white private universities report the highest grade-point averages (B), followed by Black public universities (B) and white regional public universities. The lowest grade-point averages for white students (B-) are reported by those attending public research universities. On the other hand, Figure 3.1 shows that white students attending public research universities progress through college the fastest (15.9 credit hours per term), followed by white private universities (15.7) and regional public universities (15.3), with the slowest average progression rates among white students at Black public universities (11.9).

Based on these analyses, without controlling for student abilities or background characteristics, in terms of academic performance Black students perform best when attending Black private universities. For white students, with the exception of slower progression rates at Black public universities, overall performance appears to be unaffected by type of university. Much of the reason for the slower average progression rates of white students at Black public universities is that most are older adults who attend part-time. The average age of white students attending the Black public universities in the sample is 24 compared to an average age of 21 for white students at the other types of universities.

FACTORS CONTRIBUTING TO PERFORMANCE AT DIFFERENT TYPES OF UNIVERSITIES

College Grade-Point Averages

Just as the performance levels vary across the different types of universities, so do the probable causes of performance. Student grade-point averages and progression rates at the five types of universities are predicted applying the same models as those used in Chapter 2 where the five types of universities were combined. Figure 3.2 illustrates the significant predictors of college grade-point averages at each of the five types of universities.

Only four student characteristics are significant contributors to college grade-point averages at all five types of universities. Regardless of race, students with high high school grade-point averages, high academic integration, who are highly satisfied with their university and who have relatively good study habits receive higher grade-point averages at each of the five types of universities. Students with high SAT scores and low financial need have higher grades at each type of universities except at Black public universities, where SAT scores and financial need have no significant effect upon students' grades. This is particularly interesting, because students attending Black public universities have, in fact, the greatest financial need and relatively low SAT scores among the five types of universities.

Several other variables contribute to grade-point averages at some types of universities but not at others. Perhaps the most important of these is the finding that race is a significant contributor to grade-point averages at all three types of predominantly white universities but not at the two types of Black institutions. Specifically, white students attending predominantly white universities are likely to receive higher grades than Black students at the same universities even if their SAT scores, high school grades, academic integration, study habits, and

Figure 3.2

Significant Predictors of Students' College GPA
by Type of University

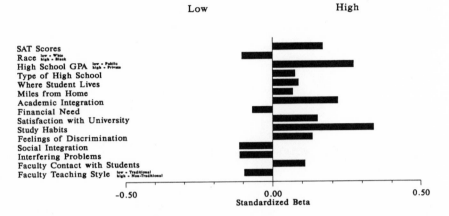

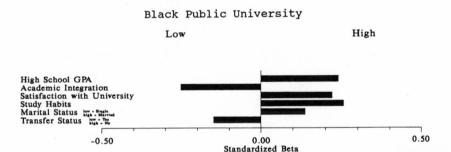

socioeconomic status are equal. Most often, researchers
conclude that when these factors are controlled, student
performance is not racially distinctive. These findings
suggest, however, (as mentioned in Chapter 2) that either
Black students attending predominantly white universities do
not aspire to receive high grades as much as white students
or that Black students are being discriminated against in
the grading process at predominantly white universities.
This in part explains why Black students attending
predominantly white universities have lower grade-point
averages despite being better prepared for college than

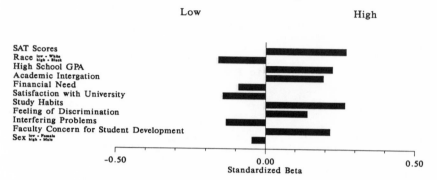

White Regional University

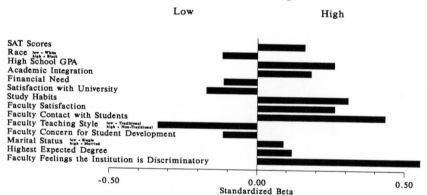

White Private University

their Black counterparts attending historically Black institutions.

Race is not a significant factor in predicting grades at historically Black institutions and does not explain why white students have higher grades than Black students at historically Black institutions. This issue is explored later in this chapter when racial comparisons are made on the significant predictor variables.

Three additional variables are significant predictors of college grade-point averages at more than one type of university but not at all. These variables include feelings of racial discrimination, interfering problems, and marital

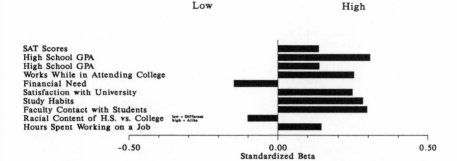

Black Private University

status.   Students attending white public research
universities and white regional universities, and who have
lower feelings of racial discrimination and fewer personal
and   family   problems,   achieve   higher   grades.   Married
students receive higher grades than single students at both
white private and Black public universities.
     Several   student   characteristics   are   significant
predictors of grade-point average at only one type of
university.   For example, at white research universities,
students with higher grades are likely to live on campus,
have relatively low social involvement, and are graduates of
private   high   schools.   At   Black   public   universities,
students who transfer in from other universities have higher
grade-point averages than students who entered as first-time
college freshmen.   At white regional universities, female
students have significantly higher grades than males.   And
at white private universities, students who aspire to attend
a graduate or professional school earn higher grade-point
averages   than   those   who   aspire   only   to   a   baccalaureate
degree.
     Faculty attitudinal and behavioral characteristics also
have varying effects upon college grade-point averages, but
none is significant at all five universities.   Chapter 2
illustrated   two   faculty   variables   that   are   significant
predictors of college grade-point averages overall.   A high
frequency of faculty contact with students and faculty with
traditional teaching styles contribute to college grade-
point averages overall.   These same two faculty factors are
also   positive   predictors   at   white   public   research
universities and white private universities but not at the
remaining three types of universities.   The three remaining
faculty factors are also positive contributors to grade-
point averages at white private universities.   In other
words,   students   at   white   private   universities   with
relatively high grade-point averages have a highly satisfied
faculty that is concerned about student development, that
has low feelings of racial discrimination, that has frequent
contact   with   students   outside   the   classroom,   and   has
nontraditional   teaching   styles.   In   contrast   to   white
private   universities,   the   faculty   factors   have   no

significant effects upon grade-point averages at Black public universities. At Black private universities, having faculty with a high level of contact with students contributes to students' grade-point averages. And at white regional public universities, having faculty that are concerned with student development contributes to students' grade-point averages.

These results indicate that some but not all strategies for increasing Black students' grade-point averages can be generalized across different types of universities. Efforts to improve Black students' college grade-point averages, regardless of types of university, should focus upon improving their precollege preparation (particularly high school performance), improving their relationships with faculty, improving their levels of satisfaction with their university, and improving their study habits. Otherwise, university officials should design different approaches depending upon the size of their institution, type of governance, and racial composition of their student bodies and faculty.

Progression Rates

Figure 3.3 illustrates the significant predictors of students' college progression rates at each of the five types of universities. A comparison of Figure 3.3 with

Figure 3.3

Significant Predictors of Students' College Progression Rates by Type of University

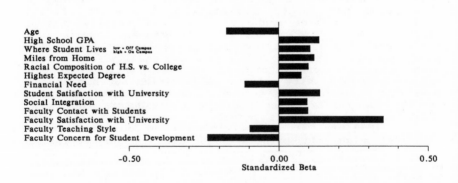

White Public Research University

Black Public University

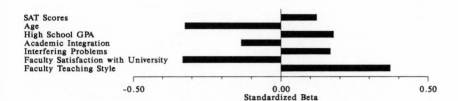

White Public Regional University

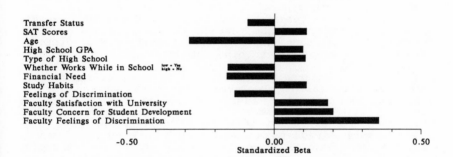

White Private University

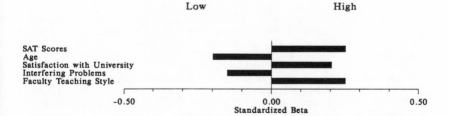

Figure 3.2 shows clearly that the determinants of progression rate are different from the determinants of grade-point average at each type of university. This is further evidence that grades and progression rates, while both are important, are two distinctly different dimensions

Black Private University

Low   High

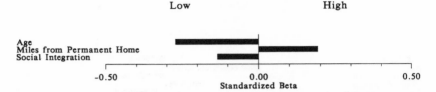

Age
Miles from Permanent Home
Social Integration

-0.50   0.00   0.50
                   Standardized Beta

of performance. The results also suggest that grade-point averages are a much more intellectual measure because the related variables are much more academic in nature.

The only variable that is a common predictor of progression rates across all five types of universities is age. Younger students are likely to have faster progression rates than older students at each type of university. This may be partially due to the fact that younger students are more likely to be full-time, traditional students who aim to complete the undergraduate curriculum in four years; whereas older, nontraditional students are likely to be more deliberate in their pursuit of a baccalaureate degree.

The public research universities where the overall progression rates are the fastest also produce the greatest number of predictors and strongest significant predictors. Figure 3.3 shows that nine student and four faculty characteristics are related to college progression rates at white public research universities. In order of importance, students with faster progression rates at public research universities: have a highly satisfied faculty, have a faculty with high concern for student development, are younger, are satisfied with their university, have high high-school grade-point averages, attend college a relatively great distance from home, have low financial need, live in on-campus housing rather than off campus, attend an institution with a similar racial composition as their high school, have frequent contact with faculty outside the classroom, have faculty with nontraditional teaching styles, have high social integration, and aspire toward pursuing a graduate or professional degree. It is somewhat surprising that at public research universities, progression rates are heavily dependent upon faculty attitudes and behaviors. It seems that if faculty are more concerned with rate of progress than depth and breadth of instruction, then progression is faster. Of course, at large public research universities faculty have a larger number of students to serve; and this finding suggests that, faculty at public research universities place greater emphasis on process and getting students through college in a timely manner rather than outcomes.

Figure 3.3 also illustrates that similar to those at white public research universities, faculty attitudes and behaviors exert a strong influence on progression rates at Black public universities but in a different way. At Black public universities, in contrast to white public research universities, students with faster progression rates have

relatively less satisfied faculty and have faculty with
traditional teaching styles. Neither the frequency of
contact with faculty nor faculty concern for student
development are significant predictors of progression rates
at Black public universities. Also, in contrast to white
public research universities, students at Black public
universities with faster progression rates have higher SAT
scores, are married, spend relatively little time working on
a job while in college, and have surprisingly low academic
integration and a large number of personal and family
problems that are normally believed to interfere with
schoolwork. Perhaps students at Black public universities
with greater problems have greater motivation to complete
college in a shorter time but not necessarily with higher
grades.

Figure 3.3 illustrates that many of the determinants of
progression rates at white regional universities are
different from the two types of universities presented
above. Like Black public universities, faster progression
rates at white regional public universities are associated
with high SAT scores and high high-school grade-point
averages. Also at public white regional universities,
students who progress faster have low financial need,
attended a public rather than private high school, work
while in college but work few hours, are transfer students
from another university, have better study habits, and,
surprisingly, have high feelings that the university is
racially discriminatory. In terms of faculty influence on
progression rates, faster progression rates at regional
universities are associated with high faculty satisfaction,
high faculty concern for student development, and high
feelings among the faculty that the university is racially
discriminatory. The effects of feelings of racial
discrimination among faculty and students at regional public
universities are especially important, because these are the
types of four-year universities that most Black students are
now attending and because faculty have the major role to
play in evaluating student performance.

At white private universities only one faculty
characteristic and four student characteristics exert
significant influence on student progression rates. Figure
3.3 illustrates that students with the fastest progression
rates at white private universities have faculty with
traditional teaching styles, have high SAT scores, are
highly satisfied with their university, are younger
students, and have relatively few interfering problems.

Figure 3.3 illustrates that only three student
characteristics and no faculty attitudes and behaviors are
associated with faster progression rates. Students who have
faster progression at Black private universities are
younger, attend college a greater distance from their
permanent home, and have relatively low social integration.

The variation among predictors of progression indicates
that strategies for improving Black students' progression
rates will differ across the types of universities. The
only academically related strategies for progression rates
appear to pertain to Black public and white public regional

universities, where precollege academic preparation (as measured by SAT scores and high school grade-point average) appears to improve students' progression rates. At the two types of white public universities, efforts to assure adequate financial aid and to achieve greater faculty satisfaction are important for timely student progression through college. Beyond these patterns, it appears that the same remedies to the slower progression rates of Black students should not be applied for all types of universities.

IMPLICATIONS OF THESE FINDINGS

The relational analyses demonstrate how the determinants of college grade-point averages and progression rates vary depending upon the type of university. However, some student academic background characteristics, attitudes, and behaviors in college have an impact upon student performance across all types of universities. These variables, significant at all universities, include students' precollege academic preparation as demonstrated by their high school grades and SAT scores and students' in-college attitudes and behaviors, as demonstrated by their academic integration, social integration, feelings of racial discrimination, and financial need. In order for Black students to compete with the higher college grade-point average and progression rates of white students, they need to have equally high precollege preparation and equally favorable in-college experiences while attending college.

Figure 3.4 illustrates the racial comparisons on two important pre-college determinants of college performance at the four types of universities where racial comparisons are made, and for Black students at Black private universities.

In terms of precollege preparation, Figure 3.4 indicates that while students report high school grades that are not racially different, they do report SAT scores that are racially different at each of the four types of universities where racial comparisons are possible. High school grades, on the one hand, are highly subjective and represent student performance in academic, general, and vocational curricula and at different types and quality of high schools. However, it appears from SAT scores, which are more objective indicators, coupled with the fact that a larger proportion of Black students are enrolled in nonacademic high school curricula, that their preparation for college is inferior to that of white students (Lee, 1985; Oakes, 1985). Efforts to improve Black students' college grade-point averages at each type of university should focus upon improving their precollege academic preparation. The racial inequality in student preparation for college may include many tangible factors beyond different high school curricula. Such factors as lower quality of instruction in elementary and high school; less family and community support and encouragement of academic preparation; failure to formulate positive behaviors and attitudes about education during preschool, elementary, and

Figure 3.4

Comparisons of Black and White Students' Precollege
Performance by Type of University

High School Grades

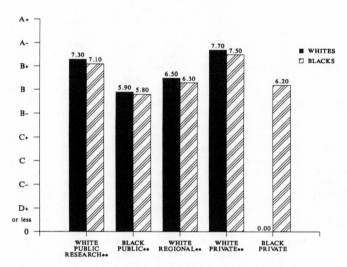

**Significant at .001 level

SAT Scores

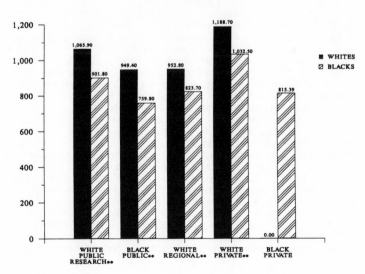

**Significant at .001 level

high school; and school-board finance policies that distribute financial and other resources inequitably are all probable contributors to the inferior academic preparation of Black students. What racial differences in the quality of instruction provided for elementary and high school students contribute to their intellectual development? What are the important racial differences in family and community support for intellectual development? What are the differences in the effectiveness of schools resulting from school finance policies that allow the allocation of fewer resources to economically poor school districts? Answers to these important policy questions are likely to provide much of the insight needed by policymakers and educators to eliminate the racial differences in precollege preparation.

The differential performance of Black and white students is apparent well before they enter college. These performance differences are exhibited by nine-, thirteen-, and seventeen-year olds on the National Assessment of Educational Progress (NAEP), by high school sophomores on the Preliminary Scholastic Aptitude Test (PSAT), and by high school seniors on the College Board's Scholastic Aptitude Test (SAT) and on the American College Testing Program's college entrance exam (ACT). Analyses of the parts of these examinations may also yield more insight into the specific intellectual skills among Blacks that are in need of greater development. Also, more focused analyses of the academic and personal background factors related to intellectual development may bring about policy change that will in turn lead to the elimination of academic performance differences. The background questionnaires administered in conjunction with these standardized tests provide a substantial data base for examining many of these important policy questions that heretofore have been unexploited for policy analyses. These background questionnaires provide such information as the type of curricula students study in high school; student performance in various types of high school courses; and family, educational, and socio-economic status.

In addition to the precollege experiences and academic preparation, the analyses presented in this chapter suggest that all types of universities are likely to contribute to the improvement of Black students' performance by improving their noncognitive experiences while attending college. Figure 3.5 illustrates that while in college, Black students have lower levels of satisfaction with their university and lower academic integration (which represents quality of relations with faculty); both are associated with lower performance. Figure 3.5 shows that Black students at predominantly white universities have relatively high feelings of discrimination and white students at historically Black institutions experience significantly high feelings of discrimination. In terms of financial need, Figure 3.5 shows that Black students at each of the five types of universities have higher financial need than their white counterparts; this, too, influences their performance in college. Efforts to address these difficulties in the college experiences of Black students as well as efforts to improve their study habits are likely to

Figure 3.5

Comparisons of Black and White Students' Behavioral
Characteristics in College by Type of University

Satisfaction With The University

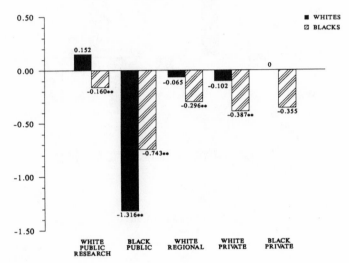

••Significant at .001 level

Academic Integration

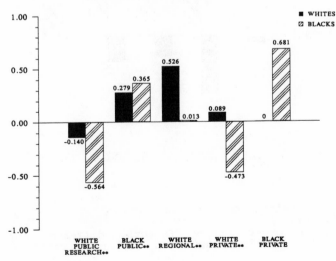

••Significant at .001 level

Feelings of Discrimination

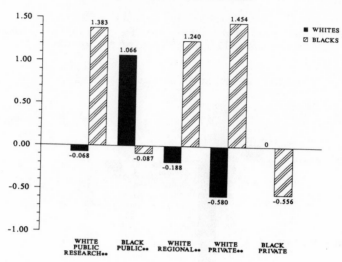

••Significant at .001 level

Financial Need

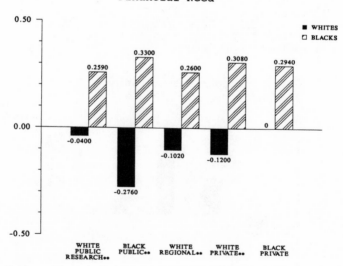

••Significant at .001 level

result in better college performance at all types of
universities.

Beyond these common factors, different types of
universities should focus upon different strategies for

increasing Black student performance. It was determined in
Chapter 2, and confirmed by data presented in this chapter,
that college grades and progression rates measure two
different dimensions of students' college performance.
Furthermore, the analyses presented in this chapter
illustrate that college performance varies by the type of
university attended. Therefore, in developing policies to
provide equality in student performance, educators must be
concerned with not only the type of performance but also the
type of university.   Universities of different size,
different academic programs and levels of degree offerings,
different racial composition, and different type of
governance can benefit from some common approaches but will
also require some unique and different approaches to achieve
equality of performance. The crisis, however, of lower
Black student performance at predominantly white
universities is especially important, because more and more
Black students are choosing to attend predominantly white
universities.   In Chapter 4, Walter Allen examines in
greater detail the performance and experiences of minorities
at predominantly white universities.

REFERENCES

Allen, W. (1986). Gender and campus race differences in
     Black student academic performance, racial attitudes,
     and college satisfaction. Atlanta, GA: Southern
     Education Foundation.

Arce, C. H. (1976). Historical, institutional, and
     contextual determinants of Black enrollment. Doctoral
     dissertation; University of Michigan.

Astin, A. W. (1977). Equal access to postsecondary
     education: Myth or reality? UCLA Educator, 19: 8-17.

Astin, A. W. (1982). Minorities in American higher
     education. San Francisco: Jossey-Bass.

Astin, A., Green, K., Korn, W., & Maier, M. J. (1985). The
     American freshman: National norms for fall 1985. Los
     Angeles: University of California at Los Angeles.

Bayer, A., & Boruch, R. (1969). Black and white freshmen
     entering four-year colleges. Educational Record, 50,
     371-86.

Blumenfeld, W. S. (1968). College preferences of able Negro
     students: A comparison of those naming predominantly
     Negro institutions and those naming predominantly white
     institutions. College and University, 43, 330-41.

Cross, P. H., & Astin, H. S. (1981). Factors affecting
     Black students' persistence in college. In G. E.
     Thomas (Ed.), Black students in higher education.
     Westport, CT: Greenwood Press.

Davis, J. A., & Borders-Patterson, A. (1973). Black students in predominantly white North Carolina colleges and universities (Research Report No. 2). New York: College Entrance Examination Board.

Gosman, E. J., Dandridge, B. A., Nettles, M. T., & Thoeny, R. A. (1983). Predicting student progression: The influence of race and other student and institutional characteristics on college student performance (Vol. 8, No. 2). New York, NY: Agathon Press, Inc.

Hartnett, R. (1970). Differences in selected attitudes and college orientation between Black students attending traditionally Negro and traditionally white institutions. Sociology of Education, 43, 419-36.

Hill, S. T. (1983). Participation of Black students in higher education: A statistical profile from 1970-71 to 1980-81. Washington, DC: U.S. Department of Education, Office for Education Research and Improvement.

Lee, V. (1985). Explaining the relationship between social class and academic achievement in public and Catholic schools. Ph.D. dissertation, Harvard University.

Lenning, O. T., Beal, P. E., & Sauer, K. (1980). Retention and attrition: Evidence for action and research. Boulder, CO: National Center for Higher Education Management Systems (NCHEMS).

Mingle, J. R. (1981). The opening of white colleges and universities to Black students. In G. Thomas, (Ed.), Black students in higher education. Westport, CT: Greenwood Press.

Nettles, M. T., Gosman, E. J., Thoeny, A. R., & Dandridge, B. A. (1985). The causes and consequences of college students' performance: A focus on Black and white students' attrition rates, progression rates and grade-point averages. A report of the Tennessee Higher Education Commission, Nashville.

Oakes, J. (1985). Keeping track: How schools structure inequality. New Haven and London: Yale University Press.

Thomas, G. E., & McPartland, J. (1984). Have college desegregation policies threatened Black student enrollment and Black colleges? Journal of Negro Education, 53(4), 389-99.

United States Department of Education, Center for Statistics. (1984). Fall enrollment report. Unpublished tabulations.

4

The Education of Black Students on White College Campuses: What Quality the Experience?

WALTER R. ALLEN

On Monday May 17, 1954, the U.S. supreme court handed down its landmark decision outlawing the doctrine of "separate but equal" in public education. The court instructed the nation to institute the desegregation of public schools "with all deliberate speed." This court order was the beginning of the transition that was intended to lead eventually to racial equality in our society. Blacks were to attend school alongside whites. Presumably they were also to experience a rapid transition to full citizenship in American society. Black Americans would achieve equality of opportunity after centuries of discrimination.

However, the stubborn persistence of racial inequality in the United States has surprised people, both lay and professional alike. Surely once the laws of the land were changed and the exclusionary procedures of key institutions altered, the blight of racial discrimination and its consequence, racial inequality, would also be eliminated. This has not proven to be the case. Despite a radical shift in their social status, Black Americans are at an extreme disadvantage in political power when compared to whites. At best, Blacks have made minimal progress in narrowing the gap between themselves and white Americans (Reid, 1982; Allen & Farley, 1986).

Nowhere is this puzzle of persistent Black inequality and limited opportunity in American society more apparent than in the field of education. Education has long been viewed as the great leveler in American society. It has been lauded as one of the few arenas where competition on the basis of merit and achievement takes precedence over personal background factors. Supposedly what matters is whether a person is intelligent, hardworking, and a high achiever - not his or her race, sex, or social class background (Davis & Moore, 1945).

The record of the U.S. educational system since 1954 and its tendency to reinforce existing racial, class, and gender inequalities has caused many to challenge the meritocratic view of education. For example, Bowles and Gintis (1976) evaluate educational systems as relatively impermeable; over the course of the education experience initial advantages of class, race, and sex are merely reinforced. There are exceptions to this pattern wherein educational achievement facilitates phenomenal upward social mobility. However, schools are frequently seen as channels for individuals to achieve previously reserved niches in the social hierarchy consistent with their origins. Thus, the sons of coal miners generally become coal miners; the daughters of college professors generally complete college; and the children of the chronically unemployed generally find it difficult to attain employment.

To the extent that U.S. institutions of higher education reinforce the status quo and insure the persistence of inequities by sex, race, and income, it can be argued that these institutions discriminate against minorities. Individuals who are not male, white, and middle-class receive fewer returns from the nation's colleges and universities. They are disadvantaged educationally in both quantitative terms (for example, average years of schooling completed, economic returns on schooling completed) and in qualitative terms (such as, satisfaction with the schooling experience, overall excellence of the education received) (Abramowitz, 1976; Blackwell, 1981; Astin, 1982).

This chapter is concerned with qualitative inequalities faced by Black Americans attending white universities. The two questions to be addressed in this chapter are: (1) What is the general quality of the educational experience of Black undergraduates who attend predominantly white state universities? and (2) How do these students fare in their social and academic relations on their campuses? The analyses in this chapter are designed to compare Black student attrition rates and equity of access with those of American Indian, Asian, Hispanic, and white students at the same universities. The salient question is this: How do Black students compare with students of other racial groups in terms of access to various fields of study, academic performance levels, and graduation rates? The answer to this question should reveal insights into the quality of education received by Black undergraduates who attend white universities.

WHAT ARE THE PROBLEMS FACING BLACK STUDENTS AT WHITE UNIVERSITIES?

When qualitative indicators of Black higher education are examined, race disadvantages revealed by quantitative indicators persist. As illustrated in Chapters 2 and 3, when compared to whites, Black college students consistently report a lower quality of college experience. This pattern is revealed by their social relationships on the campus, by their interaction with faculty and staff, by their psychological well-being, and by their academic achievements (Webster, Sedlacek & Miyares, 1979; Willie & McCord, 1972; Nettles et al., 1985). Social relationships are an integral part of the college experience; thus social involvement on the campus should serve to enhance and reinforce values and

behaviors learned in the classroom (Tinto, 1975).
     For many Black students attending white universities,
however, campus social relationships are anything but
positive. These students feel the heavy burden of racial
discrimination (sometimes subtle, but frequently not) and
face daily attempts to denigrate their personalities and
culture (Miller, 1981; Fleming, 1984; DiCesare, Sedlacek &
Brooks, 1972). Since they are often not privy to - or are
alienated from - established social networks on their
campus, these students find it necessary to spend valuable
time in the construction of Black social support systems
(Smith, 1980; Pitts, 1975). In many instances, universities
are either ignorant of and/or unresponsive to the special
needs of Black students, further complicating their
adjustment to college (Fleming, 1984; Gibbs, 1973; Peterson
et al., 1978).
     The exclusion of Black students from campus social
networks, in conjunction with unsatisfactory interpersonal
relationships, causes Black students to experience many
psychosocial difficulties and feelings of alienation;
consequently withdrawal behavior is frequent (Allen, 1986;
Fleming, 1984; Gibbs, 1974). Moreover, it is inevitable
that in the context of such structures some Black students
will begin to question or doubt themselves; their self-
concepts suffer while their aspirations and feelings of
competence decline (Fleming, 1984; Willie & McCord, 1972;
Webster, Sedlacek & Miyares, 1979). In many instances,
psychosocial, rather than academic problems, provide the
most powerful explanation of low performance and high
attrition among Black students on white campuses (Allen,
1986; Thomas, 1981).
     Two themes warrant attention with respect to this
examination of qualitative factors in the Black student's
postsecondary educational experience. The first theme
concerns the extent to which Black students on white
campuses, in general, are able to maintain positive
interpersonal relationships and to achieve satisfactory
integration with campus social networks. The second theme
focuses on the academic achievement records of Black
students in comparison to other ethnic groups on a single
campus. Together these themes define the problems for
research in this chapter. On the one hand, an overview of
Black student social adjustments is presented on
predominantly white campuses. On the other hand, a
description of modal patterns of academic achievement among
several cohorts of Black students is presented. Tinto
(1975) and Fleming (1984) argue, and this author agrees,
that students perform best academically when they are able
to maintain more positive social relationships on their
campus.

RESEARCH METHODS

     This chapter reports findings from the National Study
of Black College Students, which involves 700 Black
undergraduates attending six large, predominantly white,

state-supported universities. The study's major objective is to examine qualitative aspects of these students' educational experiences. Data were collected about the students' academic performance, relations with peers and faculty, satisfaction with the college experience, race relations on the campus, and occupational/educational aspirations. The analyses presented in this chapter begin with a general overview of findings from the total sample of students. At this stage the concern is with summarizing the general educational experiences and outcomes of Black students on white campuses. The focus then shifts to examining specific patterns on a single campus. The quality of educational experience for Black students is then compared to the expression of Asian, American Indian, Hispanic, and white students on the same campuses. The primary focus is on students' attrition rates, graduation rates, and progress toward their degrees. The chapter concludes with a discussion of the study's implications and with recommendations for the improvement of the quality of Black students' educational experiences in postsecondary institutions.

Two data sets are used in this study, one national and the other local. The national data are part of a project which examines Black undergraduate student characteristics, educational experiences, and achievement outcomes on six predominantly white state university campuses. The campuses were selected for their regional representation, for their academic reputation, and to provide historical variety. Since 60 percent of Black B.A. degree recipients are from state-supported institutions (Deskin, 1983) and 80 percent of Black students enrolled in higher education in 1982 attended state-supported institutions (National Center for Education Statistics, 1983), this study is restricted to state-supported universities. Among the states represented in this study are California, Arizona, Tennessee, Michigan, North Carolina, and New York. These data were collected during the winter of 1981 using a mailed questionnaire, to which 695 eligible students responded.

The local data set is drawn from the institutional records of students matriculating between the years 1975 and 1981 at one of the universities participating in the national study (referred to by the pseudonym Umtali State University). Since 1975 the registrar's office at Umtali State University has compiled (and updated annually through students' departures from the institution) information on entering freshmen classes. Among the items of information included in this data set are student demographic characteristics, grades, academic progress, entrance examination scores, and field of study. The data analyses included 30,806 students of which 12,066 were currently enrolled in the university. For currently enrolled students, the academic records analyzed are the students' transcript files through the fall of 1982. For the remaining 18,740 students who were no longer enrolled, the academic records analyzed include data and information up to the students' final terms of enrollment. In 60 percent of these cases, (11,163) the final term of enrollment corresponds to term of graduation.   For other students no longer enrolled (7,577), this final term represents the term when their Umtali State careers ended for reasons other than graduation (for example, dropout, transfer).

The analyses of both data sets are descriptive. Important patterns are reported in terms of percentages and proportions.   Subgroup comparisons are heavily emphasized in analyzing the Umtali State University data.   These analyses are not intended to test specific research hypotheses, but rather to provide a detailed description of the Black undergraduate educational experience (in the general as well as the specific case).   Previous research findings raise expectations that Black students experience a diminished quality of education at the postsecondary level, relative to universally desired standards and the experiences of their white peers.   Thus, this study endeavors to probe the characteristics and components of Black student disadvantages in higher education, as revealed by many qualitative indicators.

FINDINGS: THE NATIONAL STUDY

The majority of responding students perform reasonably well academically.   Figure 4.1 illustrates that Black students' college GPAS are generally far below their college GPA.   Only 6 percent report college grade point averages (GPA) of less than C (2.0), with approximately 64 percent reporting college GPAS above C+ (2.5).   However, fewer than 4 percent report college GPAS above B+ (3.5), a significant shift from the 49 percent that reported B+ averages in high school.   Black students in this study entered college with established records of high academic achievement, 80 percent report high school grade point averages above B (Figure 4.1).   Of all students, 49 percent report high school grade averages of B+ (3.5) or better.   Over half the students ranked in the top 10 percent of their graduating class, with about one-fourth ranking in the top 5 percent.   The educational aspirations of Black students in this study are high as expected.   Of these students, one-third set their ultimate educational goal at the bachelor's degree level. Another third aspire to master's level degrees, while the remaining third seek professional degrees (M.D., J.D., or D.D.S.) or doctoral degrees.   While educational goals that students expressed are evenly distributed, occupational aspirations are uniformly high.   Nearly 85 percent of the students expect to move into upper-level white-collar positions after college.

The backgrounds of Black college students in this national sample are contrary to popular stereotypes of Black college students.   Sixty- five percent of the students sampled grew up in two-parent households.   Only 15 percent are from families with annual incomes of $8,000 or less. Nearly half are from families with incomes exceeding $21,000 per year.   The pursuit of education appears to be encouraged and practiced in these students' families; 16 percent of the respondents' fathers, 19 percent of their mothers, and 28

Figure 4.1

Black Students' High School GPAs Are Generally Higher than
Their College GPAs

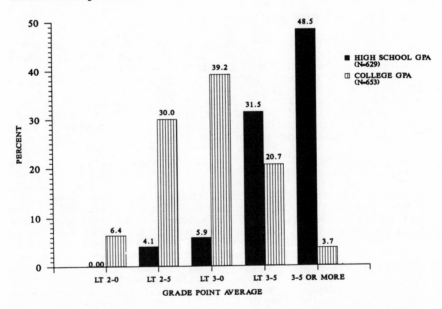

percent of their siblings hold B.A. degrees. Nine percent
of fathers, 11 percent of mothers, and 11 percent of
siblings hold advanced degrees.

The high school experiences of Black students did not
prepare them for the reality of being a racial minority in
college. Fewer than 20 percent attended high schools where
Black enrollment was 10 percent or less. To the contrary,
one-third of these students attended Black-majority high
schools (over 60 percent Black) prior to entering college.
Nevertheless, with the exception of one of the campuses
involved in this study, Black students represent less than
10 percent of the total student enrollment.

Upon entering college, these Black students are forced
to cope with the unfamiliar racial situation of being in the
minority rather than in the majority as in high school.
Considerable social adjustments result from this transition,
with apparent negative consequences for Black students.
Overall, Black students' adjustments to their universities
appear to have been awkward and generally unsatisfying.
Figure 4.2 shows how Black students rate their involvement
in campus life. Nearly 62 percent report little or no
integration into general student activities on campus. In
addition 45 percent report that extracurricular activities
on campus do not adequately reflect their interests.

Among the difficulties Black students experience in
white universities is the low number of Black students on
campus. Seventy- nine percent of the students believe that
there are inadequate numbers of Black students at their
universities. Half of the students point to limited
financial resources and inadequate high school preparation
as the most serious barriers to Black student admission and
attendance at their universities. The following comments
represent the students' views on these points: "Black
students here and at all colleges will be seriously affected
by budget cuts that result in less financial aid, and
admissions requirements that rely solely upon GPA and SAT
scores;" "No interviews or subjective criteria are examined
in the undergraduate admissions process;" "Most Black
students don't have $200 for a SAT prep course which would
improve their chances of being admitted into a selective
university."

When seeking Black faculty and/or staff aid in easing
adjustment problems, these students encounter additional
problems. Black student contact with Black faculty and
staff was found to be very limited. Sixty-seven percent of
the students report that they have little or no exposure to
Black faculty and staff at their universities. Most
students express the need for a greater number of Black
faculty and staff in order to improve their own college
experiences: "There are not enough Black faculty and staff,
especially outside of the strictly minority departments;" "I
have had only one Black professor. I think that there
should be more. I see more Black cleaning people than Black
professors and staff members;" and "I have never met a Black
faculty member, and so far I have only seen a couple of them
on campus. I had never even thought of this seriously
before and now that I have, I feel angry."

Figure 4.2

Black Students' Ratings of Their Campus Life and Extracurricular Activities

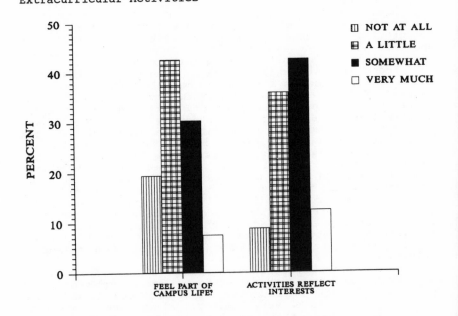

Of necessity Black students rely on white students and professors for help in making their adjustments to campus life.   Figure 4.3 illustrates the uneasiness among Black students regarding their peer relations with white students. Only a third report that white peers regularly showed high regard and appreciation of for their academic abilities. Forty-one percent report that white students often or always avoid social interactions with them outside the classroom. Just under a third (31 percent) report that white students regularly treat them as equals.

In the area of race relations, Black students reveal tensions; 60 percent report having experienced at least one incident of racial discrimination.   Of this group, 60 percent cite racial insults and negative racial attitudes as the most common forms of discrimination encountered.   The following accounts summarize the range of incidents reported: "An academic advisor told me I shouldn't take a certain class because it was extremely difficult and Blacks can't handle difficult classes;" "I was walking out of my professor's office and another professor in the office said that Black people really do look like monkeys, no wonder no one can really like them;" and, "There was a dummy in the form of a Black man dressed in white sheet with a string around its neck suspended from a lamp post in front of my dorm."

Figure 4.4 illustrates that a large number of Black students characterize the general state of Black student relations with white faculty (38 percent), white staff (34 percent), and white students (37 percent) on their campuses as being negative.   However, when questioned about their personal relationships, over three quarters report good to excellent individual relationships with white faculty (82 percent), white staff (80 percent), and white students (88 percent).   Thus, although students tended to claim positive individual relationships with whites on the campus, they rate intergroup race relations as generally poor on the campus.

Figure 4.5 shows that the majority of students (76 percent) report their white professors to show some difficulty in relating to them.   They also indicate that professors commonly avoid interaction with them outside the classroom (57 percent).   Nevertheless, a significant proportion of students report professors as encouraging them to pursue advanced studies (75 percent) and as demonstrating concern about their academic success (79 percent).   Still, over half of the students express strong doubts about their professors' fairness in evaluating Black student academic performance (52 percent).

The Black students report three common sorts of difficulties they face at white universities: academic problems (21 percent), problems of cultural adjustment or feelings of social isolation (28 percent), and problems with racism (18 percent).   In general, Black students are required to cope with a plethora of problems.   One student aptly states in summary that the major difficulties include: "discrimination by white students, the lack of sufficient finances, isolation because of the small number of Black

Figure 4.3

Black Interaction with White Peers

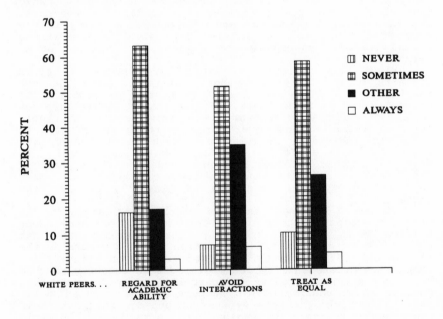

Figure 4.4

Black Students Perceive Their Personal Relationships with
Whites to be Generally Better than Overall Relationships

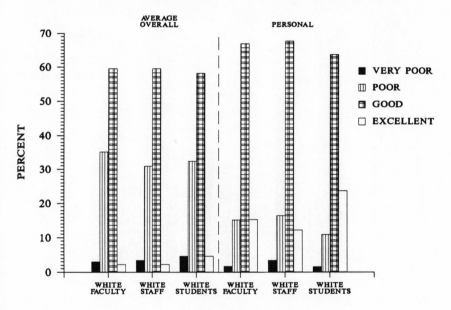

Figure 4.5

Black Students' Relationships with White Professors

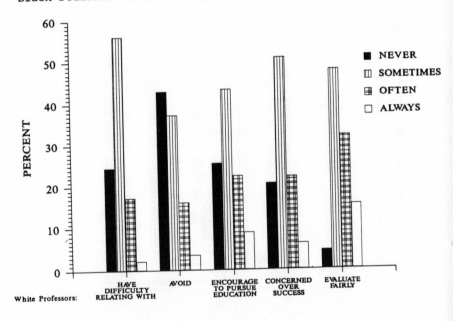

students, the grading, and work distribution - many Blacks come from lower quality high schools and are not prepared for the big advance in academic skills required in college."

With respect to the problem of financing their educations, most students identify parental earnings (41 percent) and grants or federal loans (30 percent) as their major sources of funding. Twenty-one percent of the students are not presently receiving financial aid. Of those who receive aid, over half (56 percent) consider their financial aid packages to be adequate. The remainder indicate that locating adequate financial assistance is a perennial problem. A higher proportion (52 percent) appear to be satisfied with the calibre of academic advising received, although a sizable 48 percent express dissatisfaction. A majority (57 percent) of the students consider campus remedial, tutorial, and academic services to be less than satisfactory. Black students rarely turn to university officials or personnel for help with problems (4 percent), preferring to rely on themselves (39 percent), friends (19 percent), and family (15 percent) in resolving crises.

Nearly all of the students know of other Black students who have left their university for various reasons prior to graduation. Among the reasons cited, the majority report either financial difficulties (24 percent) or academic problems (46 percent). Among the specific reasons cited are: "personal family problems, lack of motivation, lack of money to continue, didn't have the GPA to continue," and "unhappy with the atmosphere here, the pressures, the impersonal system."

Despite the rather difficult experiences of faculty and relations, Black students appear to maintain rather positive attitudes and their personal development appears unhampered. Figure 4.6 shows that Black students in this study exhibit higher than average self-concepts. They also exhibit above average attitudes about their leadership ability, self-confidence, popularity, physical well being, community perception of students, closeness with family, high school teachers' evaluations, popularity with opposite sex, and professors' evaluations. On all characteristics, except attraction to the opposite sex, well over half of the students rate themselves as above average or higher. This finding is not surprising, since the academically best prepared Black students attend white universities.

The patterns that emerge from these data are interesting and revealing. Black students on these predominantly white, state-supported university campuses enter college with strong high school records and positive family backgrounds. By all accepted standards they seem to be earmarked for success. Yet they report college grade point averages that are well below their high school grade point averages. Moreover, the students express general dissatisfaction with Black-white relations on their campuses. They are also on the periphery of campus social life and have firsthand experience with sizable numbers of their Black peers leaving school before graduation. These patterns describe the general situation for Black students

Figure 4.6

Description of Black Students' Evaluation with Regard to...

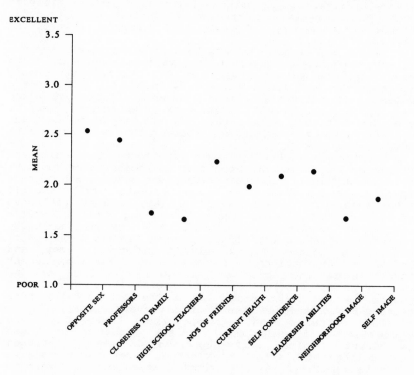

in this sample of white campuses. The focus now shifts to
the case description of one specific campus.   This
examination of Black student experiences on a single campus
will give special attention to rates of attrition, rate of
progress toward degree, and academic performance levels.
The performance of Black students will then be compared to
those of students of other racial groups on the same campus.

FINDINGS: THE CASE OF UMTALI STATE UNIVERSITY

     Whereas the national study is broad in scope, the
Umtali State University study is narrowly focused. At step
one, the population distribution across categories of the
key variables is examined (these variables include, race,
grades, enrollment status).   Second, two-way comparisons
across enrollment status and student characteristics are
illustrated (for example, race, sex, test scores).   Third,
the data are disaggregated in order to compare three groups:
dropouts, graduates, and currently enrolled students.
Finally, the experiences of a cohort of students six years
after their enrollment in the university as freshmen are
analyzed. The proportions of graduates and the proportions
of those who dropped out are then compared across
race/ethnic groups.
     Results from descriptive analyses of these data are
generally illustrative of characteristics of students who
attend this university. Results from this study may be
cautiously interpreted generalized to the category of
predominantly white, large, midwestern, prestigious, state-
supported universities.   As Figure 4.7 indicates, one-
quarter of the students enrolled as freshmen in 1975 left
school without their degrees (7,577) after six years (1975-
1981). Another 36 percent of freshman who entered school in
1975 successfully completed degree requirements (11,163).
The remaining 39 percent were currently enrolled (12,066) as
of fall 1981.   The overwhelming majority of students were
white, with 1,738 Black (5.7 percent), 116 American Indian
(.4 percent), 860 Asian (2.8 percent), and 358 Hispanic (1.2
percent).   Males were slightly more numerous than females
(55 versus 45 percent).
     Predictably, bivariate analyses showed that students
with better grades in high school, better grades in college,
and better Scholastic Aptitude Test (SAT) scores were more
likely to graduate.   The mean comparisons of the graduates
versus dropouts indicate high school grades of 3.56 for
graduates compared to 3.32 for dropouts'; college grades of
3.68 for graduates compared to 2.37 for dropouts; and 856
versus 839 combined verbal and quantitative SAT scores of
3.56 compared to 3.39.   No significant sex differences were
found in retention rates (that is, among students currently
enrolled, dropped out and graduated) despite women's higher
grades in high school (3.55 versus 3.39) and college (3.22
versus 3.12).   Males have higher combined SAT mean scores
owing to their tremendous advantage on the quantitative
section (598 versus 537).   (In interpreting the SAT scores
reported above, it should be kept in mind that scores are

Figure 4.7

Umtali State University Black Student Enrollment Status

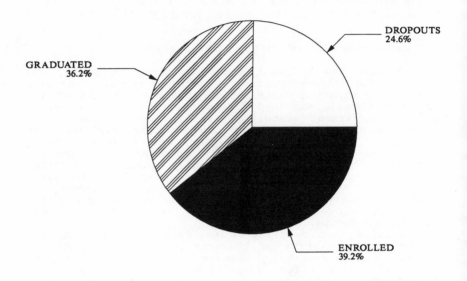

coded into ten categories and range from less than 350 to
greater than 750 by raw score. Categories are separated by
50 points, thus a score of 2 = 351 - 399, 3 = 400 - 449, 4 =
450 - 474 and so on. Mean SAT scores are reported,
therefore, in terms of categorical averages.)

Comparisons of race/ethnic groups in the total data set
revealed important differences. Asian and white student
dropout rates (21 and 23 percent) were much lower than those
of American Indians, Blacks, and Hispanics (38, 38, and 39
percent respectively). For whites this advantage translates
into a higher percentage graduating (37%), as compared with
American Indians (20%), Blacks (30%), Hispanics (30%), and
Asians (28%). The percentage of Asian graduates is somewhat
distorted, since, due to their relatively recent entry into
the university, over half the Asian students were currently
enrolled as compared to less than 40 percent of the other
groups. The proportion of Asians who graduate can be
expected to eventually equal or exceed that of whites.

Comparisons of high school grades, SAT scores, and
grades in college presage some findings from above. Asians
and whites had the highest mean high school grades (3.61 and

3.5), followed by Hispanics (3.18), American Indians (3.16), and Blacks (2.91). Mean Verbal SAT scores were highest for whites (514), followed by Asians (498), American Indians (465), Hispanics (459), and Blacks (419). Mean quantitative SAT scores were highest for Asians (578), followed by whites (550), American Indians (513), Hispanics (506), and Blacks (447). College grade differences were even more significant: mean grades were highest for whites and Asians (3.24 and 3.22), followed by American Indians, Hispanics, and Blacks (2.75, 2.65 and 2.24 respectively).

Students' final programs of enrollment also revealed clear differences by race and ethnicity. Comparing students' major field distributions and their proportional representation in the student body revealed that although Black students represented only 5.7 percent of the total enrollment, they made up 14 percent of education majors, 20 percent of majors in the arts and sciences, 7 percent of nursing majors, and 10 percent of pharmacy majors. Black students were proportionally underrepresented in engineering (3.7 percent), medicine (4.9 percent), architecture (4.3 percent), business administration (4.7 percent), and art (2.1 percent). Asian students who comprised 2.8 percent of student enrollment, were overrepresented in medicine (12.4 percent), architecture (5 percent), and pharmacy (4.5 percent). Asian students were underrepresented in business administration (1.9 percent), education (.6 percent), nursing (.9 percent), and art (1.7 percent). On the other hand, white students were overrepresented, relative to their 90 percent of total enrollment, in art (95 percent), dental hygiene (98 percent), and resource management (96 percent). At Umtali State University several programs continued to be characterized by gender bias. Females greatly outnumbered males, relative to their 45 percent of total enrollment, in art (73 percent), dental hygiene (100 percent), education (60 percent), and nursing (98 percent). At the other extreme, males (as 55 percent of the total) were significantly overrepresented in architecture (71 percent), business (59 percent), engineering (82 percent), medicine (61 percent), and resource management (59 percent). The ultimate examples of stereotyped programs are provided by nursing, which is 91 percent white female, and by dental hygiene, which is 97 percent white female.

Internal comparisons between students who dropped out, those who graduated, and those currently enrolled clarified many findings reported above. Black students were disproportionate among students who leave school for reasons other than graduation. More important, however, is the fact that Black students were twice as likely to drop out (15 percent) for academic reasons than are white (25 percent) and Asian (26 percent) students (Figure 4.8). The magnitude of male academic dropouts relative to female academic dropouts was comparable (35 percent versus 19 percent). High school grade point average, SAT scores, and college grade point average all significantly differentiated students who dropped for academic reasons from those who dropped for other reasons. The differences between academic dropouts and general dropouts follow: high school grade

Figure 4.8

Umtali State University No Longer Enrolled Status

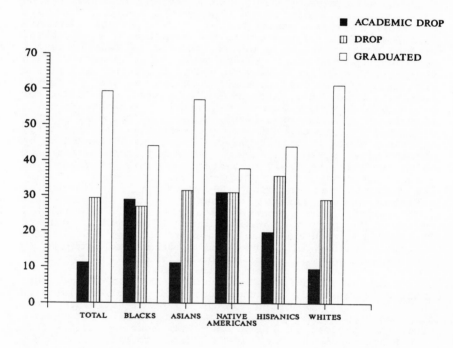

point average (3.11 versus 3.39); mean combined SAT scores
(an average between 1,000 and 1,099, combined verbal and
math scores), and cumulative college grades (1.27 versus
2.79). This pattern suggests that of these two groups, the
non academic dropout category contains the better students.
Analysis of the group of students no longer enrolled (Figure
4.8) reveals that Black, Native American, and Hispanic
students were considerably less likely than Asian and white
students to complete their programs of study successfully
(respective percentages for completion are 44, 38, 57, and
61 percent).

Graduating students are divided into categories of
those who finish: (1) early, (2) on time, (3) the summer
after scheduled graduation, and (4) later than the summer
after. Further information is provided on important
race/ethnic differences. Twenty-nine percent of Black and
Hispanic students graduated late (during the fifth year of
enrollment) as compared to 20 percent of Asians and whites.
There were also pronounced sex differences: 24 percent of
males graduate late as compared with 16 percent of females.
Rates of on-time graduation are: Asians (54 percent),
American Indians (67 percent), Blacks (57 percent),
Hispanics (53 percent), whites (65 percent), males (60
percent), and females (68 percent). As expected, rates of
on-time graduation increased in direct proportion to
increases in high school grades, rank in high school
graduating class, SAT scores, and college grades.

Within race and ethnic categories, Black females were
more likely than Black males to graduate on time (67 versus
33 percent). However no substantial sex differences were
found for the other racial/ethnic groups. Combined SAT
scores effectively differentiated early from on-time
graduates across groups. Mean combined SAT scores for
early, on-time, and late graduates by race provide a basis
for comparison: Blacks 920, 860, 860; Asians 1,197, 1,120,
1,010; American Indians 1,230, 970, 800; Hispanics 1,120,
940, 960; and whites 1,170, 1,090, 1,080.

Figure 4.9 illustrates the comparisons within the group
of currently enrolled students. Of special concern is
student degree progress. Are students ahead of schedule,
making normal progress, or behind schedule, as measured by
credit hours earned per term of enrollment? Consistent with
patterns above, Black students were overrepresented in the
category of students behind schedule, that is, students who
had fewer cumulative credit hours than the norm for their
year in school. Fewer than half the Black students (44
percent) were on schedule as compared with 75 percent of
whites, 73 percent of Asians, 65 percent of Hispanics, and
51 percent of American Indians. A slightly higher
proportion of females than males were on schedule (77 versus
70 percent). Students making normal degree progress were
clearly differentiated from those behind schedule in terms
of high school grade point average (3.56 versus 3.31),
combined SAT score (1089 versus 1050) and college grades
(3.45 versus 2.4). Comparisons across race/ethnic groups
revealed clear differences between on-schedule and late
students. The respective mean combined SAT scores were:

Figure 4.9

Umtali State University Currently Enrolled Degree Progress

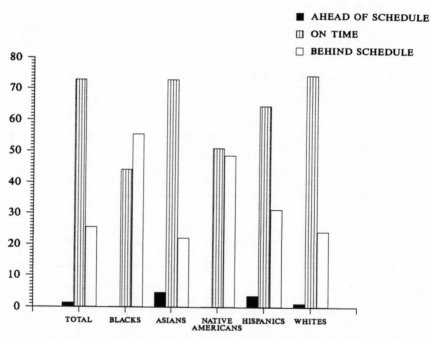

- ■ AHEAD OF SCHEDULE
- ⊞ ON TIME
- ☐ BEHIND SCHEDULE

Blacks (899 versus 873), Asians (1,110 versus 1,050), American Indians (1,000 versus 960), Hispanics (1,000 versus 920) and whites (1,095 versus 1,073). In a now familiar pattern, Black students' combined SAT scores, in the 800 range, were the lowest of the five race/ethnic groups while Asian scores, in the 400 range, were the highest.

A longitudinal analysis of the academic careers of the 18,740 dropouts was conducted. Over 50 percent of Asians and whites stayed in college through graduation and less than 50 percent of Blacks, American Indians, and Hispanics persist in college through completion. Compared to the total population, Black students were nearly three times as likely to leave college for academic reasons (29 versus 11 percent). The proportion of dropouts for academic reasons among Hispanics and American Indians was roughly twice the proportion in the total student population.

Tracing student careers in a more detailed fashion is even more revealing. For example, by the end of the first year of enrollment a staggering 35 percent of all academic dropouts among Black students had occurred. Of those who dropped out for nonacademic reasons, 27 percent left school by the end of year one. During the second year the respective percentages for Black student dropouts were 35 and 26 percent. In short, by the end of the sophomore year, 70 percent (238) of academic dropouts and 53 percent (168) of nonacademic dropouts had occurred among Black students. Equally striking in the opposite direction was the 26 percent of Black students who eventually graduated but in their fifth or subsequent years of enrollment.

Hispanic students had patterns of academic progress similar to those for Black students. Seventy-eight percent of Hispanic academic dropouts and 68 percent of nonacademic dropouts occurred by the end of the sophomore year. Of the students who graduated, 26 percent did so one year or more beyond four years. Asian and white student longitudinal academic patterns were comparable. The attrition rates after two years for academic versus nonacademic reasons are as follows: Asians (53 versus 68 percent), whites (66 versus 68 percent). In the final stages of their academic careers, 19 percent of whites and 20 percent of Asians graduated after four years of enrollment.

THE MISEDUCATION OF BLACK STUDENTS IN U.S. HIGHER EDUCATION

The extensive evidence cited and presented in this chapter raises the spectre of Black miseducation (Woodson, 1969) in U.S. higher education. Black students enter college with educational disadvantages carried over from earlier years of schooling, their grades and test scores are lower, and their occupational goals are more limited than those of white students. After college entry, Black students experience higher rates of discontinuance, lower levels of academic performance, greater underrepresentation in the more prestigious programs/institutions, and lower likelihood to pursue postgraduate studies. In addition, Black students report greater social and psychological

distress and less satisfaction with college compared to
their white peers. The profile that emerges is one which
suggests a consistent Black student disadvantage on the
nation's college campuses. When discussing the question of
Black miseducation on white university campuses, it is
important to avoid reductionist thinking. For example, it
would be absurd not to acknowledge the sizable numbers of
Black students who emerge from predominantly white colleges
and universities having had very positive experiences and
receiving high quality education. Many enter these schools
with excellent academic credentials and excel while
enrolled, going on to achieve distinction in their chosen
professions. It would also be absurd to dismiss the
historical dimension. As a process Black miseducation in
this society begins in the early years of school, resulting
in a cumulative effect that is revealed in college. Black
students are denied equal access to well-equipped schools
and highly talented, motivated teachers throughout their
elementary and high school experiences. More damaging than
these educational deficits are the spiritual deficits, which
deprive Black students of self-confidence, motivation, and
an understanding of education's transformational power.
Subtle, and not so subtle, beliefs and actions in the
schools and in the society at large encourage views of Black
Americans as ultimately uneducable. Finally one must avoid
viewing Black college students as mere reactors; in fact
they have the power - within institutionally determined
limits - to shape their own destinies. On every campus,
therefore, one will find Black students who perform well
academically despite interpersonal and institutional
barriers. In such cases their success is due to talent,
sheer persistence, and unwavering self-confidence.
     The data presented in this chapter provide a portrait
of the Black disadvantage in U.S. higher education. Black
students in the national study spoke poignantly about their
status as excluded individuals - socially, culturally, and
academically outside the mainstream of routine swirl of
campus life. They noted problems of social adjustment,
cultural alienation, racial discrimination, and strained
interpersonal relations for Black students on white
campuses. Of particular interest are the students'
reportedly awkward relationships with faculty members. Many
feel that their professors are uncomfortable in the presence
of Black students and that they tend to avoid interactions
with Black students outside the classroom. Despite these
problems Black students exhibit high self-concepts and high
attainment aspirations.
     The case study of Umtali State University elaborates on
themes from the national study. The national study compares
Black student experiences on different campuses across the
nation and uncovers patterns of experiences. The individual
college study compares Black student educational experiences
to those of students of other races on the same campus. On
average, Black students lag behind their Asian, American
Indian, Hispanic, and white peers in terms of high school
grades, SAT scores, and college grades. Black students also
drop out at one and a half times the rate for Asians and

whites. In terms of profiles, the students separate neatly
into high achievers (Asians, whites) and low achievers
(Blacks, Indians, Hispanics). As might be expected,
students in the low achieving group - where still enrolled-
are less likely to complete their program of study, to
graduate on time, and to make normal progress toward their
degrees. Relative to their proportion of total enrollment,
Black students are underrepresented in nontraditional fields
such as the sciences or engineering. (This is examined in
greater detail in Chapter 6.)
     This chapter reveals aspects of the diminished quality
of education received by Black students in U.S. higher
education. In order to understand disadvantages and to
identify causes and consequences, it is vital to observe the
broader context of this society. In many respects the
nation's colleges and universities merely inherit a
cumulative tradition. Many Black students who enter college
are products of urban school systems have failed miserably
in their responsibilities to educate them properly. Due to
financial problems, ineffective teaching, and lack of
motivation, these schools consistently graduate students who
are ill equipped to master the challenges of U.S. higher
education.
     It is important, however, that universities not be
relieved of their responsibility for the bad state of
affairs in contemporary Black higher education. American
universities are not doing all that they can to correct the
situation. One of the stated missions of public
universities is to teach students using all the techniques,
resources, and personnel at their disposal. The teaching
mission should require that state universities to adapt to
the realities of serving a diverse citizenry in terms of
cultural orientations, economic standing, and academic
backgrounds. These schools are expected to design their
programs and direct their activities so as to achieve the
worthy goal of providing effective instruction to a
representative group of students from their state and the
nation.
     Many universities appear to have lost sight of the
basic tenets which should guide their operation. The
science and art of teaching has been subordinated to the
business of grantsmanship and publication among college
faculty. In addition, there has arisen an ethic that views
higher education as the private purview of the elite. In
the extreme form these factors encourage a twisted, academic
Social Darwinism, which continues to exclude and/or hobble
individuals and groups historically relegated to the
society's periphery - Blacks, the poor, women, and other
minority group members. Faced with the smug attitude that
"higher education is not for everyone" and the accompanying
behaviors and norms meant to fulfill this prophecy, it is
not surprising that Black Americans fare so poorly in the
U.S. system of higher education.
     Solutions to the problem of Black disadvantage in the
U.S. educational system are plentiful in the literature.
Nonetheless, the situation of Black students in the nation's
colleges has shown minimal improvement on a few fronts,

while continuing to deteriorate terribly on most others. Ample recommendations to improve the status of Black higher education already exist. Were even a fraction of these systematically implemented, the quality of higher education provided Black Americans would be vastly improved. Among the insightful recommendations offered are those presented in: the final report to the National Advisory Committee on Black Higher Education and Black Colleges and Universities (NACBHEBCU, 1982); the report from the Commission on the Higher Education of Minorities (Astin, 1982); and the recommendations made by Peterson et al. (1978); Blackwell (1981); Thomas (1981); Abramowitz (1976); Wilson (1982); National Advisory Commission on Civil Disorders (1968); and Woodson (1933). Beyond the recommendations found in these sources, the following general recommendations are offered:

1. Universities must renew their commitment to increasing the Black presence at all levels on their campus. This effort will require the commitment of funding and staff resources in order to be successful. Moreover, the importance of the commitment must be explicitly communicated throughout the university with departmental, faculty, and staff cooperation being secured through a system of selective rewards and sanctions.

2. Admissions decisions must be based on the broadest possible set of academic and extracurricular indicators of student potential. Performance on standardized entrance examinations should not be accorded greater weight than high school grade point average, rank in graduating class, and teacher/counselor recommendations in the admissions decision.

3. Universities must develop comprehensive, well-coordinated support programs which meet students' academic, psychological, cultural, and health needs. These programs will need to be in tune with and responsive to the changing circumstances and needs of a student's life.

4. Universities must be willing to experiment with different approaches to teaching and learning. Individualized programs of study that allow students to strengthen themselves in areas of academic weakness and to pursue their degrees at different rates must be established.

5. Universities must retool their programs, expectations, and operations to bring these into line with the new demographic reality of U.S. society. Increasingly the pool from which new students are recruited will change from the traditional image of white youngsters fresh out of high school. In the future the pool will include more Black and other race/ethnic students, more

females, more older students returning to school, and so on. In order to survive and prosper under this new reality, universities will need to change with the times, to match the product to the consumer.

In conclusion this chapter raises questions about the fundamental character of the schooling process in the United States. It is legitimate to ask whether the nation's colleges and universities can ever hope to offer the genuine promise of equity for disenfranchised citizens. Is it within the capacity of U.S. universities to become permeable institutions, completely accessible to people different in race, sex, ethnicity, age, or financial standing from their traditional students - privileged, young white males? One must ask whether the nation's colleges and universities ever intended to define the grand experiments of the late sixties and early seventies so broadly as to entirely open up the system entirely. If one looks carefully at the responses of schools in these times of economic stringency, then the answer seems self-evident. There is a retrenchment of frightening proportions underway, a headlong rush to cut programs and to scuttle new initiatives. The end result will be to return to the time when Blacks were a rarity on white campuses.
   Improving the effectiveness of Black postsecondary education remains a pivotal issue in the future of this society.

> Education remains the primary lever by which the racial situation in this country can be controlled and changed - not simply at the college level, but also in high schools, elementary schools, and day-care centers, where today hundreds of thousands of Black youth are being separated from the elemental knowledge necessary for them to compete equally with whites when they become adults. (Ballard, 1973; p. 143)

It is therefore incumbent upon universities and the educational system in general to improve the quality of schooling received by Black Americans.
   As this paper concludes, a disturbing possibility must be entertained. What if the real issues relating to Black advancement (or lack thereof) in this society are not ultimately related to the quality of education they receive? What if they are at best only peripherally related to the educational sphere? These questions return us to the competing views of education in our society raised at the beginning of this chapter. Do educational institutions in our society provide upward mobility based on merit to otherwise excluded groups, or do they serve merely to reproduce the status quo, to validate structured inequality?
   Over the past thirty years Black Americans have made unparalleled gains in the elimination of illiteracy, in the proportion enrolled in school, and in the mean years of schooling completed (Reid, 1982). In fact by 1980 Black

Americans were indistinguishable from whites on these dimensions. However, what does distinguish Blacks from whites are the returns on their educations and the consequent, persistent economic inequities. Thus, the average white male high school graduate has earnings that exceed those of a Black male college graduate (Abramowitz, 1976; p. 204). By the same token, the 1977 unemployment rate for white male high school dropouts was equal to that for Black male college graduates (Hill, 1979).

A common response to such glaring inequities is to retreat into questions about the "quality" of education received by Black Americans (Newman et al., 1978). Hidden in this ploy is the implicit, and unacceptable, assumption that all white Americans - by virtue of their color- receive the same quality of education. Previously Black Americans were told that they did not have enough education; now the message is that they have enough education, but it is unfortunately the wrong kind. The well-founded suspicion of Black Americans toward such explanations is granted credence by Hare and Levine (1983) who state:

> the school plays a unique role in allocating people to different positions in the division of labor through routing and grading practices. Relative success in school is, in fact, the major avenue through which discrimination in the job market is justified. Given racism as well as sexism and classism in a stratified America, it can be argued that the disproportional allocation of Blacks, other people of color, women, and people of lower class origin to the lowest labor slots is functional and their relative academic failure is essential to getting the job done. (p. 19)

REFERENCES

Abramowitz, E. A. (1976). Equal educational opportunity for Blacks in U.S. higher education: An assessment. Washington, DC: Howard University Press.

Allen, W. (1986). Gender and campus race differences in Black student academic performance, racial attitudes, and college satifaction. Atlanta, GA: Southern Education Foundation.

Allen, W., & Farley, W. R. (1986). The shifting social and economic tides of Black America, 1950-1980. Annual Review of Sociology, 12, 277-306.

Astin, A. W. (1982). Minorities in American higher education. San Francisco: Jossey-Bass.

Ballard, A. B. (1973). The education of Black folk: The Afro-American struggle for knowledge in white America. New York: Harper & Row.

Blackwell, J. E. (1981). _Mainstreaming outsiders: The production of Black professionals_. Bayside, NY: General Hall, Inc.

Bowles, S., & Gintis, H. (1976). _Schooling capitalist America: Educational reform and the contradictions of economic life_. New York: Basic Books.

Braddock, J. H. (1978). Internal colonialism and Black American education. _Journal of Western Black Studies_. Vol. _2_(1), 24-33.

Davis, K., & Moore, W. (1945). Some principles of stratification. _American Sociological Review_, _10_, 242-49.

Deskin, D. R. (1983). _Minority recruitment data: An analysis of baccalaureate degree production in the United States_. Totowa, NJ: Rowman and Allanheld.

Di Cesare, P. C., Sedlacek, W. E., & Brooks, G. C. (1972). Nonintellective correlates of Black student attrition. _Journal of College Student Personnel_, _13_, 319-324.

Fleming, J. (1984). _Blacks in college_. San Francisco: Jossey-Bass.

Gibbs, J. T. (1973). Black students/white university/different expectations. _Personnel and Guidance Journal_, _51_, 463-69.

Gibbs, J. T. (1974). Patterns of adaptation among Black students at a predominately white university: Selected case studies. _American Journal of Orthopsychiatry_, _44_(5), 728-40.

Hare, B. R., & Levine, D. U. (1983). _Toward effective desegregated schools_. Unpublished manuscript, Department of Sociology, State University of New York at Stony Brook.

Hill, R. B. (1979). _The widening economic gap_. Washington, DC: National Urban League Research Department.

Miller, C. (1981). Higher education for Black Americans: Problems and issues. _Journal of Negro Education_, 208-24.

Morris, L. (1979). _Elusive equality: The status of Black Americans in higher education_. Washington, DC: Howard University Press.

National Advisory Commission on Civil Disorders Report. (1968). New York: Bantam.

National Advisory Committee on Black Higher Education and
     Black Colleges and Universities (NACBHEBCU). Higher
     education equity: The crisis of appearance versus
     reality revisited, Final Report. (1982). Washington,
     DC: U.S. Department of Education.

National Center for Education Statistics (NCES). (1983).
     Fall enrollment in colleges and universities, 1980.
     Washington, DC: U.S. Department of Education.

Nettles, M. T., Gosman, E. J., Thoeny, A. R., & Dandridge,
     B. A. (1985). The causes and consequences of college
     students' performance: A focus on Black and white
     students' attrition rates, progression rates and grade
     point averages. Nashville, TN: The Tennessee Higher
     Education Commission.

Newman, D. K. (1978). Protest, politics and prosperity:
     Black Americans and white institutions, 1940-75. New
     York: Pantheon Books.

Peterson, M., et al. (1978). Black students on white
     campuses: The impacts of increased Black enrollments.
     Ann Arbor: Institute for Social Research, University
     of Michigan.

Pitts, J. P. (1975). The politicalization of Black
     students: Northwestern University. Journal of Black
     Studies, 5(3) 277-319.

Reid, J. (1982). Black America in the 1980's. Population
     Bulletin. 37(4), 1-38.

Smith, D. (1980). Admission and retention problems of Black
     students at seven predominantly white universities.
     Washington, DC: National Advisory Committee on Black
     Higher Education and Black Colleges and Universities.

Thomas, G. E. (Ed.). (1981). Black students in higher
     education: Conditions and experiences in the 1970's.
     Westport, CT: Greenwood Press.

Tinto, V. (1975). Dropout from higher education: A
     theoretical synthesis of recent research. Review of
     Educational Research, 45, 89-125.

Webster, D. W., Sedlacek, W. E., & Miyares, J. (1979). A
     comparison of problems perceived by minority and white
     university students. Journal of College Student
     Personnel, 20(2), 165-70.

Willie, C. V., & McCord, A. S. (1972). Black students at
     white colleges. New York: Praeger.

Wilson, R. (Ed.). (1982). Race & equity in higher
     education. Washington, DC: American Council on
     Education.

Woodson, C. G. (1969). (originally published 1933).
      Miseducation of the Negro. New York: Associated Pub.

5

Some Cost and Benefit Considerations for Black College Students Attending Predominantly White Versus Predominantly Black Universities

JOMILLS HENRY BRADDOCK, II, and
JAMES M. McPARTLAND

Suppose for a moment that you are a Black person who is preparing to enroll in a four-year college degree program and who has the choice of entering either a majority Black or a majority white university. What factors would be important for you to consider in trying to reach a decision?

The racial composition of the student body and faculty of an institution are two of many college characteristics that should be considered. Other factors, such as the strength of the institution's academic programs in the area of the student's major interest, the financial assistance and other support systems available, and the academic entrance and graduation requirements are additional matters of importance in a student's college selection process. The racial composition of an institution's student body, faculty, and staff are important because they represent environmental factors that may influence how successful a minority student's college experience will be (Blackwell, 1981). In the previous four chapters Michael T. Nettles and Walter R. Allen have shown that this and the other factors constitute necessary support systems for successful academic persistence and performance in college.

A balance sheet of the potential liabilities and benefits of different college choices involves a variety of possible qualitative outcomes. In this chapter data from a recent longitudinal survey of students are used to focus upon some objective outcomes related to the educational and occupational careers of Black students. On the cost side, whether the chances of successfully completing a four-year degree for the average Black student is greater if the student enrolls in a predominantly Black institution as compared with a predominantly white institution is examined. To determine the benefits, the occupational success of graduates of white institutions are compared with that of graduates of Black institutions.

Comparisons of Black versus white university outcomes have been important in recent years because both types of institutions have undergone extraordinary transformations in their enrollments and because the federal courts through the Adams Desegregation Criteria have ordered the southern states to provide the support necessary to bring Black public colleges up to equal status of white colleges and universities. On one hand Black colleges which, prior to the sixties, enrolled nearly all Black college students, enroll less than one-fourth of Black students today. On the other hand white colleges and universities have had to adjust to the growing number of Black college students who are choosing to attend white institutions. Comparisons of the two types of institutions are important in order to indicate their respective progress as well as their continuing challenges in adjusting to major enrollment transitions. In this regard the research presented in this chapter reveals some important challenges for both Black and white colleges and universities in fostering desirable educational and occupational outcomes for Black students.

RISKS OF DEGREE COMPLETION

Any risk that a student would be unable to complete an intended four-year college degree program is a serious matter.   Completing a college degree has significantly higher occupational and income payoffs than dropping out of college before receiving a degree (Dearman & Plesko, 1980, p. 138); therefore, if Black students' risks of successful degree completion are diminished by attending one type of institution as opposed to another, they should give serious consideration to attending the institution where the odds of receiving a degree are in their favor.

There are also potential delays or redirections that a student may experience in pursuit of a college degree, which may not be as serious as failing to complete the degree program, but which may result in actual costs to the student in the job market. For example, a student may take longer at one college to complete a similar degree than at another college because of differences in financial or academic experiences. The extra time needed to complete the degree could have monetary costs. The individual who finishes sooner will gain a greater amount of valuable job experience and in addition realizing income from working on the job sooner. Another example might be students who change their major fields of study, at one or more points in time, for whatever reasons. These students may pay a price later if the income or career opportunities are less in their most recent field of study. Thus, in estimating the costs of enrolling at predominantly Black versus predominantly white institutions, it is also important to estimate whether a Black student risks delays in degree completion or is redirected away from his or her primary field of interest due to the type of college.

Estimating the actual risks to degree completion from attending different types of colleges or universities requires controlling for individual student differences in academic preparation and family circumstances, which are factors that usually influence students' performance in college. It is also important to consider those students who begin in four-year institutions apart from those who begin in two-year colleges and hope to transfer to four-year degree programs. The rate of degree completion is normally much higher in the case of the former (Astin, 1977; Tinto, 1975).

Research Method

The data for the analyses in this chapter are taken from the Black student college-bound sample of the National Longitudinal Survey (NLS) of the High School Graduating Class of 1972 conducted by the National Center for Education Statistics. This data set follows a national sample of students from the time they graduated from high school in 1972 through the succeeding seven years until 1979 and provides information on the personal background of each individual as well as their educational and occupational experiences throughout the seven-year period (Burkheimer & Novak, 1981). Degree attainment is estimated based on all Black students who entered four-year colleges or universities in the fall following their high school graduation in 1972. This involved a subsample of 230 Black males and 364 Black females. Three outcome measures are used: completion of the four-year degree within four years of initial college enrollment, completion of the four-year degree within seven years of initial college enrollment, and the students' expectations seven and one-half years after high school graduation that a four-year college degree would eventually be obtained (including those who had already received the degree). Each of these outcomes is used as a dependent variable in multiple regression analyses that include the following predictor variables: (1) an index of each person's family socioeconomic status, (2) separate scores on three standardized academic achievement tests [(A) vocabulary, (B) reading, and (C) mathematics] taken in the senior year of high school, (3) region (seventeen-state southern and southwestern region that contains most predominantly Black four-year colleges versus the rest of the nation), and (4) whether the student had initially enrolled in a predominantly white institution or in a predominantly Black institution. The multiple regression analyses are performed separately for Black males and for Black females.

Degree Completion

Are there greater risks involved in completing a degree for the average Black college student who enrolls in a predominantly white university rather than a predominantly Black institution? No significant evidence in support of this is uncovered; however, there are indications that the degree is more likely to be completed within the four-year time period at the predominantly Black university. Black four-year college students of similar backgrounds and preparation are just as likely to complete the degree by enrolling in either the predominantly white or predominantly

Black institutions, but the probability of completing the
degree within four years is somewhat enhanced for those in
the predominantly Black institutions. It may even be that
the Blacks who start in white institutions have a slightly
greater chance of eventually receiving their degree,
although they may take somewhat longer than their
counterparts who begin in predominantly Black institutions.
Table 5.1 presents the data analyses upon which these
conclusions are based. Presented are the unstandardized
regression coefficients and associated test statistics from
multiple regression analyses for the variable measuring
initial enrollment at predominantly white versus
predominantly Black universities.

Table 5.1

The Effects of Enrolling at White Versus Black Four-year
Colleges on the Degree Attainment Probabilities of Black
Students, Controlling for Socio-economic Status, Test
Scores, and Region

(b=unstandardized regression coefficient; F = test statistic)

	Black Males (N = 230)		Black Females (N = 364)	
	b	(F)	b	(F)
Probability of completing a college degree within four years	-.165*	(2.05)	-.181***	(4.60)
Probability of completing a college degree within seven years	-.098	(0.72)	-.037	(0.20)
Expectation of eventually completing college	+.125**	(3.39)	+.045	(0.49)

    * Significant at .15
   ** Significant at .10
  *** Significant at .05

The columns of Table 5.1 show a trend in size and
direction of the estimated probabilities, beginning with the
largest negative estimate, followed by a much smaller
nagative value, and then changing to a positive value. This

trend for both males and females corresponds to the
estimated effect of enrolling at a predominantly white
institution on different measures of the time needed to
finish the college degree. The top value - the effect on
the probability of finishing the degree four years following
initial college enrollment - shows that the largest risk to
Black students comes from initially enrolling at a
predominantly white rather than a predominantly Black four-
year college. The probability of prompt degree completion
is 16.5 percent less for Black males and 18.1 percent less
for Black females, controlling for region, student
background, and academic preparation. However, the middle
value - the effect on degree completion within seven years
of initial enrollment - though still negative, is much
smaller and not statistically significant. The chances for
receiving a baccalaureate degree within seven years are
estimated to be 9.8 percent less for Black males and only
3.7 percent less for Black females who enroll at
predominantly white institutions. Aside from the lack of
statistical significance, these values are so small that all
the disadvantages for Black students attending predominantly
white institutions disappear when considering the eventual
achievement of a college degree. This conclusion is
strengthened by the bottom values in Table 5.1 which show a
positive effect from starting in a white institution on
individuals' belief that they will eventually earn their
college degree. This positive probability is much larger
for Black males than Black females but suggests in each case
that measures beyond seven years after high school
graduation might actually show a slight advantage of
experiences in predominantly white institutions on the
eventual degree attainment of similar Black students.
Overall, the results suggest that the possible risks to
Black college students from initial enrollment in
predominantly white rather than predominantly Black four-
year institutions are temporary and concern the prompt
completion but not the eventual completion of the
baccalaurate degree.

Reasons for Greater Risk in Completing a Degree

        The analyses in Table 5.1 do not indicate why delay in
degree completion may occur for some Black students who
initially enroll in predominantly white institutions, but
previous research on college environments and college
student dropouts provides some possible explanations (Alwin,
1974; Alwin et al., 1975; Nettles et al., 1985; Thomas,
1981a, 1981b; Tinto, 1975; Braddock, 1981). Studies
conducted with samples of both white and Black students in
predominantly white colleges that differ in selectivity and
other environmental conditions strongly suggest that
students' experiences in both the academic and social
systems of the institution may cause them to drop out.
        College grade performance is usually the single most
important factor in predicting student withdrawal or
dismissal from college, indicating that an individual's

ability to meet the academic standards of the college is a
major determinant of successful progress toward degree
completion. The important influence that college grade
performance has on persistence in college has been shown to
hold true for all race and sex groups, and for Black college
students in both predominantly white and predominantly Black
institutions (Braddock, 1981; Thomas 1981b). Based upon
data presented in Chapter 3, Black students appear to have
more difficulty maintaining a high college grade point
average in a predominantly white institution than in a
predominantly Black institution. Comparisons of student
admissions test preformance and other admissions credentials
of college applicants show that predominantly white
institutions on the average have more academically
competitive environments than predominantly Black
institutions despite some overlap of the groups (Astin,
1982). Thus, it appears that one reason for the added risk
of delayed graduation for Black college students in white
institutions may be the more stringent level of academic
competition, which makes it more difficult for the average
Black student to maintain good grades.

Research on white college students has also shown that
a student's successful involvement in the college social
system often contributes to the student's chances of
persisting through graduation (Astin, 1977; Tinto, 1975).
Studies of Black students in white institutions (Allen,
1981; Willie & McCord, 1973) indicate numerous ways in which
Black students can feel lack of social integration with
other students and with staff in nonacademic activities and
in the general milieu of the institution. Thus, on the
average, a Black student faces more occasions for social
estrangement in a predominantly white than in a
predominantly Black college and therefore may find it more
difficult to progress at a timely and efficient rate toward
graduation at predominantly white institutions. This lack
of social integration and involvement is a major challenge
for white universities in their quest to achieve equality in
their activities and programs.

Of course Black students may find or create academic
and social support systems at predominantly white
institutions that can partially compensate for the added
risks resulting from tougher academic standards or
nonsupportive social environments. These include both
institutional academic support services provided by the
university and academic and social support systems
established by minority students themselves. Better
research and practical knowledge are needed to determine
ways in which valuable alternative academic and social
support systems can be developed and used by minority
students in predominantly white postsecondary institutions.

CAREER BENEFITS FOR DEGREE RECIPIENTS OF BLACK VERSUS WHITE
COLLEGES

Despite numerous studies of the experiences of Black
students on white college campuses, researchers have only

recently begun to consider the long-term consequences of attending predominantly Black institutions or predominantly white institutions on adult career outcomes such as income and occupational attainments (Baratz & Ficklen, 1983; Braddock, 1983; Brown & Ford, 1977; Burnim, 1980). This section reviews the existing studies and presents new results from the National Longitudinal Survey (NLS) which help fill some of the empirical gaps on the subject.

Limited indirect evidence suggests that both secondary and postsecondary school desegregation may affect Black occupational attainments. Crain (1970) observed that northern Black male graduates of desegregated high schools earned higher incomes and held higher status jobs than Blacks from segregated schools. Besides the historical time limitations of his study, which was based on retrospective reports provided by respondents whose high school experiences predated the desegregation developments of the past two decades, the sample of Blacks was restricted to residents of the North and West.

Brown and Ford (1977) found that Blacks who had earned their master's degree in business administration (MBA) from predominantly Black schools received starting salaries several thousand dollars below those Black MBA's from mixed (predominantly white) schools. However, their study focused only on a single type of graduate degree, was based on small samples, and lacked adequate controls for students' background characteristics and performance.

Braddock (1983) examined the relationship between type of college attended (predominantly Black or predominantly white) and Black occupational attainment using a national sample of recent college graduates. Although the results were mixed, there appeared to be some advantage in both annual earnings and occupational prestige favoring graduates of predominantly white colleges. Among bachelor's degree recipients, Braddock found that when controlling for college grades, region, type of job and age, Black male graduates of predominantly white institutions received nearly $600 more in annual income and held slightly more prestigous jobs than Black male graduates of predominantly Black universities. In contrast, Black female bachelor's degree recipients from predominantly white universities received nearly $450 less in income than their couterparts from predominantly Black institutions. Among master's degree recipients, the findings for both males and females showed substantial though not statistically significant gains in income- $1,800 for females and $1,500 for males - and modest occupational prestige advantages accruing to graduates of predominantly white universities. Although these findings are based on a national probability sample of recent college graduates, they must be interpreted with caution because the data do not include important background information on the respondents' social class and academic achievement test scores, which researchers have found to be related to career outcomes.

Burnim (1980), on the other hand, found virtual parity in earnings among Black men who attended predominantly Black and predominantly white univesities, but his study involved samples with severe and systematically biased nonresponse patterns (see Crain et al., 1974). Thus, the evidence on the effect of school (especially college) desegregation on Black adult occupational attainments is both limited and ambiguous. On balance, it suggests that Black graduates of predominanty white institutions have advantages in the labor market over their counterparts from predominantly Black institutions, but further research is needed to test the validity of this outcome and to identify the processes that would produce such an outcome.

The current analysis extends previous research on the relationship between degegregation in higher education and Black occupational attainment. In contrast to most previous studies, this study is based on a national rather than a regional sample and examines the relationship between desegregation and occupational attainment for both males and females, and considers a broader set of correlates of earnings - including social class and achievement test performance.

This study presents estimates of the effect of college racial composition on two measures of career success- annual earnings and occupational prestige. As in the preceding analysis, each of these outcome measures was used in multiple regression analyses that include the following six predictor variables: (1) an index of each person's family socioeconomic status, (2) combined scores on three standardized academic achievement tests [(A) vocabulary, (B) reading, and (C) mathematics] taken in the senior year of high school, (3) region (seventeen-state southern and southwestern region versus the rest of the nation), (4) college major (education versus all other fields), (5) a summated index of the number of years of full-time labor force experience, and (6) whether the student enrolled initially in a predominantly white institution or in a predominantly Black institution. Multiple regression analyses were conducted separately for Black males and for Black females in order to illustrate the difference in effects distinguishable by sex.

Table 5.2 reports the results of the regression analyses illustrating how attendance at predominantly Black or predominantly white colleges affects the annual earnings of Black male and female bachelor's degree recipients. Unstandardized beta's or metric coefficients are reported to facilitate comparisons across subgroups, such as, males versus females. These coefficients may also be interpreted as the dollar amount of annual income which may be attributed to attendance at a predominantly white institution versus a predominantly Black institution. Positive values indicate income advantages to graduates of predominantly white colleges, whereas negative values indicate income advantages to graduates of predominantly Black colleges. The regression results in the top row of Table 5.2 show that, without taking into account the effect of other factors, Black males from predominantly white universities receive roughly $1,524 more in annual income than their Black male counterparts from predominantly Black universities. Black female bachelor's degree recipients

Table 5.2

College Race Effects on Annual Income and Occupational
Prestige of Black College Graduates

(b = unstandardized regression coefficient; F = test statistic)

	Black Males (N = 103)		Black Females (N = 159)	
	b	(F)	b	(F)
Income	$1,524	(2.72)	$1,118	(0.61)
Income, controlling for five variables <u>a</u>	$2,486*	(4.56)	$ 327	(0.07)
Occupational prestige	4.6	(0.90)	1.1	(0.09)
Occupational prestige, controlling for five variables <u>a</u>	0.2	(0.00)	0.8	(0.04)

<u>a</u> five control variables are family socioeconomic status, high
school test score, region, college major, and years in labor
force

* Significant at .05 based on regression equation with
income expressed as a natural log function

from predominantly white institutions show an initial $1,118
annual income advantage. Considered alone, however, college
racial composition fails to account for a statistically
significant proportion of the variation (1 and 2 percent for
males and females, respectively) in the income of Black
college graduates.

Differences in individual earnings are determined by
factors other than the type of college or university one
attends. The second row of Table 5.2 shows how the impact
of college racial composition on income is affected by
taking into account several other important variables
(socio-economic status, standardized test performance,
region, college major, and years of labor force experience)
of earnings potential.

When statistical controls are added, sex interactions
as well as suppressor effects influence the relationship of
college racial composition and annual income of Black
college graduates. Among Black males the initial income
difference of $1,524 favoring predominantly white

institution graduates is increased to $2,487 - an increment
of nearly $1,000 - when the effects of other variables in
the model are taken into account. The suppressor effects
for males appear to result from the fact that predominantly
white college graduates - who are more likely to experience
delayed degree completion - have on the average less labor
force experience than their predominantly Black college
counterparts. Because years of labor force experience and
college race are both positively correlated with annual
earnings and are inversely correlated with each other, the
net effect of college race becomes stronger when labor force
experience is taken into account.

In contrast, among females, the initial college race
effect of $1,118 favoring graduates of predominantly white
institutions is reduced by nearly $800 - to $327 - when
other factors are taken into account. However, the adjusted
college race effect on income is statistically significant
among males only. Among females the adjusted college race
effect is trivial, indicating that college racial
composition is of minor importance in determining the labor
market success of this group when other factors are
considered. For males, on the other hand, college racial
composition has a major influence on labor market success,
accounting for nearly 20 percent of the annual earnings of
Black male college graduates.

It is difficult to explain why male graduates of
predominantly white universities show a substantial net
income advantage of $2,487 over their counterparts from
predominantly Black universities while females exhibit
virtually no gain. However, a theoretical perspective which
is discussed later in this chapter suggests that a major
part of the white college advantage may be related to the
potential integration of Black students into useful networks
of sponsorship and access to different types of job
information. The weaker results for females may indicate
that Black women on white campuses experience higher levels
of alienation and estrangement than their Black male
counterparts (Allen, 1981; Braddock, 1978; Willie & Levy,
1972) and are unable to take advantage of broader social
networks. Another possibility is that for the teaching,
health, and social service jobs, which draw most female
college graduates, a broader set of social networks and
sponsorship is not as important for getting a good job as is
the case in male-dominated professions (such as, managers).
Further research is needed to evaluate these possibilities.

The regression results in the bottom two rows of Table
5.2 show how attendance at predominantly Black or
predominantly white colleges affects the occupational
prestige of Black male and female bachelor's degree
recipients. The unstandardized betas or metric coefficients
may be interpreted as the increment (or decrement) in
occupational prestige attributable to attendance at a
predominantly white institution versus a predominantly Black
institution. Positive values indicate occupational prestige
advantages to graduates of predominantly white institutions
while negative values indicate prestige advantages for
graduates of predominantly Black institutions.

The regression results in the third row of Table 5.2 show about an advantage of 4.60 points in occupatinal prestige accruing to Black males from predominantly white institutions, while the comparable figure for females indicates a smaller advantage (1.07) for graduates from predominantly white institutions. However, neither of these unadjusted differences are statistically significant, and college racial composition alone does not account for a significant portion (2 percent or less) of the total variation in occupational prestige between either group.

The bottom row of data in Table 5.2 shows the effect of college racial composition on occupational prestige while controlling for socio-economic status, standardized test performance, region, college major, and years of labor force experience. For both males and females the inclusion of controls reduces the college race effect to almost zero (.25 and .78 for males and females, respectively). Thus, college race appears to have virtually no effect on the occupational prestige of jobs held by Black college graduates. This finding is not altogether surprising when one considers the fact that most college graduates enter fairly high-status white-collar - professional, technical, managerial, and sales - occupations. As a result, particularly among young college graduates in the early stages of their work careers, little variance in occupational prestige is explained by institutional characteristics such as college racial composition.

Reasons for Potential Added Returns

Social scientists have identified several institutional processes linked to segregation which imply that school desegregation - elementary-secondary as well as college-can have positive long-term social and economic consequences for minorities. Such processes include: (1) access to useful social networks for job information, contacts, and sponsorship; (2) socialization for aspirations and entrance into "nontraditional" career lines with higher income returns; (3) development of interpersonal social skills that are useful in interracial contexts; (4) reduced social inertia - increased tolerance of the willingness to participate in desegregated environments; and (5) avoidance of negative attributions which are often associated with "black" institutions (see Crain, 1970; Crain & Weisman, 1972; McPartland & Crain, 1980; Braddock & McPartland, 1982; Braddock, 1980). These processes are difficult to measure and investigate directly. Nevertheless, they do suggest factors that may produce individual and aggregate differences in the adult educational and career success of Blacks who attend segregated as opposed to desegregated colleges.

The results reported earlier which show potential added income returns may be understood best by the social networks hypothesis which suggests that Black students in predominantly white colleges may have greater access to useful networks of sponsorship and job information than their counterparts in predominantly Black colleges. These networks may lead to labor market advantages - including knowledge about job vacancies as well as access to better jobs.

To understand better how these processes operate, the job-seeking techniques used by the respondents in the NLS survey to obtain their present jobs were examined. Preliminary analyses reveal that although Black males and females are equally likely (39 and 40 percent, respectively) to use friendship networks to obtain jobs referrals, Black male graduates of predominantly white institutions are somewhat more likely (37 percent) than Black male graduates of predominantly Black institutions (32 percent) to have obtained their present job through friendship networks. In contrast, Black female graduates of predominantly white institutions (27 percent) are considerably less likely than Black female graduates of predominantly Black institutions (47 percent) to have obtained their present jobs through friendship networks. Also, among the respondents who reported that they did obtain their present job through friendship networks, the income and occupational prestige advantages associated with college race appear to favor Black male graduates of predominantly white institutions ($1,592 annual income and nine occupational prestige points) considerably more than they favor Black female graduates of predominantly white institutions ($663 annual income and one occupational prestige point).

Although the data analyzed here do not permit identification of the race of friends used in the job-seeking process, previous research findings on interracial contacts and simple random probabilities suggest that Black student friendship networks in predominantly white institutions are more likely to be racially mixed than are Black student friendship networks in predominantly Black institutions. Thus, these preliminary results - showing consistency in both occupational payoffs and uses/advantages of friendships in job-seeking behavior favoring males to a greater extent than females - provide important indirect support of the social networking advantage available to Black students in white colleges.

Although a number of the effects of college race on Black income and occupational prestige shown here appear small, initial occupational advantages or disadvantages may cumulate over the course of one's working life. Even assuming uniform lifetime salary and status increments among all Black college graduates, the white college advantage would not only persist but increase over time. Moreover, the contacts and sponsorship which produced the initial advantage for graduates of predominantly white institutions may influence subsequent career mobility in a similar fashion. These hypotheses cannot be examined in this study because the data were collected only on young adults at the very early stages of their work histories. Further research on the long-term consequences of attending predominantly white institutions and predominantly Black institutions is needed.

PERCEIVED DISCRIMINATION

       To parallel the analyses using objective measures of
educational and occupational success, Black college
graduates' self-assessments of their experiences of racial
discrimination in education, work, or housing are
investigated. Through this investigation other evidence of
the educational and occupational tradeoffs Black students
face by enrolling in predominantly white colleges or
universities are discovered.
       The NLS survey asked the following subjective question
of all respondents five years after high school graduation:
"Have you ever been given a special advantage or been
treated unfairly because of your race in any of the
following situations: getting a good education; getting a
job, promotion, or other work benefits; getting a house or
apartment?" For each NLS respondent, a score on this
question of +1 indicates more perceived racial advantages
than unfairness, a score of -1 indicates more racial
unfairness than advantages, and a score of zero indicates no
perceived racial advantage or unfairness. Table 5.3 shows
how Black college graduates from predominantly white
institutions differ from Black college graduates from
predominantly Black institutions on these subjective
measures, controlling for geographic region.
       The direction and size of the differences shown in
Table 5.3 depend upon the area of possible racial advantage
or unfairness being questioned. The occupational area is
the only one in which Black college graduates from
predominantly white institutions show a positive advantage
over their counterparts who graduated from predominantly
Black institutions. The values in the second row of Table
5.3, +.188 for Black male college graduates and +.184 for
Black female college graduates, indicate that less
occupational discrimination is perceived by those who
graduate from predominantly white institutions. There is no
similar perceived advantage for education or housing
discrimination. Regarding education, row 1 of Table 5.3
shows that the differences due to college race are very
small negative values, indicating no particular advantage or
disadvantage for Black graduates of white institutions.
       The third row of Table 5.3 further supports the
conclusion that the occupational area is where Black college
graduates of white institutions find the strongest positive
impact. Compared to results on employment discrimination,
the values reported in the area of perceived housing
discrimination are different in direction for Black males
and much smaller for Black females. It seems clear that
Black students who graduate from predominantly white
colleges see employment discrimination differently from the
other areas and see racial unfairness in employment to be
less of a problem than do Black college graduates from
predominantly Black institutions.

Table 5.3

College Race Effects on Black College Graduates' Perceptions
of Discrimination, Controlling for Region and Sex

(b = unstandardized regression coefficient; F = test statistic)

	Black Males (N = 84)		Black Females (N = 153)	
	b	(F)	b	(F)
Perceived discrimination in getting a good education	-.006	(0.00)	-.059	(0.35)
Perceived discrimination in getting a job, promotion, or other work benefits	+.188*	(2.34)	+.184**	(3.44)
Perceived discrimination in getting a house or apartment	-.146	(1.29)	.000	(0.00)

* Significant at .15
** Significant at .075

CONCLUSIONS AND RECOMMENDATIONS

These analyses of educational and occupational outcomes
suggest that there may be both added risks but greater
returns for Black college students enrolling in a four-year
degree program at a predominantly white institution compared
to a predominantly Black institution.   Delay in degree
attainment will often have income costs, because the extra
time spent in college study may reduce the time invested in
job experience, which is usually worth some extra income.
But taken against the risk of delay in degree completion,
the authors find indications that the degree and contacts
received from a predominantly white institution may have
somewhat greater income payoffs in the long-term market for
the average Black college graduate.   Thus, the degree from a
predominantly white institution may be worth more to the
average Black male student, but it may be more difficult to
obtain without extra time delays.

These analyses of NLS data suggest a need for further research to clarify the actual and perceived tradeoffs to Black college students of enrollment at predominantly white institutions. This chapter has examined Black college students who began in four-year institutions. There is a need for complementary reseach on Blacks who are seeking a degree at two-year colleges, as well as Blacks in postbaccalaureate programs. What characteristics of two-year colleges, including college racial composition, are related to Black students' educational progress and degree completion, controlling for students' prior preparation, family resources, geographic location, and other important individual characteristics? How is Black student enrollment or success in graduate or professional programs related to characteristics of the college or university at which the student received undergraduate training? Among both two-year college and four-year college enrollees, what are the risk factors for Black students of transferring schools or changing majors along the way toward a bachelor's degree? Does the racial composition of the college predict the probability of institutional transfers or major field changes for Black students with similar personal characteristics? What are the average occupational consequences of the final college and major field destination of Black students who follow different educational paths to the bachelor's degree? What other objective and subjective outcomes of the college experience are important in a more complete balance sheet of cost and benefit probabilities for Black students considering different types of colleges? How can these probabilities be estimated for Black students with different personal characteristics? Some of these issues can be studied with existing data sources such as NLS, but others will require larger samples and broader measures than are currently available.

These analyses also suggest certain policy recommendations for predominantly white and predominantly Black colleges that may enhance their effectiveness in meeting the needs of the current generation of Black college students. For predominantly white institutions in particular, it is essential that policies and programs be developed to facilitate Black students' integration into the academic and social subsystems of the university. Lack of Black student integration into the social and academic environment of predominantly white institutions has been associated with poor social and psychological adjustment (Fleming, 1981), dropout proneness (Braddock, 1981), and poor academic performance (Allen, 1981; Nettles et al., 1985). Policies and program remedies in this area should address several specific issues including: (1) providing adequate and nonstigmatized academic support progrms, (2) strategies to insure that the Black American experience is fairly and adequately represented in all academic offerings and extracurricular activities througout the institution, (3) clear-cut and consistently enforced institutional policies to discourage racial harrassment, (4) systematic mechanisms for fostering positive relations between

Phillips Memorial
Library
Providence College

university faculty and Black students, and (5) counseling
services which are well prepared to address special social
psychological problems arising from minority student status
in a predominantly white institution. For predominantly
Black institutions, there exists a special need to prepare
the current generation of Black students better for an
increasingly competitive and technological labor market. In
this regard policies and programs should focus on enhancing
and diversifying curricular offerings with greater emphasis
on expansion in the scientific and technical specialities
while strengthening the traditional teacher training and
social service programs. Career couseling should be
stressed to emphasize early preparation for major field
selection and student awareness of current and future areas
of greatest employmemt opportunities. Such strategies would
not only enhance the career preparation of graduates of
Black colleges but also enhance their institutional image
among employers. Both predominantly white and predominantly
Black institutions could greatly enhance Black student
success through more adequate financial aid packages,
ideally not requiring work or short-term repayment. Black
students' financial need has been well documented, and their
slower rate of progression to graduation (Thomas, 1981b;
Nettles and others, 1985) is often accompanied by patterns
of attendance discontinuities or "stop-out." When
attendance discontinuities, though temporary, lead to lender
demands for student loan repayment, reenrollment
probabilities may be diminished. Work-study
responsibilities may also impose cumulative disadvantages on
students most in need of financial assistance who already
are faced with severe academic disadvantages. Thus, grants
and scholarships appear most viable for optimizing Black
student success.

REFERENCES

Alexander, K. L., & Eckland, B. K. (1977). High school
    context and college selectivity: Institutional
    constraints in educational stratification. Social
    Forces, 56(1), 166-88.

Allen, W. R. (1981). Correlates of Black student
    adjustment, achievement, and aspirations a
    predominantly white southern university. In G. Thomas
    (Ed.), Black students in higher education: Conditions
    and experiences in the 1970's. Westport, CT:
    Greenwood Press.

Alwin, D. F. (1974). College effects on educational and
    occupational attainments. American Sociological
    Review, 39, 210-23.

Alwin, D. F., Hauser, R. M., & Sewell, W. H. (1975).
    College and achievement. In W. H. Sewell & R. M.
    Hauser (Eds.), Education, occupation, and earnings.
    New York: Academic Press.

Astin, A. W. (1977). Four critical years: Effects of
     college on beliefs, attitudes and knowledge. San
     Francisco: Jossey-Bass.

Astin, A. W. (1982). Minorities in American higher
     education. San Francisco: Jossey-Bass.

Baratz, J. C., & Ficklen, M. (1983). Participation of
     recent Black college graduates in the labor market and
     in graduate education. Princeton, NJ: Educational
     Testing Service.

Blackwell, J. E. (1981). Mainstreaming outsiders: The
     production of Black professionals. Bayside, NY:
     General Hall, Inc.

Braddock, J. H. (1978). Radicalism and alienation among
     Black college students. The Negro Educational Review,
     29, 4-21.

Braddock, J. H. (1980). The perpetuation of segregation
     across levels of education: A behavioral assessment of
     the contact-hypothesis. Sociology of Education, 83,
     178-86.

Braddock, J. H. (1981). Desegregation and Black student
     attrition. Urban Education, 15, 403-18.

Braddock, J. H. (1983). College race and Black occupational
     achievement (Report No. 349). Baltimore, MD: Center
     for Social Organization of Schools, Johns Hopkins
     University.

Braddock, J. H., & McPartland, J. (1982). Assessing school
     desegregation effects: New directions in research. In
     R. Corwin (Ed.), Research in Sociology of Education and
     Socialization, 3. Greenwich, CT: JAI.

Brown, H., & Ford, D. (1977). An exploratory analysis of
     discrimination in the employment of Black MBA
     graduates. Journal of Applied Psychology, 62, 50-56.

Burkheimer, G. J., & Novak, T. P. (1981). A capsule
     description of young adults seven and one-half years
     after high school. Washington, DC: National Center
     for Education Statistics.

Burnim, M. (1980). The earnings effect of Black
     matriculation in predominantly white colleges.
     Industrial and Labor Relations Review, 33, 518-24.

Crain, R. L. (1970). School integration and occupational
     achievement of Negroes. American Journal of Sociology,
     75, 593-606.

Crain, R., et al. (1974). Design for a national
    longitudinal study of school desegregation: Vol. II.
    Reserch design and procedures. Santa Monica, CA: Rand
    Corporation.

Dearman, N. B., & Plesko, V. W. (1980).   The condition of
    education, 1980, statistical report. Washington, DC:
    U.S. Government Printing Office.

Fleming, J. (1981).   Stress and satisfaction in college
    years of Black students. Journal of Negro Education,
    50, 307-18.

McPartland, J., & Crain, R. (1980).   Racial discrimination,
    segregation, and processes of social motility.   In V.
    Covello (Ed.), Poverty and public policy: An
    evaluation of social science research. Boston: G. K.
    Hall.

Nettles, M. T., Thoeny, A. R., Gosman, E. J., & Dandridge,
    B. A. (1985).   The causes and consequences of college
    students' performance. Nashville, TN: Tennessee
    Higher Education Commission.

Thomas, G. E. (1981a).   College characteristics and Black
    students' four-year college graduation. Journal of
    Negro Education, 50, 328-45.

Thomas, G. E. (1981b).   Student and institutional
    characteristics as determinants of the prompt and
    subsequent four-year college graduation of race and sex
    groups. Sociological Quarterly, 22, 327-45.

Tinto, V. (1975).   Dropout from higher education: A
    theoretical systhesis of recent research. Review of
    Educational Research, 45, 89-126.

Willie, C., & Levy, J. (1972).   Black is lonely. Psychology
    Today, 50, 50-53.

Willie, C. V., & McCord, A. S. (1973).   Black students at
    white colleges. New York: Praeger.

6
The Role of Colleges and Universities in Increasing Black Representation in the Scientific Professions

WILLIE PEARSON, JR.

Despite more than a century of participation by Blacks in the professional scientific community, sociologists of science have neglected the study of Black American scientists. As a result, our knowledge of Black American scientists remains very sketchy. Because of the major scientific and technological advancements in recent history, the scientific professions have become symbols of quality in America's colleges and universities. Achieving equal participation by Blacks in the scientific professions represents a major challenge to qualitative equality in American higher education. This is clearly evident in the fact that few Black college students have an inclination to major in the biological and physical sciences, engineering, and mathematics (Astin, 1982). In America's increasingly high-tech society, college major field choice has become an important dimension of equality (Pearson, in press; Cross, 1984). This chapter focuses on Black American representation in the scientific community and examines ways in which colleges and universities may bring about an increased representation of Blacks among professional scientists. To this end, this chapter (1) provides a brief analysis of Black representation in American science, (2) presents a demographic profile of Black and white American scientists, (3) presents an analysis of Black-white differences in academic preparation, (4) provides the results of an analysis of the impact of race on the development of scientific careers, and (5) recommends possible roles that postsecondary institutions can play in increasing Black American representation among professional scientists.

The research for this study involves comparative analyses of Black and white American Ph.D. scientists. (The term "scientist" as used in this study refers to individuals holding an earned doctorate prior to 1975 in anthropology, astronomy, biochemistry, chemistry, general natural science, geology, mathematics, pharmacology, political science, physics, social psychology, social science, and sociology.) The sample of white scientists is randomly selected from the 1978 edition of <u>American Men and Women of Science</u> using a table of random numbers. The sample of Black American scientists is drawn from a variety of sources: (1) various national organizational rosters, (2) individuals who keep personal files on Black American scientists in their particular discipline, (3) a snowball procedure in which letters were sent to scientists throughout the United States requesting the names and addresses of other Black American scientists, and (4) a variety of other biographic and bio-bibliographic sources.

A total of 925 Black American Ph.D. scientists was identified and mailed questionnaires, and of these, 565 (61 percent) responded. Among whites, 1,527 scientists were mailed questionnaires yielding a response rate of 686 (45 percent). One hundred sixty-seven (13 percent) of the sample are female. Natural scientists comprise approximately 64.5 percent of the sample, while social scientists account for the remaining percentage.

THE STATUS OF BLACKS IN AMERICAN SCIENCE

In a recent study, Maxfield (1982) reports that approximately 11 percent of the science and engineering doctoral population is comprised of racial and ethnic minority group members (Blacks, Native Americans, Hispanics, and Asians). Unfortunately, in far too many instances, data on minorities and Blacks are used interchangeably. This is unfortunate because minority groups differ in their rate of participation in science and engineering. For example, Asians represent the majority of the racial and ethnic minorities in science. They are more likely than members of other minority groups to be concentrated in engineering, mathematics, and physical sciences; but, they tend to be underrepresented in the social sciences (National Science Foundation and the Department of Education, 1980). In 1983 Blacks accounted for less than 2 percent of all science/ engineering doctorates. Blacks comprised 0.9 percent of mathematicians, 0.4 percent of computer scientists, 1 percent of physicists/astronomers, 1 percent of chemists, 0.3 percent of earth/environmental scientists, and 1.2 percent of biologists. They are comprised of engineers (0.6 percent), 2 percent of psychologists, and 2.5 percent of social/scientists (National Science Board, 1983; Jetter & Babco, 1984).

DEMOGRAPHIC CHARACTERISTICS OF BLACK SCIENTISTS

It is important to consider social as well as academic backgrounds of scientists as important contributors to their occupational and educational status attainment. Data on the social origins of Black American scientists (in comparison to their white peers) may provide some additional insight about those individuals who succeed in overcoming the various social barriers to enter the community of doctoral scientists. The use of a comparative sample permits an examination of similarities and differences between the backgrounds of Black and white American scientists.

In general Black and white American scientists have significantly different social origins. For instance, while Blacks are nearly four times more likely than whites to be born in the South, whites are about two and one-half times more likely to be born in the North. In fact, the South accounts for roughly two-thirds of the Black scientists, while two regions, the North and East, produce a similar proportion of white scientists. Both Black and white scientists are more likely to have grown up in racially segregated neighborhoods regardless of the region of their birth - Blacks from the West are the exception.

With regard to family background, no major differences are found in the levels of education attained by the fathers of Black and white scientists. However, this is clearly not the case for their occupational status. Overall, the fathers of white scientists are considerably more likely to be managers or professionals than the fathers of Black scientists. In short, highly educated Black fathers have not and, indeed, do not find employment commensurate with their level of education and training.

While most of the scientists tend to have their birth origins in families where the mother generally works in the home, a greater proportion of white scientists report that their mothers do not work outside of the home. Approximately one-half of the Black mothers as compared to slightly more than two-thirds of the white mothers work in the home.

Another major race difference is family size. In general, Black scientists come from families that are usually twice as large as those of white scientists. Furthermore, Blacks tend to have their origins in families that are more typically working-class or lower middle-class in status, while whites tend to come from middle-class families. Students with high scientific potential tend to have their origins in "advantaged" families with few children, have parents with high levels of education, live in relatively expensive homes, and tend to have their own rooms, desks, and typewriters (Gilmartin and associates, 1976). By and large, most Black scientists do not come from such advantaged families.

RACIAL DIFFERENCES IN THE EDUCATION OF AMERICAN SCIENTISTS

Before discussing the college undergraduate and graduate training of scientists, it may be of value to have an understanding of their high school backgrounds. Significant racial differences emerge with respect to racial composition of high school attended (p = .0001). Nearly all the whites, as compared with three-fourths of Blacks, report that they are graduates of high school where they were in the racial majority. While this pattern of racial segregation in high schools has declined over the years, the general pattern persists.

It is while in high school that most students make the decision to pursue a career in science. In an earlier study

of eminent scientists, Roe (1953) reports that most of her
subjects make the decision to pursue a career in science by
their junior or senior year in high school. The mean ages
at which the decision to pursue a scientific career is made
by individuals in this sample is 16.7 for Blacks and 18.5
for whites.

When asked why they decided to pursue a career in
science, most scientists cite personal interests and the
desire to know about the how's and why's of nature or human
nature. A greater proportion of whites (67.4 percent) than
Blacks (46.5 percent) cite this as their primary reason.
Black scientists (6.7 percent), on the other hand, are only
slightly more likely than whites (4.1 percent) to report
that they were influenced by "others." These findings,
while significant (p = .0001), simply point up the
importance of early socialization patterns.

Nearly all of the scientists performed exceptionally
well in their high school academic courses as indicated by
their senior class rank. Four-fifths of Blacks and whites
graduated in the top quarter of their senior classes, and
distributions of the two groups over the remaining three
quartiles are virtually identical.

In a study of the undergraduate origins of American
scientists, Goodrich, Knapp, and Boehm (1968) report two
major findings: (1) most are graduates of small liberal arts
colleges, and (2) the institutions which lead in the
production of American scientists are located in the
Midwest. The study does not report on racial differences in
the undergraduate origins of American scientists. Previous
studies of Black American scientists (see Jay, 1971; Young &
Young, 1974; Pearson & Pearson, 1985) show that most have
their baccalaureate origins in historically Black colleges
and universities (HBCUs). Most studies in the sociology of
science fail to include racially comparative samples and, as
a consequence, the generalizability of the findings are
limited. Fortunately this study permits a comparison of
findings across racial lines. Significant race differences
exist in the types of institutions where American scientists
have their baccalaureate origins (see Table 6.1). In
general both groups matriculate in undergraduate
institutions where they are the racial majority. But whites
are even more likely than Blacks to matriculate in racially
homogeneous institutions. Blacks having their origins in
HBCUs tend to be graduates of small privately supported
institutions as opposed to state-supported institutions.
The pattern is reversed for whites. Of those Blacks with
undergraduate origins in predominantly white colleges or
universities (PWCUs), most matriculate in state-supported
institutions. There are some rather striking cohort
variations for Black scientists with respect to the type of
undergraduate institution attended (see Table 6.2). The
proportion of Blacks having their baccalaureate origins in
PWCUs increases dramatically from the period prior to the
landmark 1954 supreme court decision, <u>Brown vs. Board of
Education</u>, to the period following the passage of the 1964
Civil Rights Act. The data also reveal another pattern,
that is, the increasing importance of predominantly Black

Table 6.1

Baccalaureate   Origins   of   American   Scientists   by   Race
(Percent)

Type of Institution	Black	White
Black Private	36.9	0.0
Black State	32.4	0.0
White Private	13.7	48.0
White State	16.9	51.8
Total %	100.0	100.0
Number of Cases	(561)	(683)
= 682.54, p = .0001		

Note: Total may not sum to 100% due to rounding.

Table 6.2

Baccalaureate   Origins   of   American   Scientists   by   Race   and
Cohort (Percent)

Type of Institution	COHORT I (Before 1955) Black	White	COHORT II (1955-1964) Black	White	COHORT III (1965-1974) Black	White
Black private	42.5	0.0	39.3	0.0	32.0	0.0
Black state	32.2	0.0	29.4	0.0	33.1	0.0
White private	12.3	52.9	12.3	42.6	18.9	49.4
White state	13.0	47.1	19.0	57.4	16.0	50.6
Total %	100.0	100.0	100.0	100.0	100.0	100.0
Number of cases	(146)	(251)	(163)	(272)	(175)	(170)
= 219.53, p = .0001 = 251.81, p = .0001 = 168.68, p = .0001						

Note: Total may not sum to 100% due to rounding.

land-grant colleges. Before 1955 Black privately supported institutions produced considerably more Black scientists than their state-supported counterparts. In the period between 1965 and 1974 however, the two types of institutions are virtually equal in the production of Black scientific talent.

Although private-supported PWCUs produced most of the white scientists earning bachelors' degrees before 1955, state-supported institutions are the highest producers from 1955 to 1974. However, differences between the two types of institutions are negligible after 1964.

Significant (p = .0001) race differences emerge with regard to undergraduate academic performance. Specifically nearly one-half of the white scientists, as compared with approximately one-third of Black scientists, report grade-point averages (GPAs) in the 3.5-4.0 range (A = 4 points); while one-half of Blacks and slightly less than two-fifths of whites report GPAs in the 3.0-3.5 range. Thus, both groups perform at the same or similar high levels that characterized their high school achievements.

Regardless of racial status, most of the scientists decide to pursue graduate studies while in undergraduate school. That decision is influenced by a variety of individuals or events. Most, however, report that a teacher influenced their decision in some manner (40.6 percent and 38.6 percent of whites and Blacks respectively). The second most frequently reported individual for whites is "self" (25.2 percent). Blacks on the other hand, equally cite an "event" (18.8 percent) and "self" (18.3 percent).

Several researchers (Bryant, 1970; Cole & Cole, 1973; National Board on Graduate Education, 1976) report that Blacks, in comparison to whites, tend: (1) to take longer to earn their doctorates, (2) to be older at the point of receiving the doctorate, and (3) to earn their doctorates at less prestigious institutions and academic departments. When reporting that Blacks take longer to complete their doctorates, the reference is usually to the lapse time between the bachelor's and Ph.D. degrees. Infrequently pointed out, however, is the fact that the actual amount of registered time in graduate school is roughly the same for both Blacks and whites (National Board on Graduate Education, 1976; Blackwell, 1981). This is quite evident in this study where Blacks and whites report that it took about eight semesters to complete their Ph.D.s. Yet the lapse time between the bachelor's and Ph.D. degrees for Blacks (10.6 years) is nearly three years longer than that of whites (7.8 years). This suggests that Blacks tend to interrupt their graduate studies or pursue their doctorates on a part-time basis (National Board on Graduate Education, 1976). It is probably equally true that such interruptions are the result of financial necessity because Black scientists have their origins in families that are less financially advantaged in comparison with those of their white peers. Naturally such interruptions influence the age at which an individual receives the Ph.D. It is not surprising, therefore, that Black scientists (x = 33.3 years) are about two and one-half years older than their

Black Representation in Scientific Professions   111

white peers (x = 30.7 years) upon receiving their Ph.D.
This finding is consistent with previous studies by Harmon
(1978) and Blackwell (1981).
    Although the scientists in this study have their Ph.D.
origins in a variety of institutions in various regions of
the United States, a greater proportion receive their
doctorates from universities located in the Midwest. This
pattern prevails even when controlling for the effects of
age. The leading regional producer of scientists of both
groups is the North (Midwest). The remaining distributions
vary along racial lines. Among Blacks, for example, the
East is the second highest regional producer up until the
cohort earning their doctorates from 1964 to 1974 where the
South assumes that position. Much of the South's sudden
rise undoubtedly is due to court-ordered desegregation in
the mid-sixties. For the first time large numbers of
southern Blacks could obtain their postsecondary education
in PWCUs in their home states. Doctorates from universities
located in the South are virtually nonexistent among Black
scientists until considerably after the 1954 **Brown vs. Board
of Education** decision. Interestingly during the period of
de jure segregation in the South a peculiar practice is
reported by Black southerners in the study - the practice of
the southern states providing financial assistance to Blacks
to pursue their graduate studies outside of their home
states. Several Black respondents who had their origins in
the South and pursued doctoral studies (usually) prior to
the mid-sixties are informative about this practice.
According to these individuals, in an effort to keep
southern graduate and professional schools racially
homogeneous, Blacks desiring to pursue advanced studies were
encouraged (required) to apply to doctoral departments
outside of their states. Once accepted, they could then
receive financial assistance from their home states. The
amount of financial assistance seems to vary from one
individual to another apparently due to home-state policies
or university expenses. For example, one Black
Mississippian reports that all of his expenses were covered,
while a Black Alabamian points out that only his tuition was
paid.
    The quality of Ph.D.-granting department for the Black
and white scientists generally reveal statistically
significant racial differences. Generally white scientists
are more likely to have received their Ph.D.s from
departments rated "prestigious" or "strong" (Roose &
Andersen, 1970). Examples of the various prestige rankings
in sociology are: (1) prestigious, University of California
at Berkeley; strong, North Carolina at Chapel Hill; adequate
plus, Johns Hopkins University; adequate, Brown University;
and unranked, the University of Kentucky. Blacks are more
likely to attend less prestigious departments (those rated
"adequate" or "unranked"). The proportion of both Blacks
and whites earning their Ph.D.s in the two highest rated
departments (prestigious and strong) steadily declines over
time, but whites continue to hold an advantage over Blacks
with respect to quality of doctoral training. There is a
corollary increase over the years in the proportion of

Blacks and whites receiving doctoral degrees from unranked
departments. Some of this increase for Blacks may be
attributed to the growing production of Atlanta and Howard
universities, two historically Black Ph.D.-granting
institutions whose doctoral programs are unranked by Roose
and Andersen's (1970) rating systems. Furthermore, some of
the increase for both groups as it relates to quality of
Ph.D. seems to be related to the increase in the number of
individuals pursuing their doctoral training in recently
established southern departments or other more recently
established departments that have emerged since the sixties.

An examination of Ph.D. departmental preferences
reveals that proportionately more whites than Blacks report
that they attended graduate departments of their preferred
choices. For example, approximately three-fourths of white
scientists, as compared to about two-thirds of Black
scientists, attended Ph.D. departments of their first
preference. Nevertheless, Blacks (95.7 percent) are equally
as likely as their white peers (95.1 percent) to indicate
that they are either "satisfied" or "very satisfied" with
their doctoral training. While these data reveal that Black
scientists are generally satisfied with their training, the
data also reveal another important fact - that Blacks
experience some difficulty in gaining admission to
departments of their choice. A number of Blacks complain
that they are excluded or denied admission to top-rated
programs because of their low Graduate Record Examination
scores. In addition, a number of southern Blacks cite lack
of total integration at southern institutions in their home
states.

Irrespective of institution of training for Black and
white scientists, all are likely to have few Black
classmates and even fewer Black professors. Black
scientists report a mean of 1.5 and .53 Black classmates and
Black professors, respectively. These statistics become
even more meager for Blacks who received their Ph.D.s in the
two HBCUs. These data further point up the paucity of Black
scientists at two critical levels: (1) among university
faculties, and (2) among doctoral students. white
respondents report even fewer Black classmates (X = .92) and
Black professors (X = .11).

As far as involvement in professional activities while
attending graduate school, Black scientists (88.7 percent)
are somewhat more likely than their white peers (83.1
percent) to report that they held membership in a
professional association. But whites (56 percent) are
somewhat more likely than Blacks (46.8 percent) to indicate
that they submitted research for publication while pursuing
doctoral studies. On the average, whites published one
predoctoral article, while their Black peers published
slightly less (.78).

Financial Support for Graduate Education

The pattern of graduate attendance by students, to a
large extent, may be influenced by their financial

situation. The extent to which this is true may explain the
differences in the manner in which Black and white students
finance their graduate education.   Significant race
differences in patterns of financing graduate science
education are obtained in this study (p = .0001). Black
scientists are more likely to be supported by a fellowship,
while white scientists are more likely to receive an
assistantship. White and Black scientists are about equally
as likely to report the use of personal or family income.
Most Blacks as well as whites cite a combination of personal
and family income, fellowships, and assistantships as major
sources of graduate support.   Blacks, however, are
considerably more likely to report "other" (usually loans)
sources of financial support. Thus, the relative financial
position of whites manifests itself.

        Postdoctoral Study

        There are no statistically significant racial
differences with respect to individuals applying for
postdoctoral fellowships. A total of 182 white scientists
and 133 Black scientists report that they applied for
postdoctoral fellowships.   Blacks are slightly more
successful in their quests for fellowships. For example,
87.2 percent of Blacks and 84.1 percent of whites report
successful applications. Differences between the two groups
are not statistically significant.
        About a third of both white and Black scientists pursue
their postdoctoral studies in distinguished departments.
Overall, one-fifth of all scientists in the study pursue
their postdoctoral studies at a nonacademic institution.
There are differences, though not statistically significant,
between Black and white scientists in terms of the purpose
of postdoctoral study. White scientists (77.7 percent), for
example, are more likely than Black scientists (74.3
percent) to cite "additional experience" as their reason for
pursuing postdoctoral studies.   Blacks (19.3 percent),
however, are more likely than their white peers (14.9
percent) to report "change of field." The major source of
fellowship funding for white scientists (64.2 percent) and
Black scientists (53.2 percent) is the United States
government.
        In their study of postdoctoral training in bioscience,
McGinnis and associates (1982) report several interesting
findings. For example, they reveal that (1) postdoctoral
trainees are more likely than others to take academic
positions; (2) prestige of postdoctoral institution replaces
doctoral prestige as the strongest predictor of the prestige
of first academic position; (3) postdoctoral training has a
positive effect on subsequent publication rates (due
primarily to the fact that postdoctorals are usually
concentrated in research-oriented sectors); and (4)
postdoctorals get over 30 percent more citations of their
publications than non-post-doctorals.   McGinnis and
associates also point out that prestige of postdoctoral
institution exerts virtually no effect on subsequent

productivity. These writers believe that one of the major
functions of postdoctoral training is that it facilitates
intellectual mobility (the time to explore new areas of
inquiry).

QUALITY OF DOCTORAL TRAINING AND CAREER OUTCOMES

Regarding first doctoral appointment, the data show
differences along racial lines which are significant, and
this pattern prevails regardless of the quality of Ph.D.-
granting department. Most of the scientists in both groups
begin their careers in academic institutions (usually in
"same race" institutions). Among Blacks beginning their
careers in HBCUs the figures range from a high of 50.6
percent with Ph.D.s from departments rated "adequate plus"
to a low of 33.9 percent with doctoral origins in
"prestigious" or "distinguished" departments. Black
graduates of distinguished departments are more likely than
their Black counterparts with Ph.D.s from less distinguished
departments to begin their careers in PWCUs or in
government. Graduates from this group are equally as likely
to take industrial positions. Prestige of Ph.D.-granting
department notwithstanding, white scientists are about
equally as likely to begin their careers in PWCUs, industry,
or government. Among whites however, employment in HBCUs
ranked last.

Because most scientists begin their careers in
academia, it is important to examine the data for racial
differences in quality of departments of first postdoctoral
appointment. An examination of the data reveals significant
race differences (p = .0001). For example, approximately
eight in ten Black scientists, as compared to about six in
ten whites, begin their academic careers in unranked
departments. At the upper level of the scale, white
scientists hold nearly a two-to- one edge over their Black
peers in careers that begin in "strong" departments (14.9
percent versus 7.9 percent) and "distinguished" departments
(9.1 percent versus 5.2 percent).

Generally a student's chances of embarking upon a
research and teaching career in a major university are
greatly enhanced if the student earns a doctorate from one
of the top-rated graduate schools (Caplow & McGee, 1965). A
student earning a Ph.D. in a top-rated department has about
a 16 percent chance of being offered employment in a
similarly ranked institution, but a student earning a
doctorate from a department outside of the top-rated
departments has only a 2 percent chance of receiving such an
offer (Brown, 1967). An examination of the quality of Ph.D.
department of origin of Black scientists reveals no
significant differences in terms of first postdoctoral
position for Blacks earning their Ph.D.s prior to 1954. In
short, a prestigious Ph.D. did not provide Black scientists
any advantage in the job market. They are about as likely
as Black graduates of less prestigious departments to begin
their careers in unranked departments mostly in HBCUs. As
is the case for Black scientists earning Ph.D.s from

departments rated "strong" or "distinguished" between 1955 and 1964, they did not have any advantage in initial placement in the job market. It is true, however, that the latter group of Black scientists exhibits entry patterns which are more diverse than those of the former group. This latter group of Blacks represents the first major shift of employment outside of HBCUs. However, the greatest shift in this direction was to occur in the next cohort, those earning Ph.D.s between 1965 and 1975, where nearly six in ten Blacks made the decision to begin their career in PWCUs rather than HBCUs. Moreover, Blacks earning their Ph.D.s between 1965 and 1975 are about twice as likely as blacks in the previous cohorts to start their careers in industry.

Overall, the data suggest Black-white variations in scientific career patterns. To a large extent, changes in the social status of Black Americans in the scientific community closely parallel those of Black Americans in the general population. For example, few Black scientists with doctorates earned before the implementation of the Brown vs. Board of Education supreme court decision of 1954 report career opportunities in other than racially segregated academic institutions. At the time Black scientists were virtually excluded from full-time appointments in industry. Furthermore, having a Ph.D. from a prestigious department did not provide Black scientists with the kinds of career opportunities available to their white peers. In short, Black scientists were restricted to employment primarily in Black settings.

With the advent of major civil rights movements, the opportunity structure for Blacks in science began to open up after 1955. This is evident in the noticeable decline over the years in the proportion of Black scientists who report their first appointments in predominantly Black settings. Despite this change, significant race differences in initial employment patterns persist. While Black scientists are entering their first positions in PWCUs industry, and government in greater numbers, white scientists are shifting their initial entries from the nonacademic to the academic sector, particularly in PWCUs. (This trend has shown a reversal in the last decade.) Black scientists entering academic employment continue to be concentrated in unranked departments, but the number beginning their careers in departments rated strong or distinguished begins to rise. Career opportunities for Blacks in the scientific labor force improved considerably after the introduction and passage of major federal civil rights legislation in the mid-sixties. As a consequence, scientists earning their Ph.D.s after 1964 report a more diverse pattern of entry into the labor force. During this period most Black scientists entering academia did so outside of HBCUs while the proportion beginning their careers in industry actually doubles (relative to that of Black scientists earning Ph.D.s prior to 1955).

In general, few white scientists report job experience in a predominantly Black setting. Most Black scientists have spent at least some of their careers in other than predominantly Black settings. Perhaps the major finding

here is that Black and white scientists arrived at their
present stations in the scientific community through
significantly different paths - paths traditionally pursued
along racial lines. After 1964 the opportunity structure
opened up considerably for Blacks, becoming, at least in
theory, more universal. That is, Blacks and whites of
similar academic origins receive similar entry level
appointments. (Unfortunately this pattern is coming about
at a time when Black student enrollment in doctoral science
programs is declining, especially in prestigious
departments.)

FACTORS CONTRIBUTING TO THE UNDERREPRESENTATION OF BLACKS IN AMERICAN SCIENCE

Black scientists agree that Blacks are underrepresented
in the sciences. Reasons most often cited for this
condition are (1) lack of early encouragement and
motivation, (2) lack of financial support and limited
opportunity, and (3) limited recruitment and institutional
racism.

Early Encouragement and Motivation

Branson (1955) believes that most of the favorable
sociocultural factors operating to attract or recruit youths
into science are virtually absent in the experiences of many
Black Americans. He contends that the aspirations of many
Blacks are probably conditioned by their participation in
the Black community where intellectual achievement has not
been traditionally emphasized. Similar conclusions with
respect to other professions have been reached by Bond
(1972). Writing on the intellectual history of Black
Americans, Bond asserts that the dearth of Blacks among
American scholars does not reflect any mental deficiencies
of the Black population as many early white scholars argue,
but rather the imperfections of the American social system.
He argues that scholars usually are more likely to have
their origins in environments that foster the use of the
written, spoken word and other primary concepts fundamental
to the learning process. Moreover, Bond believes that a
high level of family literacy is a prerequisite to the
development of a scholar.

In the recent past Black scholars had to develop their
talent in environments where illiteracy was enforced by laws
proscribing the instruction of the Black population. From
emancipation to the early seventies, the public school
curricula designed to remedy the almost universal state of
illiteracy among Black Americans were grossly inadequate and
usually ineffective. Because such a social and educational
system was not conducive to intellectual development, it is
not surprising that so few Black scholars were produced.
Early Black scholars typically emerged from atypical social
settings and educatioanl institutions which provided an
educational foundation to only a few scholars and to their

parents and grandparents (Bond, 1972).

Because of the low participation rate of Black Americans in science, Black youths have very few role models. This general absence of role models is even more acute in regions of the country outside the South, where most Black U.S. scientists reside. It has already been discussed that within the Black community there has not been a strong tradition in pursuing careers in science, at least to the same extent as such fields as the ministry, teaching, entertainment, and sports. Thus, the status of the scientist, relative to that of a physician, for example, has not been very visible. Science, for the most part, has been perceived as a difficult, unglamorous, and unrewarding profession, especially given the perceived amount of time and energy required to fill such a role. Other professions are far more visible and appealing. Black youths can readily see what a physician's work entails and realize the amount of prestige and income the position carries, but such an image of a scientist does not exist for most Black youths.

Because science is perceived to be too difficult, many Black youths, early in their educational careers, tend to avoid science and mathematics courses and take only the minimal requirements (Davis, 1986; Gilmartin & associates, 1976). Thus, the background that is so essential to subsequent training is lacking, or at best, inadequate in many instances.

It is important, however, to point out that many Black youths are systematically counseled and attracted away from or out of science and technical fields. This appears to be particularly true in many desegregated secondary schools where many Black youths are seen as incapable of thinking abstractly or solving scientific and mathematical problems.

If Black scientific talent is to be fostered, it must be encouraged in the early years (Pearson, 1986; in press). Such early encouragement will provide the kind of confidence that will serve as a motivating force in developing a keen interest in science and technology. Precisely this kind of motivation lends itself to the survival skills necessary to the successful completion of a scientific or technical program. Much of this motivation and encouragement will undoubtedly have to come from the family, teachers, and other significant individuals. Counselors will have to become aware of the career opportunities for Blacks in science in order to adequately counsel Black students. According to a study by the National Science Foundation and the Department of Education (1980), minority group members, who are already grossly underrepresented in science, are prone to misconceptions that the only individuals in scientific fields are those who have advanced degrees and are academically superior. The study recommends that the National Science Foundation (NSF) and the Department of Education (DOE) expand existing programs to provide adequate career information to minority youths beginning in the early adolescent years.

In addition to parents, teachers have a tremendously important influence on the career choices of young people.

Thus, both elementary and secondary teachers have a pivotal
role to play in the increased production of Black
scientists.   Currently there is a need for new and
innovative science curricula that will stimulate the
interest of a broad spectrum of students and can be
especially directed toward Black students.   Ideally, these
new curricula should be offered during the middle-school
years.

Recruitment and Retention

In order to understand better the current status of
Blacks in scientific professions, it is necessary to review
the available pool of talent or the pool from which
professional (doctoral) scientists are recruited.
Obviously, the fewer Black Americans with bachelor's
degrees, the more restricted the pool of talent for graduate
student recruitment.   And to understand this situation, it
is important to examine briefly the position of Blacks in
higher education.
    The proportion of Black Americans now enrolled in U.S.
colleges and universities increased tremendously in the last
two decades but has levelled off in recent years.   Between
1966 and 1976 Black college student enrollment increased 175
percent (from 282,000 to 1,062,000) (Durham Morning Herald,
1978).   Today about 60 percent of all Black college students
were enrolled in two-year institutions such as community and
junior colleges or technical and vocational schools.
Unfortunately it is precisely these students who tend to
have attrition rates that exceed those of students enrolled
in four-year colleges and universities.   Furthermore in
these schools students are unlikely to be recruited for
further raduate study.   Of the remaining 40 percent, less
than one-half attend one of the HBCUs, while the remainder
are enrolled in PWCUs.
    Although most Black college students are now enrolled
in PWCUs, it is estimated that as many as 70 percent fail
to graduate from these institutions (Fiedlein, 1979).   As a
consequence, HBCUs will probably continue to have a
differential influence on the preparation of Blacks for
postbaccalaureate training (Trent, 1984).   Regardless of the
racial characteristics of their undergraduate institutions,
considerably more Black students must graduate if the
available pool of Black graduate students is to increase.
Despite the progress and success of HBCUs in the production
of Black undegraduates, most available information indicates
that there has not been a spillover effect at the doctoral
level.
    There are of course, other factors that limit the pool
of prospective Black scientists.   Finances are a major
problem for many.   In their study of Black college seniors
at HBCUs, Gurin and Epps (1975) found that Black college
students were considerably more likely than white college
students to report finances as the principal reason for not
continuing their education beyond the baccalaureate level.
Another factor is related to poor academic backgrounds.

Boyd (1974) reports that while more than one-half of all Black college students desire to continue their education beyond the baccalaureate, only about one-fourth have the grade point average necessary to be accepted for further study. Of those expressing a desire to pursue graduate studies, only one-tenth plan to continue on to the doctorate. In addition many Black students do not score well on standardized tests, which, in turn, limits their educational options, especially in distinguished departments (Thomas, 1986). These and related factors greatly reduce the available pool of Black talent for graduate study.

Among the Black students continuing to the doctoral level, many tend to concentrate in the field of education. The situation is compounded by the fact that Blacks are more likely than whites to switch disciplines as they ascend the academic ladder. For example, an examination of the 1973-1974 U.S. doctoral cohort by the National Board on Graduate Education (1976) shows that of Blacks with undergraduate majors in the life sciences, about one-half (52 percent) continue in that field at the doctoral level. In contrast, 80 percent of comparable whites earn a doctorate in the same field as their undergraduate major. Predictably, education is the preferred choice of those Blacks switching disciplines. Again, these factors further contribute to the underrepresentation of Blacks in the scientific professions.

For those Blacks who manage to clear the various hurdles in pursuit of doctoral studies, the course is often unsettling. Nearly one-half of the Black scientists, as compared with about one-third of whites, receive their doctoral training in the two lowest-rated departments. At the upper end of the scale, slightly more than one-half (53.9 percent) of white scientists, as compared with slightly more than a third (36.0 percent) of Black scientists, attend the two highest-rated programs.

In summary, a sizable proportion of Black scientists earn their Ph.D.s in departments that are far removed from the frontiers of scientific discovery. Racial discrimination and variations in quality of doctoral training account for the two-to-one advantage white academic scientists hold over their Black peers in terms of first postdoctoral positions in departments rated "strong" or "distinguished." However, the data on younger academic scientists, Ph.D. recipients after 1965, show a narrowing of the gap. In fact, no significant race differences emerge for these younger academic scientists with respect to first academic position.

INCREASING BLACK REPRESENTATION IN THE SCIENTIFIC COMMUNITY

If Black representation in the scientific community is to significantly increase, much of the responsibility will necessarily have to be placed upon the shoulders of colleges and universities. The roles that these postsecondary institutions play in the development of Black scientific talent are pivotal and, therefore, require both public and private support. There is evidence that some colleges and universities are responding to the problems of low Black representation in science with a variety of innovative programs (Prodgers, 1980; Pearson & Pearson, in press). Nevertheless, there is much that postsecondary institutions can and should do to address the issue of Black underrepresentation in the sciences.

First, by increasing the number of Black science enrollments and lowering their attrition rates, the proportion of Blacks in science can be significantly improved. In general, Black college students have higher withdrawal rates than their white peers. However, between 73 and 88 percent of the Black withdrawals are for nonacademic reasons (National Science Foundation and Department of Education, 1980). This suggests that financial support plays a major role in the attrition process. To address this problem, more public and private funding needs to be directed toward those undergraduate departments enrolling large numbers of Black students and those with proven records of producing Black scientific talent. Today Black students are more likely to attend four-year PWCUs. As a consequence, it is probably more cost-effective to provide funding support to those institutions, irrespective of racial makeup, that are most successful in producing Black scientific talent, as well as to those committed to that goal. (For a list of some of the colleges and universities, see Pearson & Pearson, in press.) If Black representation in science is to increase, PWCUs will have a major role to play.

Second, colleges and universities must develop stronger ties with secondary schools. A variety of collaborative endeavors are possible. Interested college professors, especially Blacks, could present lectures and conduct experiments in the schools. This will not only permit college professors to have pre-college student contact; but it will enable college professors, in collaboration with pre-college teachers, to develop within Black students those abilities that are conducive to academic persistence and accomplishment in science (Prodgers, 1980). Because it is vitally important that training in mathematics and science be both sequential and uninterrupted, college professors could reinforce this in their visits (Davis, 1986; Smith, 1980). Another advantage of this approach is that it exposes young Black students to role models while permitting young white students to see Blacks who have achieved a high status in a prestigious occupation. It is also important to stress that a similar role may be played by nonacademic scientists. This cooperative endeavor will provide college mathematics and science professors with a more accurate assessment of entering college students' basic knowledge of science and mathematics. Apparently, many of the suppositions held by college professors that their students have an adequate basic knowledge of biology, chemistry, and mathematics are erroneous (Prodgers, 1980).

Third, colleges and universities can and should devlop more innovative math and science, reading and writing programs for schools and colleges. These innovative programs should also draw on the growing body of literature in the humanities, math/science education, and social studies of science. Fortunately, some college science programs are now doing this (Prodgers, 1980).

Fourth, because of the scarcity of up-to-date laboratory equipment in many schools and colleges, especially at HBCUs, more collaborative ventures are needed. For example, colleges within close proximity can not only share human resources and equipment but can pool their financial resources to purchase expensive laboratory equipment. Furthermore, appeals can be made to private industries in and around the community to donate equipment. Along these same lines, scientists can develop joint courses or summer institutes that would be opened to high school and college students. (An added incentive for college professors could be recognition and credit toward tenure and promotion for these types of activities if they result in greater production of minority scientists.)

Counselors at both schools and colleges should become better acquainted with career opportunities for Blacks in science, mathematics, and engineering. In addition, they should be aware of programs designed to strengthen minority students who plan to enter science or engineering. Programs such as Mathematics, Engineering, and Science Achievement (MESA) and Minority Engineering Education Effort (ME3) are designed to identify and assist minority students who demonstrate academic promise (Smith, 1980) There are also various other state, regional, and national programs. (For a listing of some of these intervention programs, see Malcom, 1983.)

Fifth, while these recommendations will do much in the way of arresting the problems of low enrollments and attrition confronting Blacks up to the undergraduate level, additional steps are required to increase Black representation among doctoral trained scientists. Currently, Blacks make up decreasing proportions of degree recipients as they ascend the academic degree ladder (Astin, 1982; OTA, 1985; Wilson & Melendez, 1984). It is imperative that undergraduate professors encourage talented Black students to continue their training beyond the baccalaureate degree. Far too many Black undergraduate science majors enter the labor force (or leave science altogether) after earning their bachelor's. Most are attracted by lucrative salary offers from private industry. Unfortunately most do not return to pursue advanced study leading to the Ph.D. degree. In short, Black college students must be made aware of the long-term benefits of a doctorate in science, mathematics, or engineering. Those who pursue doctoral studies will do well to become involved in teaching and research activities. Teaching and research skills provide invaluable training and experience which will ultimately prove vital to success in a scientific or technical career whether academic or otherwise. In the long run such skills will enhance career development and career mobility (Blackwell, 1981).

Sixth, an increase in Black representation in the scientific profession will provide additional role models for the next generation of Black scientists.

In summary, Blacks have made unquestionable gains toward achieving equity at the baccalaureate level but their proportion in science remains negligible. At the doctoral level, substantial progress is needed. A considerable amount of time and a strong commitment on the part of all parties involved will be required to accomplish this goal. Efforts to involve more Blacks in science are justified not only on the basis of equity but also of societal necessity. With the declining number of college-age students, this country can ill afford to waste any creative talent (Turnbull, 1983; Prodgers, 1980). Without comprehensive and dedicated efforts on the part of decision makers in colleges and universities, government, and private industry, Blacks are unlikely to achieve parity in the scientific community.

REFERENCES

Astin, A. W. (1982). Minorities in American higher education. San Francisco: Jossey-Bass.

Blackwell, J. E. (1981). Mainstreaming outsiders: The production of Black professionals. Bayside, NY: General Hall.

Bond, H. M. (1972). Black American scholars: A study of their beginnings. Detroit: Balamp.

Boyd, W. M., II (1974). Desegregating America's colleges: A nationwide survey of Black students, 1972-73. New York: Praeger.

Branson, H. R. (1955). The Negro scientist. In J. H. Taylor, C. Dillard, & N. K. Proctor (Eds.), The Negro in science. Baltimore, MD: Morgan State College Press.

Brown, D. G. (1967). The mobile professors. Washington, DC: American Council on Education.

Caplow, T., & McGee, R. (1965). The academic marketplace. Garden City, NJ: Anchor Books.

Cole, J. R., & Cole, S. (1973). Social stratification in science. Chicago: University of Chicago Press.

Cross, T. (1984). The Black power imperative. New York: Falkner.

Davis, J. D. (1986). The effect of mathematics course enrollment on racial/ethnic differences in secondary school mathematics achievement. Princeton, NJ: Educational Testing Service.

Fiedlein, K. (1979, September 9). Slow fade to white integration's price: Black colleges? The Charlotte Observer.

Gaston, J. (1973). _Originality and competition in science_. Chicago: University of Chicago Press.

Gilmartin, K. J., et al. (1976). _Development of scientific careers: The high school years_ (Final Report). Palo Alto, CA: Americn Institutes for Research.

Goodrich, H. B., Knapp, R. H., & Boehm, G. A. W. (1962). The origins of U.S. scientists. In B. Barber & W. Hirsch (Eds.), _The sociology of science_. New York: Free Press.

Gurin, P., & Epps, E. (1975). _Black consciousness, identity, and achievement_. New York: Wiley.

Harmon, L. R. (1978). _A century of doctorates: Data, analyses of growth and change_. Washington, DC: National Academy of Sciences.

Jay, J. M. (1971). _Negroes in science: Natural science doctorates, 1876-1969_. Detroit: Balamp.

McGinnis, R., Allison, P. D., & Long, J. S. (1982). Postdoctoral training in bioscience: Allocation and outcomes. _Social Forces, 60_, 701-22.

Malcom, S. M. (1983). _An assessment of programs that facilitate increased access and achievement of females and minorities in K-12 mathematics and science education_. Washington, DC: Office of Opportunities in Science, American Association for the Advancement of Science.

Maxfield, B. D. (1982). _Science, engineering, and humanities doctorates in the United States: 1981 profile_. Washington, DC: National Research Council, National Academy Press.

National Board on Graduate Education. (1976). _Minority group participation in graduate education_. Washington, DC: National Academy of Science.

National Science Board. (1983). _Science indicators, 1982_. Washington, DC: National Science Foundation.

National Science Foundation and Department of Education. (1980). _Science and Engineering: Education for the 1980's and Beyond_. Washington, DC: National Science Foundation and Department of Education.

Number of women, Blacks take big jump at colleges. (1978, June 11). _Durham Morning Herald_, p. 2A.

Pearson, W., Jr. (1985). _Black scientists, white society and colorless science: A study of universalism in American science_. Port Washington, NY: Associated Faculty.

Pearson, W., Jr. (1986). Black American participation in American science: Winning some battles but losing the war. Journal of Educational Equity and Leadership, 6, 45-59.

Pearson, W., Jr. (in press). The flow of Black scientific talent: Leaks in the pipeline. Humbolt Journal of Social Relations.

Pearson, W., Jr., & Pearson, L. C. (1985). The baccalaureate origins of Black American scientists: A cohort analysis. The Journal of Negro Education, 54, 24-34.

Pearson, W., Jr., & Pearson, L. C. (in press). Race and the baccalaureate origins of American scientists. Journal of the Association of Social and Behavioral Scientists, 32, 149-64.

Prodgers, S. B. (1980). Increasing minority representation in science. Regional Spotlight, 13, 1-8.

Roe, A. (1953). The making of a scientist. New York: Dodd, Mead.

Roose, & Andersen, (1970). A rating of graduate programs. Washington, DC: American Council on Education.

Smith, E. J. (1980). Career development of minorities in nontraditional fields. Journal of Non-white Concerns, 8, 141-56.

Thomas, G. E. (1986). The access and success of Black and Hispanics in U.S. graduate and professional education. Washington, DC: National Academy of Sciences.

Trent, W. T. (1984). Equity considerations in higher education: Race and sex differences in degree attainment and major field from 1976 through 1981. American Journal of Education, 41, 280-305.

Turnbull, W. W. (1983). Schooling for the age of technology: Where does America stand? Statement before the Joint Economic committee, Congress of the United States, Washington, DC.

Vetter, B. M., & Babco, E. L. (1984). Professional women and minorities. Washington, DC: Scientific Manpower Commission.

Wilson, R., & Melendez, S. E. (1984). Minorities in higher education. Washington, DC: Office of Minority concerns, American Council on Education.

Young, H. A., & Young, B. H. (1974). Scientists in the Black perspective. Louisville: Lincoln Foundation.

7
The Role and Responsibility of the Federal Government: Strategies for Achieving Qualitative Equality at the National Level

CYNTHIA G. BROWN

During the past thirty years, educational opportunities and achievement have increased dramatically for Black Americans. Indeed, actions to open access to and increase equity in public education for Blacks and other victims of discrimination have triggered substantial improvements in the entire education system of this country. These actions were propelled by:

■ federal law enforcement - first by powerful court interpretations of the Fourteenth Amendment, and subsequently, through the enforcement of antidiscrimination statutes enacted by Congress in the sixties and seventies1; and,

■ federal education grant-in-aid and loan programs.2

The results have been dramatic, especially at the elementary and secondary school levels. For example:

■ Most southern schools formerly segregated by law are now desegregated. In 1964 less than 1 percent of southern Black youngsters attended predominantly white schools. By 1980 43 percent of these students were in predominantly white schools and only 23 percent were in schools with 90-100 percent minority student enrollment (Orfield, 1982).

■ Segregation in the assignment of Black and white elementary and secondary school teachers has been virtually eliminated.

■ Black enrollment in postsecondary institutions increased 92 percent between 1970 and 1979; Hispanic enrollment more than doubled and the enrollment of women increased by two-thirds over the same time period. These figures compare with an 8.3 percent increase in white male postsecondary enrollment between 1970 and 1979 (NCES, 1980, 1981; Jeffries & Associates, 1980).

■ Black students have increased their rate of educational attainment faster than white students over the past decade. This is true for reading and math scores at the elementary and secondary school levels and Scholastic Aptitude Test (SAT) scores for entering college freshmen. However, a significant gap between Black and white educational performance still exists.

While federal court and executive branch efforts appear to be closing the gap between Black and white student access to education and achievement in elementary and secondary schools, progress of Blacks relative to whites is less evident at the postsecondary level. Expanded opportunities in higher education have not yet resulted in:

■ equal college graduation rates. In 1979 only 4.5 percent of Blacks twenty-five years or older had completed four years of college while 17.2 percent of whites in that age group had completed four years of college (The Chronicle, October 20, 1980, p. 2).

■ equal performance and equal quality of experiences for Black students in America's colleges and universities. It has been illustrated in the first three chapters of this book that Black students' grades are lower than their white counterparts and their college experience is not as enjoyable.

■ continuing growth in Black enrollment in undergraduate and graduate schools. Between 1982 and 1984 Black undergraduate enrollment in four-year colleges and universities declined by 3.5 percent (NCES, 1984). Black graduate student enrollment declined from 65,000 in 1975 to 62,000 in 1980 (Blackwell, 1982).

■ elimination of the maldistribution (let alone low number) of doctoral degrees earned by Blacks. Over half of the doctoral degrees earned by Blacks annually are in education while less than 2 percent are in engineering (Blackwell, 1982).

■ equal job opportunities for college graduates. In 1982 Black college graduates were more than twice as likely to be unemployed as white college graduates; 7.1 percent of such Blacks and 2.8 percent of such whites were unemployed (U.S. Department of Labor, 1982).

These differences in the quality of the higher education experience for Blacks and whites persist despite intensive federal government activity over the past two decades.

The federal effort to expand postsecondary educational opportunities for Blacks and other minorities has been a two-pronged approach. First, the federal government has enforced Title VI of the Civil Rights Act of 1964 in order to desegregate higher education institutions, especially in those nineteen states that maintained separate public colleges for Blacks and whites. Second, it has provided

financial aid chiefly to students, but also in a more
limited fashion to institutions through such programs as
Title III of the Higher Education Act, which provides aid to
developing institutions, most notably historically Black
colleges.

This chapter examines federal law enforcement action
aimed toward improving the quality of higher education for
Blacks and aimed toward expanding educational opportunities
for Blacks in southern and border states. It describes
federal government activities over the past two decades and
attempts to explain why these activities occurred. The
chapter concludes with recommendations for more effective
federal government activity in the future.

FEDERAL CIVIL RIGHTS ENFORCEMENT IN PUBLIC HIGHER EDUCATION INSTITUTIONS

It is well established by law and tradition that
primary operational responsibility for public education at
the postsecondary as well as elementary and secondary school
levels resides with state government. It is also firmly
established that public, and to a somewhat lesser extent
private, educational institutions are subject to federal
government requirements mandated by the Constitution and
congressionally enacted statutes applicable to federal fund
recipients, which prohibit discrimination on the basis of
race, color, national origin, sex, handicap, or age. In the
case of nineteen states,3 - most of which previously denied
Blacks admission to their traditionally white institutions,
and all of which established and still maintain public
colleges whose original missions were to serve Black
students - federal civil rights requirements apply to the
removal of vestiges of former statewide dual systems of
public higher education.

The Office for Civil Rights (OCR), which since 1980 has
been located in the U.S. Department of Education (and
formerly was in the Department of Health, Education, and
Welfare), for over sixteen years has pressured several state
systems of higher education to desegregate pursuant to OCR's
responsibility to enforce Title VI. The OCR's pressure has
varied from year to year and has been directly related to
events in federal court litigation challenging its
performance, such as <u>Adams v. Bennett</u> (originally styled
<u>Adams v. Richardson</u>).

Students of the <u>Adams</u> litigation and OCR activity
frequently charge that government officials, and perhaps the
<u>Adams</u> plaintiffs as well, were/are merely interested in
quantitative measures of desegregation rather than the
quality of educational programs available to Black students,
Black student performance in postsecondary institutions, and
the benefits Blacks receive from college educations. The
thesis of this chapter is that federal efforts to dismantle
dual systems of higher education:

■ have focused on quantitative desegregation performance
  measures by institutions in the belief that improvement in

the quality of education for Black students would automatically follow;

■ have been limited in part because of the lack of federal case law on the subject; and

■ have been too narrow in approach and consequently provided inadequate assistance and incentives to states and institutions to assure the success of desegregation efforts.

Before examining these points, it is important to describe briefly the history of federal enforcement activities to expand postsecondary educational opportunities for Blacks, particularly through the desegregation of dual public systems of higher education.

FEDERAL EFFORTS TO DESEGREGATE HIGHER EDUCATION

The illegality of government-sanctioned school segregation was proclaimed definitively by the Supreme Court in its famous 1954 decision in Brown v. Board of Education. Though the Brown case concerned elementary and secondary schools, the decision applies with equal force to de jure segregation in postsecondary education. Perhaps ironically, however, while a series of key supreme court decisions which led to Brown involved the denial of graduate and professional education programs for Blacks (for example, Missouri ex rel. Gaines v. Canada in 1983; Sipuel v. Board of Regents in 1948; Sweatt v. Painter in 1950; and McLaurin v. Oklahoma State Regents in 1950), no education desegregation decisions issued by the supreme court subsequent to Brown have addressed higher education. As a result, theories regarding appropriate responses to the finding of illegal discrimination are much more developed for public lower education than for higher education (Dimond, 1982).

The effect of Brown was by no means immediate in elementary and secondary schools or postsecondary institutions in the seventeen southern and border states with de jure segregated education systems. Because of lack of progress in school desegregation and other areas of discrimination against Blacks, Congress passed the Civil Rights Act of 1964. Title VI of the act states:

No person in the United States shall, on the ground of race, color, or national origin, be excluded from participation in, or be denied the benefits of, or be subjected to discrimination under any program or activity receiving federal financial assistance.

HEW (now the Department of Education) was charged with enforcing Title VI as it applies to educational institutions, and by 1965, was engaged in vigorous efforts to desegregate southern schools. Title VI procedures require that HEW attempt to secure voluntary compliance by institutions with the statute and the federal courts nondiscrimination standards. If such attempts fail, it provides institutions with the opportunity for a quasi-judicial administrative hearing, the loss of which could lead to the termination of, or refusal to grant, federal financial assistance. As an alternative, the procedures allow HEW to refer the matter to the Department of Justice so that it can file suit in federal district court.

In 1969 HEW's Office for Civil Rights (OCR) turned its attention to postsecondary education in addition to elementary and secondary education. In 1969 and 1970 OCR notified the ten states of Arkansas, Florida, Georgia, Louisiana, Maryland, Mississippi, North Carolina, Oklahoma, Pennsylvania, and Virginia that they were in violation of Title VI because they had not dismantled their dual systems of higher education which had previously been segregated by law or other state action. All ten either refused to submit statewide desegregation plans or submitted inadequate ones. However, OCR did not initiate enforcement proceedings as required by Title VI. As a result of this and failure to enforce Title VI in other areas, the NAACP Legal Defense and Educational Fund, Inc. (LDF), filed the Adams suit in 1970.

In 1973 HEW was ordered by the Adams court either to negotiate acceptable corrective action plans or to begin enforcement proceedings.4 In 1977 the same court ordered HEW to issue formal guidance on the essential ingredients of acceptable statewide desegregation plans. It also ordered HEW either to renegotiate plans it had accepted or to start enforcement proceedings. In 1977 HEW responded by publishing guidelines entitled the Criteria Specifying the Ingredients of Acceptable Plans to Desegregate State Systems of Public Higher Education (Criteria), and in early 1978, published Revised Criteria to apply to all states that OCR might later determine to have failed to remove vestiges of de jure segregation in their higher education systems.

OCR negotiated and accepted plans from five of the six states cited in the 1977 order. When negotiations broke down in 1979 between the state of North Carolina and OCR, OCR notified the state that enforcement proceedings were being initiated. The administrative hearing on North Carolina began in 1980 and was suspended upon negotiation of a plan in 1981.

Subsequent to the 1977 court order, OCR began investigations of eight other states (Alabama, Delaware, Kentucky, Missouri, Ohio, South Carolina, Texas, and West Virginia), which appeared to have remaining vestiges of formerly illegally segregated systems of higher education. Because OCR delayed in both notifying these states of its findings and in negotiating plans, LDF returned to court regularly.

Interactions of the Adams court, OCR, and, more indirectly, the Department of Justice is by no means over. However, by the end of 1985, all but three of the nineteen states - Alabama, Mississippi, and Ohio - were operating under desegregation plans accepted for the time being by OCR or federal courts.

The legal postures of postsecondary desegregation in Tennessee, Maryland, and North Carolina are different than those of the other states. Tennessee is the only one of the nineteen states in which the higher education desegregation issue has never been directly addressed by the executive branch.5 Maryland and North Carolina are examples of two states which successfully thwarted Title VI action. Many would argue that desegregation issues are the most difficult in these two states, since they have the largest number of historically Black public colleges - five in North Carolina and four in Maryland.

Maryland was one of the original states investigated by OCR in 1969. However, it sought and obtained from a federal district court a preliminary injunction against OCR proceedings. The preliminary injunction in the Maryland case was in effect for ten years. While OCR and the Justice Department actively considered reopening the case during the Carter administration, negotiations were not initiated until the last days of the Carter administration. They continued in the Reagan administration and OCR finally negotiated a plan in June of 1985.

North Carolina also turned to the federal courts to escape federal pressure. Its success was tied to national politics. Throughout the Carter years the toughest and most public battle about higher education desegregation occurred over North Carolina.6   When OCR announced that it would begin enforcement proceedings and hold up future federal funding on new projects pending the outcome of an administrative hearing, University of North Carolina (UNC) officials, like those in Maryland, sought to enjoin the proceedings. They only partially succeeded. The judge retained jurisdiction but allowed the executive branch administrative hearing to go forward. The hearing commenced in July 1980 and continued for five months into the Reagan administration. In June 1981 the Reagan administration accepted a desegregation plan, which it filed in the North Carolina federal court in the form of a consent decree. Former OCR officials denounced the plan as "'significantly worse' than plans repeatedly rejected by the Carter administration" (Washington Post, July 11, 1981, p. A5). The LDF unsuccessfully petitioned the Adams court to prohibit the entry of the plan into a federal court as a consent decree. This petition also failed with both the appeals court and the supreme court.

THE CRITERIA

For reasons that can only be speculated about and that will be discussed in more detail later, OCR neglected to set forth publicly written guidlines for state higher education officials regarding acceptable desegregation plans until ordered to do so by the Adams court. OCR did not exhibit such reluctance with regard to Title VI requirements for elementary and secondary schools, but published written guidlines for acceptable school desegregation plans in 1965,

1966, and 1969 and for acceptable bilingual education programs in 1972.

In 1977 OCR published the _Criteria_ for acceptable corrective plans to eliminate the vestiges of former statewide dual systems. It noted three categories of vestiges that had to be addressed:

1. The proportionately fewer Blacks than whites who enroll in and graduate from southern postsecondary institutions.

2. The continuation of separate systems of higher education with traditionally white institutions enrolling and employing overwhelmingly white students and faculty and with traditionally Black institutions enrolling and employing predominantly Black students and faculty.

3. The continuation of narrow missions and inadequate resources for traditionally Black institutions as well as programs which often are duplicated by nearby white institutions.

The _Criteria_ are divided into two parts - the preamble and elements of a plan. The preamble makes several important points about the legal and policy context in which guidance regarding desegregation plan substance is provided:

■ states must "take affirmative remedial steps" and "achieve results in overcoming the effects of prior discrimination";

■ there must be a statewide approach to desegregation;

■ goals and timetables must be established to measure progress in eliminating the vestiges of illegal segregation and in providing equal educational opportunities for all citizens;

■ OCR should take into account the differences between elementary and secondary education in developing strategies to eliminate inequality in higher education-especially important are the voluntary rather than compulsory nature of higher education, and the statewide and the regional influencs of higher education which are more pronounced than elementary and secondary education; and

■ states must recognize the "special problems of Black colleges" and the "transition to a unitary system must not be accomplished by placing a disproportionate burden upon Black students, faculty, or institutions."

QUANTITY   VERSUS   QUALITY   IN   THE   FEDERAL   GOVERNMENT
ENFORCEMENT EFFORT

Quality Higher Education and its Availability to Blacks in
the South

It is well recognized today that attainment of a
college degree is the surest way to secure desirable and
higher paying jobs. Indeed, the correlation between income
and education level is widely documented and reaffirmed by
the recent findings of Braddock reported in Chapter 5.
     The American higher education system has developed over
three centuries. Educational programs in the liberal arts
and professions such as the ministry, medicine, and law grew
in number initially through the development of private
institutions. Access to that system has historically been
based upon socioecoomic status, primarily income. But with
the change from an agrarian to industrial and now to a
technological and information-oriented society, the need has
emerged for a more broadly educated populace. The push for
a better educated citizenry led to the development of great
statewide systems of public colleges and universities.
Expanded financial support, provided partially by federal
funds, was intended to allow every person with the desire
and requisite ability to obtain a college education
regardless of family income.
     While barriers to higher education based on income have
been substantially reduced, reductions in other access
barriers - namely, those based on minority group status-
have come more slowly. In the South where Blacks are most
highly concentrated, during the past century separate public
colleges were established for Blacks.   These colleges
received fewer resources than their white counterparts and
were allowed to offer a very limited number of educational
programs. While resources for Black colleges were limited,
historically white campuses were expanded greatly in the
sixties and seventies as were the public universities in the
Midwest, North, and West.
     Even though postsecondary institutions existed for
Blacks, Black participation rates in higher education were
far below white rates as late as 1970. Consequently, in
1970 when _Adams_ was filed, there was a twofold challenge to
expand educational opportunities for Blacks: (1) to
desegregate higher education institutions, and (2) to
increase the number and proportion of Blacks in public
colleges and universities.
     The difference in educational opportunity for Blacks
and whites in the South was astounding.   In 1960 the
majority of the American Black population was concentrated
in the seventeen southern and border states.   It is
estimated that in 1960, historically Black institutions
enrolled 96 percent of the Black college students in the
South (Mingle, 1978). At that time as well as today, no
public Black college had a medical or dental school; only
two had pharmacy schools; two had law schools; two
engineering schools; and none could provide terminal or

near-terminal degrees in any other fields except education.
None today has a comprehensive research and development
capability (Berrian, 1982). In other words, higher
education for Blacks in the South was separate and unequal.
     Indeed, such inequality continues for many students
enrolled in historically Black colleges. The federal
government, through OCR, charges that failure to make Black
colleges equal to historically white colleges in the
quality of educational opportunity perpetuates racial
segregation. It has specified actions against institutions
that continue this illegal condition. In 1980 it detailed
such illegalities in the case of one state, North Carolina
(while acknowledging that the state had taken some steps to
dismantle its dual system and that many of its actions were
facially "race-neutral" and might have been legal if "all
things had been equal"):

> Respondents have perpetuated racial duality,
> discrimination, and their colleges' racial
> identifiability in numerous ways: e.g., by
> maintaining racially identifiable student bodies,
> faculties, administrative staffs, and governing
> boards . . . by maintaining more limited and
> restricted institutional missions at TBIs
> [traditionally Black institutions] compared to
> TWIs [traditionally white institutions]: by
> confining TBIs within lower and more restrictive
> institutional "categories"; by placing a more
> limited quantity, range, and level of academic
> program offerings at TBIs as compared to TWIs; by
> permitting more rapid and extensive enrollment
> growth and program development at TWIs; by
> maintaining and reinforcing a statewide system of
> racially duplicated colleges and academic program
> offerings; by perpetuating an overall pattern of
> superior resource allocation to TWIs as compared
> to TBIs; by permitting the development of
> predominantly white two-year community colleges
> and technical institutes, which by their locations
> and program offerings have competed successfully
> with TBIs for white and other students; by
> perpetuating a pattern of less adequate and less
> attractive campuses, grounds, buildings,
> laboratories, and other physical facilities at
> TBIs compared to TWIs; by perpetuating disparities
> in the "passrates" of TBI and TWI graduates taking
> professional licensure examinations; by
> perpetuating disparities between TBIs and TWIs in
> their reputation for overall academic quality; by
> maintaining a pattern of relatively lower monetary
> compensation for faculty at TBIs as compared to
> TWIs, and for Black faculty as compared to white
> faculty; by providing faculty at the TBIs who have
> lesser academic credentials than the faculty at
> TWIs; by the placement and development of the vast
> bulk of the system's "remedial" education programs
> at TBIs and by additional means to be demonstrated

at trial. (Government's Pre-Trial Brief in Administrative Proceeding Against the University of North Carolina, 1980, p. 17)

The _Criteria_ and "Quality"

OCR has spoken through the _Criteria_ about objectives that states must seek and commitments they must make to eliminate the vestiges of formerly dual higher education systems and to expand educational opportunities for Blacks. The _Criteria_ call for desegregation not merely in terms of eliminating the racial identity of institutions by changing the racial composition of students and faculty but also by increasing access to education for Blacks. The authors of the _Criteria_ intended such affirmative action. As one student has pointed out, "When defined in terms of enlarging access, both numerically and proportionately, desegregation promises both better opportunities for individual students, a more national distribution of systemwide resources, and the institutional development of Black public colleges" (Preer, 1979, p. 34).

Nevertheless, it is charged by many that the _Criteria_ and the federal effort are concerned with quantitative and procedural goals (for example, numbers of Blacks and whites attending and graduating from institutions, and elimination of educationally unnecessary program duplication) as opposed to qualitative goals (equality in a variety of outcome measures concerning academic experience and performance as well as usefulness of the college degree.)

The charge is largely unfair. As is discussed in greater detail below, federal officials suffered from two major problems, neither of which were clearly recognized at the time the policy approach of the _Criteria_ was developed. First, they were constrained by the legal environment. No federal court had provided clear guidance on remedial standards to desegregate a statewide system of public higher education. And courts concerned with other civil rights questions in elementary and secondary schools were generally reluctant to consider outcome measures of educational performance and post-high school success as final indications of the elimination of the effects of past illegal discrimination. Second, federal officials developed too narrow an approach to solving the postsecondary education segregation problem in the South. No doubt political and financial obstacles played a major part in relying on a strategy based chiefly on executive branch law enforcement, but hindsight calls into question the narrowness of the original decisions.

In any event, the federal authors and implementors of the _Criteria_ were concerned with the quality of desegregated and expanded educational opportunities for Blacks. They assumed that quantitative goals and objectives could only be met if steps were taken to assure that qualitative goals would be met as well. This appears to be sound reasoning about how to meet the ultimate goals, despite the fact that federal actions were inadequate. There are early

indications at some institutions that qualitative and
quantitative goals are inextricably linked. Examples are
included in the following section:

Increasing Quality of Public Black Colleges

Those traditionally Black institutions striving to
increase their public appeal are attracting increased
numbers of white students and are improving educational
opportunities for Blacks. There are at least two current
examples: The University of Maryland Eastern Shore and
South Carolina State College.

The University of Maryland Eastern Shore (UMES),
founded in 1886 and located on the Eastern Shore of the
Chesapeake Bay in the county with the lowest per capita
income in the state, is the Black land grant college of
Maryland. It is the only Black college of Maryland's four
public Black colleges that has ever been a part of the
Univesity of Maryland system. By the late seventies it was
losing enrollment and proposals were often made that it be
merged with nearby Salisbury State University, a
predominantly white public institution (not part of the
University of Maryland) in which most state resources had
been invested for development of higher education on the
Eastern Shore.

UMES's future prospects changed dramatically in 1978
when the University of Maryland Board of Regents adopted a
comprehensive plan to make UMES its major presence on the
Eastern Shore. As a result, ten new high-demand programs,
not duplicated at Salisbury State, were introduced at UMES.
These programs include computer science, poultry technology
and management (to complement the billion dollar per year
poultry industry on the Eastern Shore), physical therapy,
environmental science, construction management technology
(second home and retirement homes are increasing on the
Eastern Shore), hotel and restaurant management (to respond
to growing bay and ocean recreation activities), and
engineering technology. In addition, an honors program,
planned and implemented with the professional schools at the
University of Maryland at Baltimore, was started (Young,
1980).

As a result, UMES has changed dramaticaly in the past
few years.

■ It has increased enrollment of both Black and white
students, growing 7.5 percent between fall 1981 and fall
1982 (Thrasher, 1983).

■ It has made substantial desegregation progress with white
students constituting 25 percent of current enrollment,
all in regular day courses (Thrasher, 1984).

■ It has also attracted Black and white students with
significantly improved test scores. Once SAT scores of
entering UMES freshman were below those of freshman at the

other three historically Black colleges in Maryland; but, as Table 7.1 illustrates, today they are the highest.

Similar changes appear likely at South Carolina State College (S.C. State).   In 1981 South Carolina officials negotiated a desegregation plan with OCR which provided a $14 million "enhancement package" for S.C. State.   The package included a new business school, computer science program, an expanded engineering technology program, and transfer from the University of South Carolina of the doctor of education professional degree program for education administration.   As at UMES, white enrollment is increasing at S.C. State, and in the 1981 summer session, after the enhancement package had received much public attention, white graduate enrollment at S.C. State reached 24 percent and white undergraduate enrollment 14 percent (Bass, 1982).

Table 7.1

Combined Verbal and Quantitative SAT Scores for the Four Historically Black Colleges in the State of Maryland

			Institution		
	Year	UMES	Bowie State	Coppin State	Morgan State
Fall	1979	654	621	571	634
Fall	1980	681	639	579	631
Fall	1981	704	615	581	620
Fall	1983	696	619	610	643

Achieving Admissions and Retention Goals

Quantitative desegregation goals of admission and retention are not being met at most traditionally white institutions because appropriate "qualitative" steps to welcome Black students and help them to succeed are not being undertaken on a comprehensive basis.   Derek Bok, president of Harvard University, has pointed out that:

A number of studies have shown that minority students tend to perform below the levels predicted by their prior grades and test scores and that Blacks and Hispanics are often clustered at the bottom of their class.   At present, however, we simply do not know the explanation for

these findings . . . one would expect minorities
with the lowest grades and scores to fall furthest
below their predicted peformance, since these
students would presumably feel the most inferior
academically. But the evidence fails to bear out
this hypothesis and even suggests that the
opposite is often true. Hence, other factors
would appear to have more to do with the
performance of minority students. In today's
society, Blacks, Hispanics, and American Indians
have tended to come from inferior schools and have
had to cope with obvious burdens and difficulties
in adjusting to predominantly white institutions.
Thus, the failure of many minority students to
perform according to expectations may well result
from pressures and problems in the university
environment. If this is true, the proper solution
is to improve the environment for minority
students or provide them with effective remedial
help, not to exclude them from the university.
(Bok, 1982, pp. 102-3)

Many colleges and universities have implemented
developmental education programs for underprepared students
and special counseling programs to help students adjust to
their college environments. It is very important to
evaluate the effectiveness of these programs.

Desegregating Enrollment

While white students are increasing their enrollment in
traditionally Black colleges with high-quality and high-
demand programs, they are not enrolling at those Black
colleges with weak programs and well-publicized high failure
rates of their graudates. Low pass rates on state licensure
examinations are especially common for graduates of nursing
and education programs. For example, Florida A & M
University's (FAMU) College of Education graduates had a
pass rate on the teacher certification examination of only
27 percent in 1981 (Clark et al., 1982). As a result of low
pass rates at other colleges as well as FAMU, in 1982 the
Florida state legislature enacted a requirement that 80
percent of a school's education graduates must pass the
teacher certification test or the school's accreditation
will be withdrawn. Desegregation progress at the FAMU
undergraduate level has been nonexistent.

Reasons Why the Federal Government Has Failed to Achieve Quantitative or Qualitative Desegregation

It is evident from the discussion above that federal
activity directed toward desegregating higher education
institutions was substantial during the seventies and
continues into the eighties. However, the _Adams_ plaintiffs,
the _Adams_ court, and the Reagan administration have all

judged the progress to be inadequate both in terms of desegregation and expanded access to higher education for Blacks. Neither "quantitative" or "qualitative" goals have been met. State plans continue to be renegotiated and closely monitored by concerned parties in the hopes that the goals that have been elusive to date can be attained eventually.

By any measure, desegregation progress has been greater in southern elementary and secondary schools than in southern colleges and universities. This progress in public schools <u>can</u> be tied to federal enforcement action. No doubt some of the difference in success of federal action relates to differences in the nature of the two types of educational institutions especially the compulsory aspect of school attendance and the voluntary choice process in higher education. But this basic difference does not account for all of the difference in federal action. Consequently, it is important to examine why federal enforcement actions aimed at dismantling dual systems of higher education have enjoyed limited success in achieving racial equality.

There seem to be at least three major reasons why federal civil rights activity in this area has been inadequate - too few federal court precedents, a very narrow executive branch strategy, and underestimation by federal officials of state resistance. A fourth factor may be the political ramifications of the pressure from many public Black college officials and their constituents to retain Black colleges primarily for Blacks.

<u>Lack of Federal Court Precedents</u>. In the thirty-two years since <u>Brown</u>, the supreme court has not addressed the question of higher education desegregation and has spoken on the issue of expanded opportunities for minorities only in terms of what resulting acceptable limits in opportunities are for majority students, as in <u>California Board of Regents v. Bakke</u>. Federal courts have ruled on cases involving parts of higher education systems in Alabama, Arkansas, Georgia, Tennessee, and Virginia, but none have spelled out specific constitutional principles of relief for dismantling dual systems. As Dimond points out, (1982) the supreme court has made clear that for elementary and secondary schools, "group discrimination against Blacks as a class (as well as denial to individuals of meaningful access to particular schools) is prohibited by the Consitution . . . [while] the tension between theories of group relief and individual access has not been resolved for higher education" (p. 132).

The significance of this unresolved issue is especially important for the fate of historically Black colleges. If federal courts adopted a constitutional approach of equal access for individuals, they would require a state that had restricted access to higher education on the basis of race to take affirmative steps to assure that Blacks were no longer effectively excluded. However, Dimond explains that the access principle does not require states to upgrade traditionally Black colleges so long as they are <u>now</u> funded on a race-neutral principle and have nonracial admission and hiring standards.

A group relief theory offers better prospects for traditionally Black colleges. Under group relief provisions, a state that operated a dual system must develop an effective desegregation plan that results in a unitary system of "just schools" without racial identifiability, addresses the past effects of segregated education, and does not place the burden of desegregation disproportionately on Blacks or their institutions. This priciple is adopted in the Criteria.

In the area of civil rights enforcement, the executive branch rarely gets far ahead of the federal courts. Indeed, the school desegregation initiatives of the federal government taken in the late sixties and early seventies were routinely endorsed by the federal courts. Such has not been the case in higher education. No court has specifically embraced the Criteria and applied them to a particular state system of higher education. The Adams court has found them to be acceptable guidance from the federal government but has not spoken specifically on their substance or the process they employ. For example, neither the Adams court nor plaintiffs have challenged the procedural weaknesses of the Criteria - the fact that they rely on "commitments" to take appropriate steps rather than on specific "measures" to accomplish the desired end results.

In other words, the executive branch through the OCR Criteria adopted the goal of group relief but, probably in part because of the lack of court support, was reluctant to require forcefully that states spell out how they would reach the goal. If this is so, dramatic progress as a result of OCR action may not be realized until some court addresses in concrete terms the nature of appropriate relief to dismantle former dual systems of higher education.

Narrow Executive Branch Strategy. Unlike other areas of civil rights enforcement in education, the federal approach to the desegregation of higher education has been too narrow. There has been no use of compliance incentive mechanisms, little technical assistance, and inadequate data analysis or other research. The reason for this is perplexing. It may be due to the regional nature of the problem and the little knowledge of, or concern about, the issue that the public outside the South has. Such lack of interest by the public has not been true for elementary and secondary schools.

Whatever the reason, beginning in 1964 with the Civil Rights Act, Congress provided for a broader federal approach to elementary school desegregation. Title IV of that Act provided federal funding for technical assistance "regarding effective methods of coping with special educational problems occasioned by desegregation." By 1980 $45 million in Title IV funds was appropriated annually with the widespread implementation of court and OCR-ordered school desegregation plans, Congress recognized the need for another "carrot" to accompany the enforcement "stick." It enacted the Emergency School Aid Act (ESAA) in 1972 to help school districts to plan carefully, to support special programs to facilitate the desegregation process, and to encourage the "voluntary elimination, reduction or prevention of minority group isolation."7 Title IV and ESAA were limited to addressing civil rights problems in elementary and secondary schools, and use a "carrot-and-stick" approach never tried with regard to segregation in higher education.

In the latter seventies OCR awarded technical assistance contracts on a variety of civil rights issues. In 1981 it awarded its only contract to aid in the higher education desegregation process. However, the need for such technical assistance help has been well documented, particularly by the contractor who received this award, the consulting firm headed by Kenneth Clark - Clark, Phipps, Clark & Harris, Inc. (CPC&H).

Any civil rights technical assistance program has a difficult beginning. Institutions are suspicious of the contractor's or grantee's relationship to the enforcement role of OCR. However, technical assistance is readily sought by education officials when an institution's need for help is clear as a result of strong and consistent OCR enforcement and when financial incentives for compliance are provided, such as under ESAA. CPC&H found this same pattern.

It appears that technical assistance activiies have promise in assisting the higher education desegregation process, but the questions remain as to why they were not tried earlier and why they now appear to be abandoned. In the Carter years OCR officials proposed an ESAA-like program as well as technical assistance. But within HEW and the Department of Education, these recommendations never rose above other priorities or budget limitations to appear in budget requests to Congress. The Reagan administration is even less interested in multiple approaches to solving civil rights problems. It carries out its legal responsibilities which, because of the Adams case, are substantial in this area. But it is doing little to assure real progress toward the goals of desegregation and expanding higher education opportunities for minorities. Indeed, CPC&H (1982, p. 147) noticed indications of change in Adams state officials as a result of Reagan administration actions: "in general, the officials of the Adams states seem to be 'hunkering down' for a long haul with respect to effecting major changes in the basic desegregation picture in their respective states and . . . a significant change has occurred in the priority given to desegregation as such."

The executive branch has also engaged in minimal data analysis or research into the obstacles to successful higher education desegregation. Neither OCR nor the Office for Educational Research and Improvement (formerly the National Institute for Education) has funded major research on this issue. Yet both have supported extensive research on a variety of civil rights problems in elementary and secondary schools including school segregation, bilingual education, and the misclassification of minority students as disabled.

OCR's data collection efforts in higher education- including the special efforts in the Adams states - are of low quality in contrast to its collection and analysis of data concerning participation and treatment of minorities, women, and the disabled in elementary and secondary schools and vocational education programs. As a result, the data collected are incomplete, are available long after they are collected, are not analyzed in narrative form, and are not disseminated routinely to interested parties. Without data and research reports, higher education officials and concerned citizens are discouraged from initiating programs and activities to aid in the processes of desegregation and expansion of educational opportunities for minorities.

The federal government has approached civil rights enforcement concerning dual systems of higher education in an almost haphazard way. Since 1969 OCR officials have tried valiantly to mount aggressive enforcement programs in this area. But all have failed to one degree or another to gain the broad-based higher-level support they need for a sustained, effective program. To some extent they could not gain that support because of the absence of federal court rulings supporting their positions and because of political resistance of both white and Black higher education officials in the South (see below). However, full explanations are not obvious; this area provides fruitful ground for more public policy analysis.

Underestimation of State Resistance. While adequate court support and a narrow approach has limited the effectiveness of federal actions, federal success has also been thwarted by fierce state resistance to pressure to eliminate the vestiges of their dual higher education systems. Federal officials seemed to underestimate this resistance and to be somewhat surprised by it. State resistance occurs for a variety of reasons including:

- heightened federal activity, which coincided with a demographic downturn in expected growth in student enrollment and faculty position openings;

- a general unwillingness of state officials to enhance traditionally Black institutions at the expense of nearby traditionally white four- and two-year institutions (This is especially true in states like North Carolina and Maryland which appear to have overbuilt their systems or built them too fast based on either faulty projections of student enrollment growth or assumptions that the dual system could be maintained. However, all nineteen states dramatically expanded their higher education systems during the sixties and seventies with the exception of their traditional Black colleges, few of which grew at all.);

- lack of federal financial incentives to plan and implement programs to address this problem;

- unwillingness of state higher education and elected officials to address systematically the poor educational preparation of many Black high school graduates;

■ intransigency of state legislatures dominated by rural interests unsympathetic to strong support of education and resistant to federal pressure;

■ general, but relatively recent, public support (by whites) for equal access to traditionally white institutions for Blacks and whites, but still little support for enhancement of traditionally Black institutions which are often viewed as unfortunate remnants of a segregated past.

Still, southern state resistance to public school desegregation was even more forceful. But, what was present in the case of school desegregation was strong guidance from the federal courts, no ambivalence by the federal government, and resolve of the northern public that this level of education - for which attendance is compulsory and recognized as vital for the future happiness and self-sufficiency of all children - be desegregated and equally accessible.

Pressure from Black College Officials. Finally, the fourth factor that has affected federal civil rights activity in this area is the difference in views among Black educators and political leaders about where federal emphasis should be placed in expanding higher education opportunities for Blacks. The most vocal group on the desegregation issue has been public Black college officials and their constituents who want to retain Black colleges primarily for Black students. They have used the political process to gain support for their position at both the federal and state level. Their position has been readily accepted by many white higher education officials who sometimes use it as an excuse not to make greater desegregation progress at their own institutions. The fact that very few Blacks have been appointed to the highest positions at historically white schools confirms the fear of Black college officials that if they "lose" the Black colleges, they will lose leadeship positions in all public higher education.

THE FUTURE: RECOMMENDATIONS FOR A MORE EFFECTIVE FEDERAL EFFORT

Even though the Reagan administration is less aggressive than previous federal administrations in pursuing civil rights compliance goals, there are some positive developments which may yet spell progress in increasing educational opportunities for minorities. Such promising activities include new state leadership, useful research, and continuing litigation.

State Leadership

In some southern states leaders are emerging who want to put segregated higher education behind them as they did for elementary and secondary segregation. Such leaders are found in universities. An example is Dr. John S. Toll,

president of the University of Maryland, who has initiated
and sustained the effort to develop the University of
Maryland Eastern Shore as a full high quality partner in the
University of Maryland system. He also has recruited an
outstanding scientist and educator, Dr. John B. Slaughter,
as chancellor of the university's largest campus at College
Park. Dr. Slaughter is the first Black to be appointed as
the chief executive of a flagship university in a southern
or border state.

Other important leaders have been governors, of whom
the best example is Governor Richard W. Riley of South
Carolina. Richard Riley participated in the struggle of his
state to desegregate its public schools. As governor, he
wanted his state to address with less difficulty the
desegregation of higher education. He is quoted as seeing
postsecondary desegregation as "an opportunity to show the
people in the world and the United States and the Southeast
that South Carolina was at such a stage that we could take
on a major race issue, handle it quickly, handle it fairly,
and without emotional involvement" (Bass, 1982, p. 29). He
and other South Carolina officials did that. On the heels
of the Reagan administration retreat in North Carolina,
Governor Riley submitted a strong desegregation plan to OCR
in 1981.

Research

Good research is starting to appear on the problems and
needs of minority students in postsecondary institutions.
While the federal government still is not financing relevant
research in this area, private foundations like the Ford
Foundation, the Lilly Endowment, Inc., the Mott Foundation,
the Carnegie Corporation of New York, the Rockefeller
Foundation, and the Southern Education Foundation have
sponsored useful research projects.

Continuing Litigation

The Adams case remains active with the Adams court
continuing to pressure OCR with regular orders. The recent
1983 order spurred more timely submission of desegregation
plans from some states and the renegotiation of plans with
other states which had failed to make adequate progress
under previous plans.

Recommendations for Improved Federal Efforts

While the gap is closing between Black and white
college students in access to and benefits from
postsecondary education, the differences remain substantial.
Inadequate levels of financial aid for students are one
major problem. Another problem is the continuing failure to
desegregate higher education in those nineteen states that
maintained public colleges on the basis of race. As of

1978, 43 percent of all Black students in postsecondary education attended institutions in the nineteen <u>Adams</u> states (Blackwell, 1982).

Federal government pressure remains the key to desegregating higher education and expanding postsecondary education opportunities for minorities. The Constitution and Title VI mandate that the federal government assume such responsibility at least through its civil rights enforcement procedures. But such a legalistic approach by itself is probably neither adequate nor sensible today. While the courts to date have not provided sufficient support to the executive branch, there are signs that state education and elected officials might respond positively to a broader federal strategy of expert assistance and financial incentives.

If this is so, what is needed is renewed federal commitment to expand postsecondary educational opportunities and to eliminate continuing segregation of Blacks. This commitment should be an articulated priority by the highest level federal officials. These federal officials should overtly encourage state elected and education officials to join in partnership with federal officials to plan, enact, and implement a multi-faceted program to reach specific goals in established time periods. This expanded and improved program to address the issue of Black participation in higher education should include:

- a written assessment, preferably by a presidential commission, of the status of minorities in higher education and the federal responsibility to improve the situation;

- a reinvigorated OCR enforcement program leading to the negotiation of state desegretgation plans which are based on the <u>Adams Criteria</u> and include specific steps with real promise of success.

- expanded financial aid for low-income students;

- a temporary, competitive grant program to provide assistance to public colleges and universities, both traditionally Black and white, in the nineteen <u>Adams</u> states for planning and implementing innovative programs to meet desegregation plan goals (Given the proportion of Blacks working throughout the country but educated in these states, it should be possible to sell this as a national need.);

- a variety of technical assistance programs including, for example, federally funded experts to provide on-site help; sponsorship of conferences and workshops for elected and education officials and for representatives of interested Black and white student, parent, faculty, administrative, and alumni groups; preparation of case studies and models of effective programs to desegregate and increase Black participation in higher education; and support for institutional staff to address these problems full-time;

■ timely collection, analysis, and dissemination of relevant
  data; and

■ research studies on how best to address specific problems.

   However, the essential ingredient is not such a broad-
based program, but clear, visible, and sustained leadership.
With such leadership the plodding progress of the past can
be replaced with crisp movement forward and expanded
opportunities, participation in, and benefits from higher
education for Blacks and all minorities.

REFERENCES

Babcock, C. R. (1981, July 11). U.S. accepted desegregation
    plan once rejected for N.C. colleges. The Washington
    Post, p. A5.

Bass, J. (1982). Something's happening in South Carolina.
    Atlanta: Southern Education Foundation.

Berrian, A. H. (1982). Toward desegregation and
    enhancement. In R. Wilson (Ed.), Race and equity in
    higher education. Washington, DC: American Council on
    Education.

Blackwell, J. E. (1982). Demographics of desegregation. In
    R. Wilson (Ed.), Race and equity in higher education.
    Washington, DC: American Council on Education.

Bok, D. (1982). Beyond the ivory tower: Social
    responsibilities of the modern university. Cambridge,
    MA: Harvard University Press.

Brown, C. G. (1983, July 27). Civil rights: Losing the
    tools to do the job. Education Week, p. 16.

Califano, J. A. (1981). Governing America: An insider's
    report from the White House and the Cabinet. New York:
    Simon and Schuster.

Clark, Phipps, clark & Harris, Inc. (1982, October).
    Technical assistance on higher education desegregation:
    A report. Submitted to Office for Civil Rights, U.S.
    Department of Education, Contract No. 300-81-0402.

Dimond, P. R. (1982). Constitutional requirements. In R.
    Wilson (Ed.), Race and equity in higher education.
    Washington, DC: American Council on Education.

Jeffries & Associates, Inc. (1980). Facts about Blacks
    1980-81. Los Angeles, CA.

Mingle, J. R. (1978). Black enrollment in higher education:
    Trends in the nation and the South. Atlanta: Southern
    Regional Education Board.

Orfield, G. (1969). The reconstruction of southern
    education: The schools and the 1964 Civil Rights Act.
    New York: John Wiley.

Orfield, G. (1981). Why it worked in Dixie: Southern
    school desegregation and its implications for the
    North. In A. Yarmolinsky, L. Liebman, & C. S.
    Schelling. Race and schooling in the city. Cambridge,
    MA: Harvard University Press.

Orfield, G. (1982). Desegregation of Black and Hispanic
    students from 1968 to 1980. A report to the
    Subcommittee on Civil and Constitutional Rights of the
    Committee on the Judiciary of the U.S. House of
    Representatives. Washington, DC: Joint Center for
    Political Studies.

Preer, J. (1979). Lawyers v. educators: Changing
    perceptions of desegregation in public higher
    education. Paper presented at the 1979 North Carolina
    Desegregation in Higher Education Conference, Raleigh,
    NC.

Proportions of Americans who have attended college rose
    during the 1970's, Census Bureau reports. (1981,
    October 20). The Chronicle of Higher Education, p. 2.

Thrasher, G. Director of Institutional Research, University
    of Maryland Central Administration, Adelphi, Maryland.
    Conversations of September 22, 1983, and January 4,
    1984.

U.S. Department of Education, National Center for Education
    Statistics. (1980). Digest of education statistics
    1981. Washington, DC: Author.

U.S. Department of Education et al. (1980, May 31).
    Government's pre-trial brief. In administrative
    proceeding in the matter of the state of North Carolina
    and the board of governors of the University of North
    Carolina at al., ED Docket No. 79-VI-I.

U.S. Department of Education, National Center for Education
    Statistics. (1984). The condition of education 1984.
    Washington, DC: Author.

U.S. Department of Education, Office for Civil Rights,
    (1982). 1980 elementary and secondary schools civil
    rights survey: National summaries. Arlington, VA:
    DBS Corporation for the Department of Education, Office
    for Civil Rights.

U.S. Department of Education, Office for Civil Rights.
    (1982, December 6). Data processing and analysis of
    the seventh report on progress in implementing
    statewide higher education desegregation plans:
    Undergraduate entry rates, enrollment, graduate and

professional entry rates, and faculty data by race/ethnicity, Volume I of II. Arlington, VA: DBS Corporation under subcontract to Opportunity Systems Incorporated for the Office for Civil Rights, Department of Education.

U.S. Department of Health, Education, and Welfare, Office for Civil Rights. (1978, February 15). Revised criteria specifying the ingredients of acceptable plans to desegregate state systems of public higher eduction. Federal Register, 43(32).

U.S. Department of Health, Education, and Welfare, National Center for Education Statistics. (1980). The condition of education for Hispanic Americans. Washington, DC.

U.S. Department of Labor, Bureau of Labor Statistics, (1982, August 10). News. Tables 1 and 2.

Wilson, R. (1982). Race and equity in higher education. Washington, DC: American Council on Education.

Young, R. H. (1981). Campus in transition: University of Maryland Eastern Shore. Adelphi, MD: the University of Maryland.

NOTES

   1. The antidiscrimination statutes affecting education institutions include four statutes that prohibit discrimination on the basis of race, color, national oigin, sex, handicap, or age by recipients of federal grant funds: Title VI of the Civil Rights Act of 1964 (race, color, national origin); Title IX of the Education Amendments of 1972 (sex); Section 504 of the Rehabilitation Act of 1973 (handicap); and the Age Discrimination Act of 1975. Two other statutes applicable to education institutions address employment discrimination alone: Title VII of the Civil Rights Act of 1964 (race, color, national origin, sex) and the Equal Pay Act of 1976 (sex). In addition, Executive Order 11246 prohibits employment discrimination on the basis of race, color, national origin, sex, or religion by federal contractors, including education institutions. Federal contractors are forbidden from discrimination in employment on the basis of handicap under Section 503 of the Rehabilitation Act of 1973.

   2.   Important federal education programs at the elementary and secondary school level include Chapter 1 of the Education Consolidation and Improvement Act, the Bilingual Education Act, and the Education of the Handicapped Act. Postsecondary education level programs include Pell Grants and Guaranteed Student Loans.

3.   Alabama, Arkansas, Delaware, Florida, Georgia, Kentucky, Louisiana, Maryland, Mississippi, Missouri, North Carolina, Ohio, Oklahoma, Pennsylvania, South Carolina, Tennessee, Texas, Virginia, West Virginia.

4. It accepted plans for eight states and referred the two states with unacceptable plans, Louisiana and Mississippi, to the Department of Justice, which subsequently filed suit. In 1975 the plaintiffs in the Adams case returned to court charging that the accepted plans were inadequate and were not being implemented, and that HEW was continuing to shirk its responsibilities to assure compliance with Title VI.

5. In 1968 private citizens filed suit to enjoin the expansion of the predominantly white University of Tennessee - Nashville, (UT-N). The Department of Justice and LDF both intervened in the case, Geier v. Alexander (formerly Geier v. Dunn). Several orders have been issued in both the Geier case and a related case, including a 1977 order to merge UT-N and the historically Black institution, Tennessee State University, because of inadequate desegregation progress. While chiefly Fourteenth Amendment cases, Geier is important for Title VI activities because it provides most of the judicial guidance about what constitutes acceptable steps to desegregate and to appropriately measure desegregation progress.

6. For a partial history and interpretation from one perspective, see Joseph A. Califano, Governing America: An insider's report from the White House and Cabinet (New York: Simon and Schuster, 1981).

7. The $298.5 million in funds ESAA provided annually by 1979 became an essential ingredient in successfully integrating school systems, first in the South and later in the North and West. The Reagan administration proposed and convinced Congress to abolish the EASS program and to fold it into the education block grants bill enacted in 1981, The Education Consolidation and Improvement Act (ECIA). Money spent on desegregation-related activities dropped to 8 percent of its former level - from $298.5 million under ESAA in 1979 to an estimated $25.2 million on similar activities under ECIA 1982 (Brown, 1983).

8

The State Role in Achieving Equality
of Higher Education

JOHN B. WILLIAMS

INTRODUCTION

State governments have played a major role in determining
the status of racial equality in higher education. Because
of state segregation laws and exclusionary policies prior to
1960, nearly 100 percent of Black college students attended
Black colleges in the nineteen southern states. These Black
college students in southern states represented 75 percent
of all Black college students in the United States (Mingle,
1981). Today less than 25 percent of all Black college
students attend Black colleges. This transition in Black
student enrollment over the past two decades can be traced
through the federal courts which have eliminated segregation
laws and exclusionary policies over the past two decades.

Despite the enrollment transition, however, educators
and policymakers of all political persuasions agree that
desegregation in education is a vague public policy.
Despite extensive case law, recent public policies, and the
growth in applied social science research, remedies for
racial inequalities in higher education remain uncertain.
At the elementary and secondary levels such remedies as
mandatory busing or special compensatory treatment for
minority school children are controversial because of the
great difficulty and inattention to precisely measuring the
impact such policies have upon individuals and institutions.
The unresolved issues are effectiveness and fairness.
Recent research, however, indicates that at the higher
education level, numerous inequalities continue to exist
because of vague public policies and the failure of public
policies to address many remaining inequalities that have a
negative effect on Black students.

Title VI of the 1964 Civil Rights Act is particularly
vague. Judge Wisdon (1964), for example, writing for the
Fifth Circuit Court gave the following interpretation of
Title VI:

> Title VI.requires all federal agencies
> administering any grant-in-aid program to see to
> it that there is no racial discrimination by any

school or other recipient of federal financial aid
. . .

To make Title VI effective, the Department of
Health, Education and Welfare (HEW) adopted the
regulation, "Nondiscrimination in federally
assisted programs." This regulation directs the
commissioner of education to approve applications
for financial assistance to public schools only if
the school system agrees to comply with a court
order, if any, outstanding against it, or submits
a desegregation plan that is satisfactory to the
commissioner. (United States v. Jefferson County
Board of Education 372 F2d 836[5th Cir 1966])

It appears that Title VI was intended to allow the
administrative branch of the federal government maximum
flexibility in undertaking the difficult and largely
unprecedented task (in 1964) of regulating state and locally
controlled public segregated elementary, secondary and
higher education systems (Orfield, 1969). The great
flexibility during a period of broad political support for
school desegregation in 1964 is viewed as a mechanism for
optimum success. On the other hand, during periods of
increasingly broad skepticism over desegregation as a social
policy, such as in the eighties, lack of clarity has proven
to be a liability to efforts to achieve educational
equality. Title VI is difficult to implement because it:
(1) does not specify proofs needed to connect past de jure
practices with current patterns of racial isolation, (2)
does not apply in de facto segregation circumstances which
now include qualitative inequalities such as student
performance, and (3) does not offer guidance for
establishing remedies or delineate responsibility for
undertaking remedies.
Title VI and other racial equality policies and
statutes are concerned with equalizing education for white
and minority children. An important aspect of the vagueness
of these statutes has to do with the definition of equality
used to judge adequate compliance. Is equality concerned
with equalizing the outcomes of schooling for Black and
white students, with equalizing resources used to provide
education for Blacks and whites, or with treating Black and
whites through equal means in their process of obtaining an
education? Each of these policy options underlies certain
aspects of American social policy though not necessarily
where education is affected. But all three of these areas
are not necessarily compatible. As Alexander Heard, the
former Chancellor of Vanderbilt University, argued in the
early stages (the sixties) of recruiting Black students at
his institution, in order to treat Blacks equally, his
institution needed to treat them specially. One
interpretation of his comment is that in order to equalize
the outcomes of college attendance at Vanderbilt,
institutional resources needed to be allocated
disproportionately in favor of Blacks. Or, the same process
was unlikely to lead to the same outcomes for Black students

and white students attending white universities.

A full account of the debate over the true meaning of educational equity underlying Title VI and similar provisions of law lies beyond the scope of analysis in this chapter. It is important to recognize, though, that Title VI regulation of higher education incorporates two of the three policy options. Implementing Title VI, particularly where higher education is concerned, appears to incorporate achievement of equal resources and achievement of equal treatment (or processing) as standards for integrating state systems of higher education, but very little concern for equalizing outcomes has been specified in existing public policies. This is to say that, to the extent that Title VI is concerned with equalizing higher education offered Black and white students, the operable definition of equality involves measuring resources and processes, but not student learning and outcomes.

By not focusing upon elements of students' higher education experience and outcomes, purveyors of Title VI regulatory policy leave themselves open to the charge that they are unconcerned with improving the quality of college education provided for Blacks. The reluctance on the part of policymakers to concern themselves with student outcomes is consistent with an unwritten law among government officials.concerned with higher education: that quality of the college experience measured in anyway is an inappropriate concern for government. Colleges and universities have striven in recent years to retain autonomy in the area of quality and qualitative equality arguing that these matters are not within the purview of government responsibility. And among academicians, little agreement exists over appropriate and accurate methods for measuring college outcomes regardless of whether the purpose for doing so includes making determinations about racial equality. State and federal policies have, however, evolved since 1965 toward achieving procedural and resource equality with less resistance from college administrators and faculty than is the case with student achievement and outcomes.

These circumstances, however, have changed a bit over the past two or three years. State-government-initiated reforms have involved making assurances of uniform college outcomes as a means of satisfying concern for high quality. The assurances have amounted to setting minimum test scores which all students must achieve in order to progress through college and graduate. This change has come about for a number of reasons. In general, lawmakers and policy officials have come to realize the liability of avoiding determinations of the quality of higher education, and educators have abdicated this responsibility.

Unfortunately, requiring students to pass standardized tests in order to graduate constitutes only a limited response to the quality problem. Arguably, the fallacies of the minimum test-score approach are: (1) inability to show that the college experience imparts ability to pass outcomes tests, (2) inability to demonstrate that specific aspects of the college experience more than others impart ability to pass outcomes tests, and (3) inability or unwillingness to

demonstrate that the college experience is race-neutral, or
that Blacks and whites are equally imparted the skills and
knowledge needed to pass the tests. Assuming the accuracy
of the tests, there exists additional disagreement over the
issue of whether standardized testing of college students
measures that set of academic skills and basic knowledge
that colleges ought to impart.

The limitations imposed upon higher education
institutions as a result of the quality movement impedes the
enforcement of Title VI regulations because Blacks are
disproportionately excluded from college by failing to pass
entrance and/or graduation examinations. On the other hand,
Title VI does not in turn require states to use test scores
as measures of the achievement of desegregation. Such a
requirement would demonstrate more inequalities in higher
education than the courts now deal with. Because Title VI
is concerned primarily with procedural equality and with
equalizing resources, it has hardly examined the inequality
in the qualitative facets of higher education. This chapter
is concerned with the limited ways in which states have
implemented Title VI toward achieving equality in
educational processes and resources. Measures of outcome,
particularly changes in student academic performance and
accumulated knowledge, are infrequently considerations by
state government to determine progress toward compliance
under Title VI, and therefore represent a challenge in
gaining a place on the agenda of policymakers and federal
judges. Whether they should be incorporated into the
compliance process and how are also matters of consideration
in this chapter.

THE STATE GOVERNANCE SYSTEM UNDERLYING TITLE VI REGULATION
OF HIGHER EDUCATION

States hold primary responsibility by constitutional
provision or by statute for public higher education. They
exercise this responsibility by operating colleges and
universities as special agencies of the administrative
branch of state government. Not unexpectedly then, state
laws and constitutional provisions offered the basis for
racial discrimination in public higher education as it was
practiced prior to the Brown v. Board of Education (court
decision 347 U.S. 483 [1954]).

A widely known example is the 1904 "Day Law," named for
its originator in the Kentucky General Assembly, which won
support on appeal from the U.S. Supreme Court in Berea
College v. Kentucky (211 U.S. 45 [1908]). The Day Law aimed
"to prevent contamination of Kentucky's white children"; it
made it "unlawful for any person, corporation, or
association of persons to operate any college, school or
institution where persons of the white and Negro race are
both received as pupils for instruction" (Act, Kentucky,
1904, Chapter 85, p. 18). This law and others like it
clearly had the effect of allowing state policymakers who
were so inclined to distribute fewer public resources for
higher education for Blacks than for whites (Trueheart,

1980). Such laws also permitted other inequalities - like not permitting certain courses of study to be offered at Black colleges and universities - to characterize governance of public higher education systems in states today affected by Title VI (Browning & Williams, 1978).

Not unexpectedly the states guilty of adopting such laws and policies and of operating racially segregated higher education systems did not on their own take giant steps toward remedying past actions once segregation laws were abolished in the fifties and sixties. On the contrary, one can easily recall the specter of Governor George Wallace physically confronting U.S. Attorney General Nicholas Katzenbach to prevent Blacks from enrolling at the University of Alabama; or the several days of violent rioting which accompanied James Meredith's forced admission to the University of Mississippi. While a few offender states, consistent with national trends, mounted nondiscriminatory admissions policies and established scholarship programs for low-income students, and while other states marginally increased funding for traditionally Black colleges, few state officials offered genuine leadership in the direction of formally ending discrimination in public higher education. This was the case despite _Brown_ and other progressive judicial opinions. Impetus for achieving equality in previously segregated public higher education systems stems from a combination of federal legislative and judicial action. As a result of the passage of Title VI, the Office for Civil Rights (OCR) at the U.S. Department of Education (DOE) has, since 1969, attempted to regulate state government policy in previously de jure segregated states in the direction of creating remedies for past actions. With changing administrative leadership at the White House, OCR's role has been one of varying reluctance to implement Title VI. When this fact was brought to the federal judiciary's attention through litigation, the district court in Washington required OCR to assume a more energetic regulatory posture. Periodically over the past sixteen years, the court has pressed OCR to implement desegregation in states affected by Title VI.

Thus the real energy for ending segregation in the nineteen state higher education systems guilty past de jure laws comes from federal, not state government. On the other hand, state governments involved in the problem are central for actually ending segregation, since they alone operate public college systems. Even if state governments on their own had chosen to desegregate higher education beyond offering scholarships and requiring nondiscriminatory admissions policies, they would have needed to do so with great constraint. State governments have traditionally exercised limited oversight of public higher education because of the deeply held tradition of academic freedom and independence from interference from all forms of government. This tradition has characterized the development of both public and private higher education in American society, and it extends far beyond Title VI regulation. These factors complicate Title VI regulation and enforcement. The complex system of governance of public higher education renders

Title VI regulation a problematic and unpredictable undertaking. Reports on the experience of implementing Title VI (including court findings support) this interpretation.

THE TITLE VI REGULATORY PROCESS IN HIGHER EDUCATION

A brief description of the federal-state regulatory process is necessary for understanding the state role within the web of higher education governance. First of all, the current, sixteen-year-old Title VI regulatory process is based upon the unarguable existence of past segregation laws and policies and upon evidence of little change in the racial representation of students, faculty, and staff within the states' public higher education institutions. Of central importance in producing such results is the continued existence of at least one predominantly Black public institution which was established to facilitate racial separation in each state system.

The following excerpts from a 1969 letter to the governor of Virginia from the director of the Office for Civil Rights illustrate the basis for the federal government's finding of continued effects of past segregation laws:

(T)he State of Virginia is operating a non-unitary system of higher education. Specifically, the predominantly white state institutions providing four or more years of higher education have an enrollment which is approximately 99 percent white. The predominantly Black institutions have an enrollment which is predominantly Black in similar proportions. In addition to this situation which prevails in individual institutions throughout the state, the two land grant colleges, Virginia Polytechnic Institute and Virginia State College, technical colleges, one for Blacks and one for whites, remain structurally separate and predominantly of one race, the latter Black and the former white. Another manifestation of the state's racially dual system of higher education is evident in the City of Norfolk in which are situated two large institutions, predominantly white Old Dominion University and predominantly Black Norfolk State University, the enrollment of which is 98 percent Negro. (Letter from Leon Panetta, director, Office for Civil Rights to Mills E. Goodwin, Governor of Virginia, December 2, 1969, p.1)

Reflecting such findings, the current federal regulatory process involves requiring the administrative branch of the affected state governments - usually the governor's office and that of the chief state higher education officer - to undertake three related tasks: (1) to define the problems underlying observed, continuing patterns of racial segregation, (2) to plan remedies for

such problems which promise to result in more integrated
distributions of students, faculty, and administrators, and
(3) to implement remedial strategies. Individual colleges
and total college systems both constitute units of analysis
and of action for purposes of designing, implementing, and
measuring.progress in the above three tasks. In this way
the process acknowledges the importance of action at the
campus level, but clearly assigns the central coordinating
agencies and the governors primary accountability for
remedying de jure segregation. No uniform process seems to
exist across states for involving individual institutions in
planning and implementing desegregation and little if any
information is contained in the star plans about how
institutional involvement took place.

As a result of Adams v. Califano (480 F. Supp. 121
[D.D.C. 1977]), the states must follow guidelines or
"criteria" the Office for Civil Rights has provided for
diagnosing segregation problems and for planning and
implementing remedies. OCR issued these higher education
desegregation "criteria" in July 1977 and received court
approval of them in February 1978 (Federal Register 1978,
43(32), 6658-64). The guidelines identify four major
elements that must be reflected in state higher education
desegregation plans: (1) restructuring dual systems
(enhancing traditionally Black colleges and universities),
(2) increasing Black enrollments at predominantly white
institutions and increasing white enrollment at
traditionally Black institutions, (3) increasing "other
race" faculty, administrators, nonprofessional staff, and
trustees, and (4) reporting and monitoring requirements.

In order to "disestablish the structure of the dual
systems," the guidelines require in each state desegregation
plan: (a) "definition of the mission of each state college
and university on a basis other than race," (b) "specific
steps to eliminate educationally unnecessary program
duplication among traditionally Black (TBIs) and
traditionally white institutions (TWIs) in the same service
area," (c) "steps . . . to strengthen the role of
traditionally Black institutions in the state system," and
(d) "prior consideration to placing . . . new . . . degree
programs . . . at traditionally Black institutions."

Where increasing Black enrollment is concerned, the
guidelines require delineation of strategies to be used to
accomplish an increase system wide and also at traditionally
white institutions. Specifically, the proportion of Black
high school graduates in a state who enter the state college
and university system should at least equal the percentage
of whites who graduate and similarly matriculate. At each
traditionally white, four-year institution and in the system
as a whole, specified annual increases in the proportion of
Black undergraduate enrollment should occur. Where graduate
enrollment is concerned, the guidelines require goals for
equalizing the proportion of white and Black bachelor's
degree recipients who enroll in graduate and professional
programs in the state systems of higher education. Separate
annual and total goals must be established for each major
field of study at the graduate and professional levels.

According to the guidelines, numerical goals for increasing the percentage of white students at traditionally Black institutions should only take place when: (1) increases in Black student enrollment at traditionally white institutions is demonstrably improved, (2) specific steps to enhance traditionally Black institutions are successfully undertaken, (3) when competing instructional programs at geographically proximate Black and white institutions within the same system are eliminated, and (4) when a complete assortment of new instructional programs has been assembled at traditionally Black institutions. Goals for white enrollment at traditionally Black institutions were required on September 1, 1979, assuming that the aforementioned changes had occurred.

The third substantive area addressed in the guidelines is the desegregation of faculty, administration, nonprofessional staff, and governing boards within the affected state systems. In general, the Criteria ask state officials to establish employment goals that equal Black graduation rates in postbaccalaureate programs, or the proportion of Blacks with the required credentials in relevant labor market areas, whichever is greater. In other words, if 10 percent of the persons earning M.A. degrees in biology at public universities in the state in 1978 were Black, then 10 percent of employees in jobs requiring a biology M.A. in the state system should also be Black (Federal Register 1978, 43(32) 6663-64).

Where systemwide and institutional governing boards are concerned, the racial composition of the state or area served must be reflected in board composition. Timetables are required for accomplishing all these outcomes. The final area of the guidelines specifies requirements for the submission of plans, deadlines, and timetables for monitoring progress.

CHANGES IN THE STATE ROLE IN IMPLEMENTING TITLE VI

Implementation of Title VI through the system just described has been characterized by subtle changes in states' roles. Initially states took a largely inactive stance. When the Office for Civil Rights first notified ten states in 1969-1970 that their higher education systems stood in violation of Title VI, only five responded as requested with systemwide desegregation plans for achieving compliance. The well-known Adams v. Richardson (480 F.2d 1159 [D.D.Cir. 1973]) court case placed increased pressure upon state governments to expand their roles in achieving desegregation in public higher education. Plaintiffs in the Adams case wanted appropriate agencies of federal government, the Adams defendant, to exert greater pressure upon the states. Simply put, they wanted the Department of Health, Education and Welfare to obey federal civil rights statutes that require remedies for past segregation and other civil wrongs.

In 1974 after the appeals court upheld the original Adams decision (356 F. Supp. 92 [D.D.C. 1973]), the Office for Civil Rights again requested plans from the ten states which continued to operate segregated higher education systems. Showing evidence of increased cooperation, nine of the ten submitted them as requested: one plan was rejected and eight were approved. Having failed to receive a cooperative response, OCR referred the states of Mississippi and Louisiana to the Justice Department for further action through the courts.

But submitting state plans may only have indicated willingness to go through the motions on the assumption that little additional effort would be required. The state plans that were approved in 1974 did not promise to accomplish a great deal. Most consisted of vague promises to achieve very general results such as increasing Black enrollment, but with no mention of how much of an increase, in what manner new students would be enrolled, nor how much money would be allocated. Their submission and approval did not, therefore, signal a more enthusiastic response to the states than in 1969-1970, nor did the plans symbolize or portray a more fulsome role for state government in pursuing compliance.

A variety of evidence supports these conclusions. In a published statistical assessment of the 1974 plans, Terry Wildman concludes that:

> (E)ven a generous appraisal of plans by southern states to desegregate their higher educational systems must conclude that by 1980 not a single state will have removed "all vestiges of a dual system of education." This is true, first, because these states will not be enrolling students in equal representative proportion by race at all levels, and second, because to remove past inequalities would require a quantum jump in the numbers of Blacks being educated - something not proposed in any plan. Third, no one plan was specific or detailed enough to enable HEW to determine whether proposals were actually attainable. And fourth, even if proposals were manageable in terms of planning specificity, funding needed for implementing plans have not been assured. (Wildman, 1975, p. 69)

Additional evidence consists of a decision by plaintiffs in the _Adams_ case to petition the district court for further relief with arguments similar to Wildman's after their own review of the 1974 plans. The District of Columbia District Court, which holds jurisdiction in the original case, agreed with the plaintiffs. Like the original decision, the court in 1977 criticized both the U.S. Department of Health, Education and Welfare and the state governments involved for playing nonconstructive roles and for attempts to obfuscate Title VI regulation of higher education. To correct this continuing problem, the court ordered OCR to request additional desegregation plans from the eight states that had satisfactorily submitted them in 1974. OCR was ordered to prepare guidelines for the states to use in designing the new plans (<u>Adams v. Califano</u>, 430 F. Supp. 118 [D.D.C. 1977]).

While the case was being decided and the guidelines or "criteria" were being approved, some states underwent a less than subtle change in their roles in the desegregation process. Some became actively rebellious against federal regulation. The governments of North Carolina and Maryland undertook court actions, arguing that federal intrusion into the governance of public higher education traditionally left to the public colleges and universities themselves or to state government had gone too far. But moves toward active recalcitrance by Maryland and North Carolina, similar to Mississippi and Louisiana earlier in 1974, did not proliferate. Most states did not change their compliance postures. Six of the original ten, having seen their desegregation plans approved in 1974 and later repealed, agreed to.submit new ones in 1977-1978. Moreover, nine of the additional ten states notified by OCR in 1980-1981 of continued violation of Title VI also submitted plans. Of the states notified in 1980-1981, only Ohio followed the example set by Mississippi, Louisiana, Maryland, and North Carolina.

Not actively rebellious, the response or role of most affected states - most clearly the six which submitted plans as called upon in the past - was nonetheless described by the federal district court in 1983 as insufficient, unsubstantial, and unproductive. The court responded to yet another petition by plaintiffs for further relief on the grounds that the state plans approved in 1977-1978 had not accomplished much, did not require suitable remedies, and did not increase the role of state government in pressuring colleges and universities to comply. In particular, statistics showed convincingly that Black enrollment had in most cases remained unchanged, but that in other cases, Black enrollment decreased; moreover, that employment of Black faculty and administrators had not improved and/or decreased; and that promised enhancements at Black colleges and universities had not materialized.

In March 1983 the court concluded that where Arkansas, Georgia, Florida, Virginia, Oklahoma, and the community college system of North Carolina are concerned:

1. The <u>Revised Criteria Specifying the Ingredients of Acceptable Plans to Desegregate State Systems of Public Higher Education</u> (43 Fed. P 6658 - February 15, 1978) require each of the above states to desegregate its system of public higher education over a five-year period culminating in the 1982-1983 academic year.

2. In 1978 and 1979 the Department of Health, Education and Welfare accepted plans to desegregate formerly <u>de jure</u> segregated public higher education systems from Arkansas, Florida, Georgia, Oklahoma, and Virginia, and from North Carolina's community college system. The plans expire at the end of the 1982-1983 academic year.

3. Each of these states has defaulted in major respects on
its planning commitments and on the desegregation
requirements of the Criteria of Title VI. Each state has
not achieved the principal objectives in its plan because
of the state's failure to implement concrete and specific
measures adequate to ensure that the promised
desegregation goals would be achieved by the end of the
five-year desegregation period (Adams v. Bell, D.C. Civil
Action No. 3095-70, March 1983, p. 2).

In view of his findings, Judge Pratt issued an
injunction requiring the above states: (1) to submit
another plan by June 30, 1983, which promised actions
leading to the goals established in their earlier plans, (2)
to choose strategies which would meet with success by the
fall of 1985; and (3) to submit a progress report by
February 1, 1984. In the injunction the court ordered the
Office for Civil Rights to: (1) institute formal Title VI
enforcement proceedings by September 5, 1983, if plans were
not submitted, and/or (2) evaluate the progress reports by
April 1, 1984, (Adams v. Bell, 1983).

The court also noted that Pennsylvania, having failed
to reach agreements with plaintiffs and DHEW, had also
refused to submit a desegregation plan as ordered by the
Office of Civil Rights in 1981. The court ordered
Pennsylvania to propose a plan which included remedies
affecting so-called "state-related" institutions. Observing
that the Office for Civil Rights had not begun enforcement
proceedings since 1981, Judge Pratt in another injunction
ordered proceedings against Pennsylvania within 120 days of
the hearing unless a plan was submitted. Since then,
Pennsylvania has completed and obtained approval for its
desegregation plan (Adams v. Bell, 1983).

Evidence of a changing, more substantial role of state
government emerges in the states' written amendments of the
1978 desegregation plans which were approved by the Office
for Civil Rights in 1983. One might well expect that, after
more than twelve years of Title VI regulation in Arkansas,
Florida, Georgia, North Carolina; Oklahoma, Pennsylvania,
and Virginia, the court and other parties might become
impatient and make more convincing efforts to achieve
results. The amendments, recently required by the court
after rendering its March 1983, findings, are more detailed
and seem to provide more appropriate and potentially far-
reaching remedies.

The following is a summary of specific commitments for
remedies in Florida's January 1978 desegregation plan, State
University Systems for Equalizing Educational Opportunity in
Public Higher Education in Florida (Florida State Board of
Regents, February 1978) and in its 1983, Revised Plan for
Equalizing Educational Opportunity in Public Higher
Education in Florida (Florida State Board of Regents May
1983). These documents provide evidence of an emerging
trend toward a more substantive state role. The Florida
plan exemplifies similar evidence in other recent state
plans and amendments.

Synopsis of The Florida Desegregation Plan, 1978

The 1978 Florida plan begins by reporting that each college and university in Florida's upper division and community college system holds a mission defined in ways unrelated to race. A review of role and scope was to be completed for the upper division institutions by April 30, 1978.

The plan next reports the following steps taken to enhance Florida A & M University (FAMU), the state's only public traditionally Black institution (TBI): (1) placement of high demand business, pharmacy, architecture, and journalism programs to attract white students; (2) funding of $615,000 for a white student incentive grants program; and (3) supplemental funding of $17.6 million for facility renovation and construction, $944,000 for academic programs, and $187,000 for a visiting scholar program.

As a result, the student enrollment at FAMU is 14 percent white, with 29 percent white faculty. The plan promises to finish revising FAMU's mission by April 30, 1978, and to continue providing "equitable allocations" of funding resources. The plan offers further assurance that three generic higher education governance processes will serve to enhance FAMU in accordance with Title VI requirements: a systemwide, periodic instructional program review by the regents' staff, the systemwide role and scope study mentioned earlier, and the state instructional program authorization process which "considers state and student needs" when locating new degrees. Along the same line the plan points out that funding is accomplished by a student enrollment driven formula. FAMU receives an equitable share and has received substantial supplemental allocations which have brought its facilities up to par.

The plan promises to employ an ongoing review process to determine program duplication especially where Florida State University, the University of Florida, and FAMU are concerned. If necessary, duplication will be eliminated in ways that favor FAMU. Priority will also be given to FAMU-proposed instructional programs, but fewer new approvals are expected overall during the next decade. Desegregation impact assessments will be undertaken when important system changes are anticipated.

Where student enrollment is concerned, the plan commits the state to continued enrolling of first-time Black and white freshmen in equal proportions to their representation in the state population. It agrees to increase enrollment of Blacks at upper-division TWI's until this proportion approximates the proportion of Blacks who complete lower-division work. The state will enroll first-time graduate and professional students in Black/white ratios which equal ratios of Black/white B.A. recipients in the Florida system. Beginning in 1979 numerical goals would be established to increase white enrollment at FAMU.

If any disparity exists in the proportion of Blacks and whites graduating from community colleges and universities, steps would be taken by the state to reduce the disparity. (Since Florida operates a higher education system consisting

of two-year lower-division and two-year upper-division
institutions, completion of a four-year degree depends upon
unimpeded movement from two-year to four-year institutions.)
The plan expresses the system's intention to maintain
extensive access and mobility between the lower-division and
the upper-division institutions and to continue its open
admission policy at the lower-division institutions.

The plan promises that the hiring rate for Blacks at
public institutions will not fall below the proportion of
Blacks holding appropriate credentials in relevant labor
markets.   The proportion of Blacks holding positions on
governing boards would continue to be equal to their
proportion in state and regional populations.

The following summary of the 1983 Florida addendum
contains important and notable differences from the original
plan:

The Florida Plan Addendum, 1983

The 1983 Florida addendum asserts that between
January 1978 and September 1983, eleven new
instructional programs will have begun at FAMU.
The FAMU budget reportedly increased by 60 percent
between 1979-1982 while authorized staff and
faculty positions have increased by 8.7 percent.
Nine positions and $430,000 above the formula-
generated base of support for new academic
programs was awarded for 1983-1985.   The fiscal
year (FY) 1985 FAMU budget also includes $286,000
for construction of an allied health instructional
facility and $293,000 for a special outreach
program to strengthen the academic preparation of
high school students in the FAMU service area.   In
addition to the 1978 program enhancement
commitments, a joint FAMU/Florida State Institute
for Engineering was established in Spring, 1982.

Since 1978 the Florida legislature appropriated
over $32 million for renovation and construction
at FAMU.   This money was earmarked for two new
academic buildings, new facilities for womens'
athletics, seven other athletic facilities still
under construction, and renovation of old
structures.   The addendum promises that FAMU will
benefit from policies and measures adopted in the
new state system ten-year master plan for
strengthening undergraduate education.

Where student enrollment is concerned, the
addendum asserts that the regents have taken steps
to end declines at FAMU - a 20 percent decrease
since 1977.   A 1981-approved student enrollment
goal suggests that FAMU student enrollment should
increase by 40 percent in unduplicated, high
demand programs by 1983.   Strategies to accomplish
this goal have included providing educational
programs for military personnel, providing evening

programs for associate degree students at
Tallahassee's community colleges and the
community-at-large, additional recruitment
activities including the establishment of an
enrollment committee to examine factors affecting
recruitment, and to design strategies which also
reduce attrition by 25 percent before 1978.
Systemwide Black student enrollment declined from
10.4 percent in 1977-1978 to 8.9 percent in 1981-
1982. Reportedly, this was caused by statewide
declines in Black high school graduation rates,
sharp declines in Black enrollment in community
colleges, higher Black enlistment in the military,
and reductions in federal student aid. In
response to this problem, each institution will
continue to implement recruitment and admission
strategies described in an earlier 1981 addendum.
Provisions will also be made for sharing
information about prospective students among
colleges. The state's 10 percent exception
admission policy will be extended to enable upper-
division institutions and graduate and
professional schools to admit underprepared
students up to a limit of 10 percent of their
total program enrollment. The board of regents has
also committed to provide an increase in financial
aid and expects each university to establish
strategies to meet enrollment goals.

The state system office will also augment two
statewide programs designed to increase Black
graduate and professional school enrollments: (1)
the State University System Special Summer Program
for Black graduate and professional students
provides 140 Black students with orientation to
the state's universities, academic advisement, and
stipends each year; and (2) the Graduate Student
Grant-In-Aid Program provides $4,500 per year per
student with priority to students in high demand
academic areas and an increased appropriation from
$101,250 in 1982-1983 to $310,000 for 1983-1984.

The plan also promises to address the problem of
high school/college articulation. A postsecondary
school academic/career exploration program was
developed by FAMU upon request from the board of
regents to facilitate the retention in and
completion of high schools by Black students. For
Summer 1983, 120 high school students were
selected, and a budget of $293,000 was approved
for the period 1983-1985. Similarly, the Florida
Institute of Education Precollegiate Program was
established in 1982 to improve the preparation of
college-bound Black high school students. The
institute coordinates precollege programs over
five geographically defined regions of Florida.
Its tasks include: (1) training public school

personnel to assist with Black students'
preparation for college, (2) training of selected
college and high school personnel to use
recruitment strategies and the university system's
admission procedures, (3) disseminating
information about college admissions, (4)
monitoring efforts by high schools to modify their
course offerings toward improved college admission
and aspiration, (5) monitoring Black student
enrollment in college preparatory high school
courses, and (6) providing assistance along with
the Department of Education to community groups
that offer to assist in identifying potential
college students and in providing these students
with educational enrichment services.

Insofar as faculty and staff hiring are concerned,
the addendum reports a second consecutive annual
increase in the number and proportion of Blacks
hired by the Florida systems of higher education.
In 1981 the regents adopted a new resolution
requiring annual progress reports from university
presidents, but later amended it to require that
presidents establish numerical goals and review
them with the chancellor. Each president did so
by March 31, 1983. For 1983-1984 a projected
Black employees rate of 16.7 percent was adopted
and broken down to indicate: 11.4 percent
executive/administrative/ managerial, 10.7 percent
faculty, 15.1 percent professional, 19 percent
skilled crafts, and 37.8 percent service
maintenance.

The addendum also indicates two other important
actions: (1) each university will annually
establish an "appropriate" number of teaching and
research assistantships for Black graduate
students; and (2) the names of Employee Grant-In-
Aid and Graduates Student Aid Program recipients
will be publicized widely. The Florida chancellor
has provided criteria and a format for organizing
desegregation impact assessments. The
chancellors' Office of Equal Opportunity Programs
receives the assessments, and the regent reviews
them. A variety of actions by the Florida
legislature and the regents, the addendum asserts,
have required impact assessments. These are: (1)
inauguration of a college level academic skills
test to assess the academic achievement of
students (policies for assisting students who fail
have been adopted by the regents); (2) teacher
education admission requirements have been
increased, probably resulting in fewer Blacks
entering the profession; and (3) upper-division
admission standards were raised including those at
FAMU, and universities are required to develop
alternative plans to lessen the negative impact on

Black student enrollment, including the use of the
10 percent exemption policy.

To further assess the impact of these new
policies, the state university system and OCR
conducted a survey in 1983 to determine the
distribution of high school students by race in
the state. Also procedures for collecting data by
race on the teacher education admission test were
inaugurated. For reporting and monitoring
purposes, the regents approved formation of a
statewide desegregation advisory committee in May
1982. Teams of advisory committee members conduct
on-site visits to college campuses to review EEO
activities.

Based upon a comparison of the original 1978
desegregation plan and the 1983 addendum, the Florida role
shows improved clarity. A close inspection indicates
increased levels of specificity about Florida desegregation
problems and about proposed remedies in the addendum. The
1983 document, more than the 1978 plan, presents specific
actions taken by FAMU and funding appropriated to conduct
these actions. The addendum presents clearer data
indicating systemwide enrollment declines and program
funding to remedy this problem. In addition, hiring goals
are calculated in the manner required by the guidelines and
are accompanied by monitoring provisions.

Increased specificity as a criterion seems to describe
Florida and the other states' analyses of the educational
equality and desegregation problems they face. Perhaps
because greater information is required to establish
remedies, or perhaps because remedies are not easily reduced
to a single set of strategies, specificity of planned
strategies to end racial inequality did not significantly
improve in the addenda.

Beyond specificity one area of improvement in the 1983
remedies involves first-time attempts to address student
outcomes rather than just the process and inputs that have
traditionally been considered. Some of the state amendments
propose programs and program elements that seem to be aimed
not only at greater access for Blacks, but also at Black
students' achievement and improvement of their lives on
campus.

The 1983 Oklahoma amendment, Compliance with Title VI
of the Civil Rights Act: Extended Revised State Plan
(Oklahoma State Regents, June 1983), provides several
examples of programs of this kind. Programs described in
the document for implementation at the professional and
graduate school level propose: (1) hiring minority
counselors to assist student adjustment on campus, (2)
changing curricula at the law school to introduce civil
rights law practice as a component in the curriculum, (3)
expanding procedures for early identification of students
who encounter academic difficulty, and (4) offering part-
time employment for Black doctoral students in entry-level
jobs at the university. Such evidence in the Oklahoma

addendum and others are noteworthy although not abundant.
State plans that are designed to achieve equality of
educational outcomes should be considered with advisement.
No matter how detailed and consistent with the guidelines
planned remedies appear to be, many go unimplemented, and
many others are not implemented as planned. Moreover, it
should be pointed out in a spirit of candor - which has not
always accompanied discussions of Title VI regulation - that
increased specificity and other perceived differences
between 1978 plans and 1983 amendments may really reflect
the states' increased capacity to collect and present
compliance data. Even when a plan suggests improvement in a
state's willingness to confront a racial equality problem
with knowledge and candor, implementation does not
necessarily follow.
Subtle changes in the state's role in the direction of
greater candor and specificity, at least in defining higher
education equality problems, may instead reflect greater
assurance on the part of state officials that only limited
solutions will be required, at least in the near future by
federal government. This interpretation most clearly holds
where the regulatory experience of more actively
recalcitrant states have come under review. From the
perspective of the states involved - Mississippi, Louisiana,
Maryland, and North Carolina - there may well have been some
benefit derived from refusing to submit and/or rewrite
desegregation plans as required by the federal government.
The clearest benefit from the point of view of these states
is that they have not had to expend much effort over the
past several years to desegregate their higher education
systems. Moreover, by waiting until President Reagan was
elected before settling their dispute with the judiciary,
these states were able to reach agreements which may require
less action to achieve compliance. In a sense, such
agreements constitute an indication and approval by federal
government of a less substantial state role in Title VI
regulation during recent years.

Synopsis of The North Carolina Consent Decree of 1981

The July 1981 consent decree between the University of
North Carolina system and the U.S. Department of Education
provides the best evidence of recent state movement in a
less substantial direction. The decree came about when the
University of North Carolina asked the U.S. district court
for the eastern district of North Carolina to enjoin the
department from withholding federal funds to the university
until an administrative hearing in accordance with Title VI
could be held. The purpose of the administrative hearing
was to determine whether the university system stood in
violation of Title VI as the department alleged in its
"Notice of the Opportunity for Hearing" on April 24, 1979,
and whether the university had to revise its 1978
desegregation plan adhering to the Office for Civil Rights
guidelines. The district court granted the university's
request, and the administrative hearing began in July 1980.

The consent decree entered by both parties to the hearings-
the university and the department - specifies that:
    Specifically, the university does not waive its
contention that the Amended Criteria Specifying Ingredients
of Acceptable Plans to Desegregate State Systems of Public
Higher Education, (42 Fed. Reg. 40,780 [1977]), and the
Revised Criteria Specifying the Ingredients of Acceptable
Plans to Desegregate State Systems of Public Higher
Education, (43 Fed. Reg. 6,658 [1978]), are both statutorily
and constitutionally defective; that the government does not
have the right to prescribe, guide, or evaluate curricula,
programs, program content, or the institutional location of
program or course offerings, it being the position of the
university that such decisions are reserved to the
university by the First Amendment of the Constitution and
laws of the United States; that the government's actions
have denied North Carolina its right of constitutional
equality and have denied the students, faculty, and
administrators of the university due process and equal
protection of the law as guaranteed by the Fifth Amendment
of the Constitution of the United States. Moreover, by
consenting to the provisions of this decree, the university
does not concede that numerical assessments of the racial
composition of the university or its constituent
institutions are constitutionally or statutorily permissible
measure of compliance with the fourteenth amendment or Title
VI, it being the position of the university that such
numerical assessments are constitutionally and statutorily
prohibited or unauthorized. (Consent Decree, North Carolina
v. Department of Education; filed April 24, 1979, p. 6-7)
    The important commitments the university made in the
consent decree to accomplish desegregation can be summarized
in a few paragraphs.
    First, the decree lists a variety of information
dissemination activities aimed at increasing Black
enrollment and employment:

1. Two separate brochures describing the ingredients of
    equal educational opportunity, undergraduate, and
    graduate/professional degree programs;

2. A manual describing two- and four-year college
    transfer policies and procedures;

3. Video cassettes offering basic information about the
    UNC system, featuring its multiracial charter;

4. Video cassettes of a similar kind for each
    institution;

5. Recent institutional catalogues distributed to
    public and private high schools and colleges in
    North Carolina with equal education opportunity
    assurances highlighted in them;

6. TWI brochures for minority students. In cooperation
    with the North Carolina State Department of Public

Instruction, the University of North Carolina System general administration will sponsor workshops for high school counselors to be held at each higher education institution in the system. The workshops will focus upon student recruitment and preparation for college. Also, where student recruitment is concerned:

1. Each TBI will attempt to hire at least one white admissions officer, and vice versa at TWI's.

2. Each institution will conduct high school visits and, where practical, "other-race" admissions officers will contact "other-race" students for a systemwide total of more than 4,282 visits.

3. TWIs with 4,000 or more students must visit 100 public high schools with 15 percent minority enrollment.

4. A listing by race of North Carolina high school students who took the PSAT will be used by TWIs to recruit Black students.

5. Each institution will solicit names of potential minority enrollees from its minority alumni and current students.

6. Each institution will annually visit community colleges, technical institutes, and private junior colleges in their geographical area and make special efforts to contact minority students.

7. TWIs will use the college board's listing of outstanding minority community college graduates to recruit.

8. The university system will continue to assist the Joint Committee on Community College Transfer Students.

9. All minority students admitted shall be contacted and encouraged to enroll.

10. Each TWI will invite prospective minority students to visit the campus.

Where graduate and professional enrollments are concerned, major universities shall make at least one recruitment trip to a public or private TBI. Deans of the schools of medicine, dentistry, and public health will send representatives to TBIs, and graduate and professional schools will transmit information about their programs to institutions with large minority populations. Institutions with graduate schools will also contact public high schools to acquaint them with their programs.

The decree announces four scholarship programs for minority students: (1) a Minority Presence General Grants Program funded at $720,000, (2) a Minority Presence Doctoral Study for Minority Students enrolling in medicine, veterinary medicine, and law, (3) the Board of Governor's Medical Scholars Program, and (4) the Board of Governor's Dental Scholars Program.

The decree promises that by 1986-1987 minority enrollment shall equal or exceed 15 percent of the total combined head count enrollment in the TWIs. The president of the system's administrative council shall monitor progress where employment is concerned. Each institution's affirmative action plan expires October 1, 1983, and will be revised and extended to December 31, 1986, to comply with Executive Order 11246.

Where TBI enhancement is concerned, the decree notes that state funding ranged from 4 percent - 17 percent higher at TBIs from 1972-1981. The university commits itself to provide financial support consisting of appropriations and tuition receipts to each TBI at least equal to the weighted average of the financial support provided to TWIs in the same institutional type category. Student faculty ratios at TBIs have remained comparable with TWIs and shall remain at least equal to the most favorable ratio of any TBI.

State appropriations for TBI faculty salaries are at parity with TWIs, except for those at the East Carolina School of Medicine, the North Carolina Central Law School, and the University of North Carolina at Asheville. The appropriations shall be maintained. All TBI library facilities, as promised in 1974, meet minimum state standards and will remain that way. Where summer sessions, student financial aid, and tuition rates for regular session students are concerned, parity between TBIs and TWIs shall be maintained. The decree reports that a comprehensive capital improvement program of new facilities and major renovations has been funded and begun at TBIs.

Concerning TBI faculty development, the decree commits the system to achieve parity and notes some progress. To continue such progress: (1) a faculty doctoral study assignment program shall continue at current $400,000 funding and will provide priority placement for TBI faculty; (2) the system shall require all new full-time faculty at TBIs and all faculty requesting tenure to hold doctoral degrees except in exceptional cases; and (3) annual conferences with deans at the TBIs to review academic personnel policies will be held by the general administration. The decree also promises that the general administration will seek to improve the administration and management of TBIs holding conferences with appropriate administrators and by December 31, 1986, providing funds to establish senior administrative positions for institutional development at three of the five TBIs. The TBIs, like TWIs, will establish development plans that include new degree program proposals. The president of the system is assigned responsibility to monitor the above activities and to

request institutional reports. Annual reports will be filed
with the court during the month of December through 1986.
     Obviously from this summary, while the consent decree
centers upon the three basic areas contained in the Title VI
guidelines - student desegregation, desegregation of
employment, and traditionally Black college enhancement - it
does not diagnose desegregation problems and propose
remedies in the manner prescribed by such diagnoses.   For
example, an appendix to the decree entitled, "Commitments
and Major Accomplishments of the university, 1972-1980,"
contains data describing the discrepancy between college
entrance rates of Black and white North Carolina high school
graduates: in 1980, 20.5 percent for Blacks and 25.5
percent for whites.   These data bear no clear relationship
to the Black enrollment goal established in the body of the
decree - "15 percent of total combined head count
enrollment" in the TBIs and at least "10.6 percent for total
combined head count enrollment" of the TWIs.   At issue since
1978 between OCR and the university system had been the
notion of establishing numerical enrollment and employment
goals, a practice university officials termed "arbitrary"
and "unrelated to any principle" in the 1978 desegregation
plan (University of North Carolina, Board of Governors, May
1975).   Notably, where student enrollment is discussed, the
decree often refers to "minority" enrollment, perhaps
suggesting less responsibility to recruit Blacks as long as
other minorities are enrolled.
     For the record, although the decree itself contains no
enrollment data, data in the appendices suggest the
following facts about desegregation trends within the
system: (1) the proportion of Blacks in the university's
total undergraduate enrollment grew only by 1.9 percent
between 1972-1980; (2) "minority enrollment" at TWIs
increased from 3.1 percent to 7.4 percent between 1972-1980
with most of the growth taking place at three or four
institutions in urban areas; and (3) the percentage of total
Blacks in North Carolina public higher education who were
enrolled at TWIs rose from 13.3 percent to 31.5 percent over
the same period.   The enrollment trends described by these
data are not impressive.
     The decree also does not use data on Black employment
to establish goals, a procedure advocated in the Title VI
guidelines.   It refers instead to institutions' affirmative
action plans that are already approved, but are soon to be
renewed; it agrees to revise these plans so that they comply
with Executive Order 11246, not the Title VI guidelines.
Black faculty employment in tenured or tenure-track jobs
rose from 1.5 percent in 1968 to 2.1 percent in 1980; 4.1
percent of new faculty hired between 1977-1980 were Black.
White faculty at TBIs ranged from 11 percent 30 percent in
1975, and from 19 percent - 38 percent in 1980.   If these
figures are exemplary of U.S. Labor Department pressure to
desegregate faculty at the university, there may be some
advantage to the university in pursuing faculty
desegregation via the affirmative action route.   On the
other hand, OCR has not required a great deal of other
states on the employment desegregation problem, so the

university in this instance may simply have seized upon an opportunity to exert its free will in defiance of government orders.

The decree rejects the basic assumption of the guidelines that compensatory treatment is necessary for TBIs to achieve equity. The theory underlying the decree is that the university need only match resources between white and Black institutions and that almost everything necessary has been done to accomplish this goal. Conspicuously absent from the discussion of TBI enhancement in the decree and its appendices is the problem of program duplication. Since there are five public TBIs (more than any other state) and only ten public TWIs within the state system, and since many of these public institutions are located in the Greensboro-Raleigh-Durham area, one might reasonably expect duplication to emerge as a problem. The fact that so many TBIs exist may be interpreted as evidence on the state's determination to serve its comparatively large percentage of Black citizens prior to the Brown decision, or it may constitute evidence of the state's determination to segregate them. Robert Dentler reports that throughout the 1980 administrative hearing, the problem of duplication persisted as a bone of contention. The issue was eventually decided in the favor of the university system. One of the issues OCR and the university could not resolve prior to the hearing and which led the university to risk fund withdrawal was the program duplication problem (Dentler, 1983).

But lack of attention to the duplication problem is consistent with what seemed, in its other aspects, an important assumption of the decree. The assumption underlying the university's proposed student desegregation programs and its decision not to treat the duplication problem is that no discrimination exists within the university system; that discrimination may have existed in the past, but through passage of equal educational laws the problem has been remedied. The 1978 North Carolina desegregation plan is less circumspect where this assumption is concerned. It asserts in no uncertain terms that Black students fail to enroll at the university: for "historical" reasons; because they do not have information; because they mistrust the university; because they are academically unprepared; and because they lack motivation and money to attend. The enrollment of Blacks is low for these reasons alone, and the university assumes no responsibility for remedying the situation except that it is acknowledged to exist in these terms (North Carolina Board of Governors, May 1978). No remedies reflect the fact that Blacks may be treated poorly within the multicampus system of the university or that race discrimination may continue. The duplication problem is ignored for similar reasons: no racism was previously or is currently involved in the placement of instructional programs within the system, therefore no remedies reflecting this problem are viewed as necessary.

PREDICTING THE FUTURE STATE ROLE IN TITLE VI COMPLIANCE

     Both trends in the state role in Title VI regulation of
higher education can be expected to continue. Some states
will propose and implement clearer, more substantial
strategies, perhaps emphasizing outcomes of the college
experience for ending de jure segregation, while others will
continue both active and passive means of maintaining the
status quo. Both trends are possible because Title VI
regulation is a complex, multifaceted policy intervention
that is difficult to implement. It involves activating the
gigantic federal bureaucracy, to pressure nineteen state
bureaucracies which in turn exert influence over diverse
colleges and universities that value their independence and
autonomy. Viewed in this way, from an implementation
perspective, some of the most salient factors that will
affect the state role become clear.
     First of all, the federal role in Title VI is changing
and is losing clarity in the process. It is unreasonable to
expect nineteen different states to respond independently of
each other, but along roughly similar dimensions, if the
federal government cannot agree upon clear signals about
what ought to be accomplished. This assertion differs from
earlier observations that Title VI is a vague statute.   I
refer now to the disagreement among federal agencies over
the correct interpretation of the true meaning of Title VI.
The open-endedness of Title VI makes it more important for
agencies to reach some semblance of an agreement.
     At stake is a broad change in major civil rights policy
by the current federal administration. Assistant Attorney
General William Bradford Reynolds described the change in a
speech at the Southern Education Foundation on February 10,
1983:

     The Civil Rights Division's enforcement activity
     is of single purpose, and that is to achieve
     quality education in a desegregated environment .
     . . At the primary and secondary levels, mandatory
     assignment programs requiring extensive
     dislocations of students have, in educational
     terms, seriously harmed school systems across this
     land, particularly in the larger metropolitan
     areas. Nor do you need me to tell you that the
     gradual erosion of public education that occurs at
     the preparatory grade levels has an equally
     distressing impact on our public institutions of
     higher education . . . Our efforts in the Civil
     Rights Division have thus been to strive for a
     greater degree of sensitivity to the educational
     needs of particular communities that must respond
     to the constitutional and moral imperative of
     desegregation . . . Not surprisingly, employing a
     similar philosophy to desegregate institutions of
     higher learning has met with considerably less
     resistance, principally because forced busing is
     not a viable option at this level . . . The states
     of North Carolina, Louisiana, and most recently

Virginia, have entered into amicable settlements,
and several other states are close to a final
resolution of their higher education cases. A
principal reason for these positive results is
this administration's attitude toward Black
colleges and universities in this country . . .
Unlike our predecessors, we believe the effort
should be made to preserve and enhance
predominantly Black institutions, while promoting
desegregation, rather than looking to merge them
with white colleges or discontinue them altogether
. . . As with elementary and secondary education,
at the centerpiece of our higher education
desegregation program is the guiding hand of
educational quality. An effective dismantling of
dual systems of higher education depends upon
eliminating all barriers that deny equal access to
any public college or university in the state . .
. With respect to predominantly white
institutions, we have employed a variety of
techniques to increase other-race enrollments.
Considerable emphasis has been placed on programs
designed to inform students of available
educational opportunities and to recruit other-
race students. Developmental or remedial
educational programs have been used to reduce
Black attrition rates. Cooperative efforts
between geographically proximate institutions have
been required, including faculty and student
exchanges and joint degree programs. These and
other measures that we have adopted help to ensure
equal access for all students, regardless of race,
to a quality educational institution of their own
choosing. (Reynolds, 1983, pp. 10-11)

Evidently the current administration's policy involves
establishing equal access as the desegregation goal - a
focus upon process, not outcomes. Translated into action,
this means that predominantly white institutions are now
asked to emphasize student recruitment with remedial
programs to reduce attrition without serious attention to
the achievement of numerical enrollment goals. Black
institutions will be enhanced because, in order to improve
the quality of the new desegregated public system, TBIs must
offer high-quality programs like their white counterparts.
Where program duplication becomes an issue, the new approach
involves caution "against adding new degree offerings in low
demand courses that were available at other colleges in the
system. At the same time, where student demand justifies
it, duplicating an existing program - such as the nursing
school (a bone of contention in both North Carolina and
Louisiana) - (is) considered sound from both an educational
and desegregation standpoint" (Reynolds, 1983, p. 11). In
both North Carolina and Louisiana where the nursing school
placement issue arose, the Justice Department favored
placement at the white institution or at both white and
Black institutions in the same region. Notably, where the

new policy is concerned, no mention is made of Black
employment problems.
    Antecedents of this new approach are less than vaguely
apparent in the North Carolina plan and consent decree. If
current disagreement between agencies of federal government
- specifically between the Justice Department's new approach
and OCR Title VI guidelines - is resolved along the lines of
Reynolds' statement, expansion of the state role toward
desegregation goals seems unlikely.
    Another broad issue which may have an effect
independent of disagreements at the federal level is the
emerging movement toward quality in higher education. A
seven-member panel was appointed in September 1983 by the
director of the National Institute of Education to
scrutinize higher education in the same way that primary and
secondary schooling has been scrutinized in recent years.
The panel issued a report with findings that the quality of
undergraduate education nationally has been seriously
compromised by the "strains of rapid expansion, followed by
recent years of constricting resources and leveling
enrollments . . . The realities of student learning,
curricular coherence, quality of facilities, faculty morale,
and academic standards no longer measure up to our
expectations" (Quoted in Chronicle of Higher Education Vol.
39, No 9, p.1). Several states have already begun to
establish policies and new standards aimed at improving
higher education.
    Among supporters of desegregation, the initial reaction
to the rapidly advancing quality of higher education
movement is one of deep skepticism. A rush to improve
quality may turn limited and already diminishing attention
away from desegregation in Adams states. More disagreements
in federal policy will emerge. Assistant Attorney General
Bradford Reynolds's thinly disguised argument for the
pursuit of quality rather than desegregation, defined in
terms other than access, is likely to be taken up by
opponents of Title VI. Undoubtedly desegregation will be
blamed, as Reynolds seems to suggest, for lowered quality,
and the always simmering debate over perceived
contradictions between quality and equity may result in
reductions in state effort.
    Viewed more narrowly, the quality issue holds other
implications for Title VI regulation. The quality of
strategies proposed to end segregation and beyond that to
achieve so-called quality dimensions could be improved if we
knew more about how to make campus-level changes that
improve the lives of both Black and white students. Among
the least of these is improvement in the distribution of
students by race throughout the systems of state public
institutions. Since desegregation involves changing such
voluntarily defined distributions, information about the
determinants of Black students' choices of institutions
would be welcomed. But very little of the growing research
literature on student choice (why students enroll in college
and why they choose to enroll at the institutions they
choose) deals with Black student populations.
    Another continuing and not easily resolved constraint

upon the state role is the traditional taboo of government
involvement in the governance of higher education. Even
where state government is moved to exert greater control or
pressure for change, its hands remain tied in many state
systems. The magnitude of state government control over
higher education is symbolized by the size and authority of
higher education coordinating and planning agencies within
the executive branch of the state government. In a recent
study of state coordinating agencies, researchers at the
Education commission of the states reported that most are
small, are recently established, and hold responsibility in
three areas: budget review and/or approval, program review
and approval, and long-range planning. Great variance exists
where the extent of their authority in these areas is
concerned.   Although the growth of such agencies has
increased in the past two decades, a trend seems to have
emerged in the opposite direction more recently (Burnes et
al., 1983).   Concern about outcomes which support equality
but also increase campus involvement is less likely to
receive attention of state coordinators and governance
officials under circumstances like those described in this
study. On the other hand, other public officials seem to be
forcing attention to a determination of outcomes as a means
of measuring improved quality.

CONCLUSION

     A vital role by state government is essential for
formulating and implementing Title VI regulations in public
higher education. Evidence exists showing movement toward a
more abundant and more clearly defined role of state
government in Title VI regulation and yet at the same time a
diminishing state role is apparent. The most recent state
desegregation plans include more detailed analyses of
desegregation problems and, to a lesser extent, more
detailed remedies aimed at clearly defined desegregation
goals. For example, after careful analyses of institutional
needs under changing economic conditions, the most recent
progress made in achieving enrollment goals and enhancement
commitments contained in the 1980-1985 plan. As a result of
these analyses, the new desegregation plan for Maryland's
public higher education institutions provides new strategies
for achieving desegregation goals that were not achieved
during the first five years of the plan (Maryland
Desegregation Progress Report, 1985-1989).
     On the other hand, some states have successfully
circumvented requirements established in the Title VI
guidelines and show only modest movement toward weakened
standards with evidence of less state government influences.
For example, the annual progress report for Tennessee simply
describes the changes in student enrollment towards
obtainment but fail to explain the reasons for such changes
and also does not present plans for producing more favorable
results (the Tennessee Desegregation Progress Report, 1987).
The U.S. Department of Education's Office for Civil Rights,
which is responsible for providing leadership in the

enforcement of Title VI, has recently contributed to the
passive treatment of outcome. In 1987 for example, the OCR
produced a report showing progress by the Adams States in
enforcing Title VI.   This report has come under widespread
criticism for its failure to do more than simply describe
the progress of the states without offering analyses and
opinions about these outcomes (Chronicle of Higher
Education, Vol. 33, No. 28, March 1987).
     Several factors will exert an impact upon future
changes in the state role. Among those recognized are: (1)
resolution of disagreements over Title VI requirements at
the federal level, (2) increasing concern for improved
quality of higher education, (3) increased knowledge about
how to conduct successful desegregation remedies, and (4)
changes in the authority of state higher education
coordinating agencies and state boards of higher education.
     Two specific events will affect the future state role
where racial equality is concerned. First of all, the
Department of Education must decide whether the states whose
desegregation plans expired in 1985 and 1986 have achieved
compliance.   The states involved are Arkansas, Florida,
North Carolina's community college system, Oklahoma,
Virginia, Georgia, West Virginia, South Carolina, Missouri,
and Delaware.   In a recent news release the Department of
Education described its preliminary compliance reports
undertaken to determine whether further regulation is
required. According to the release, the recent compliance
"reports detailed efforts made by the ten states to
desegregating their systems of higher education . . . They
do not express a conclusion as to whether the states have
been successful in desegregating the affected systems . . .
or what additional measures might be necessary in cases
where a system has not been fully desegregated" (U.S.
Department of Education, March 30, 1987, p. 1). Clearly a
finding of compliance by the department can result in less
pressure to remedy the problem, if seemingly inevitable
court challenges by the plaintiffs in the Adams case fail.

REFERENCES

Act, Kentucky 1904, Chapter 85.

Adams v. Bell D.C. Civil Action No 3095-70 (1982).

Adams v. Richardson 480 F. 2d 1159 (D.C. Cir. 1973).

Adams v. Richardson 356 F. Supp. 92 (D.C. Cir. 1973).

Adams v. Califano 430 F. Supp. 118, 119 (D.C.C. 1977).

Berea College v. Kentucky 211 U.S. 45 (1908).

Board of Governors. (1978, May). The revised North
     Carolina state plan for the further elimination of
     racial duality in public higher education systems,
     phase II; 1978-1983. Mimeo, University of North
     Carolina, Chapel Hill.

Brown v. Board of Education 347 U.S. 483 (1954). Donald W.
     Burnes,Robert M. Palaich, Aims McGuiness, and Patricia
     Flakus-Mosqueda. State Governance of Education: 1983.
     Denver: Education Commission of the States, 1983.

Browning, J. S., & Williams, J. B. (1978). The history and
     goals of Black institutions of higher learning. In C.
     V. Willie and R. R. Edmonds (Eds.), Black colleges in
     America. New York: Teachers College Press.

Chronicle of Higher Education. Vol. 29, No. 9, October 24,
     1984, p. 1.

Dentler, R. A., Baltzell, D. C., & Sullivan, D. J. (1983).
     University of trial. Cambridge, MA: Abt Associates.

Federal Register. (1978). 43(32), 6663-64.

Florida Board of Regents. (1983, May). Addendum: Revised
     plan for equalizing educational opportunity in public
     higher education in Florida. Mimeo, State University
     System, Tallahassee.

Florida Board of Regents. (1978, February). State
     university system of Florida revised plan for
     equalizing educational opportunity in public higher
     education in Florida. Mimeo, State University System,
     Tallahassee.

Oklahoma State Regents for Higher Education. (1983, June).
     Compliance with Title VI of the Civil Rights Act:
     Extended revised state plan. Mimeo, State Capitol,
     Oklahoma City.

Orfield, G. (1969). The reconstruction of southern
     education. New York: Wiley.

Reynolds, W. B. (1983). The administration's approach to
     desegregation of public higher education. American
     Education, 19(4), 9-11.

State of North Carolina v. Department of Education, Eastern
     North Carolina Civil Action No. 79-217-CIV-5, Consent
     Decree, July 17, 1981.

Trueheart, W. E. (1980). The consequences of federal and
     state resource allocation and development policies for
     traditionally Black land-grant institutions.
     Unpublished Ed.D. dissertation, Harvard University,
     Graduate School of Education.

U.S. Department of Health, Education, and Welfare. Amended
    criteria specifying the ingredients of acceptable plans
    to desegregate state systems of public higher
    education. Federal Register, 43(32), 6658-64.

U.S. v. Jefferson County Board of Education 372 F2d 836 (5th
    Cir. 1966).

Wildman, T. (1976). A statistical review of state plans
    submitted in response to the Pratt Decision. In P.
    Mohr (Ed.), Equality of opportunity in higher
    education: Myth or realty? (pp. 28-69). Lincoln, NE:
    Southern Network.

9
The Role of Private Interest Groups in Achieving Equality for Black Students in Higher Education

REGINALD WILSON

The higher ground in conducting research on the qualitative dimensions of equality in higher education has quite properly been occupied by the education agencies of federal and state governments. Apparently applying the same rationale behind the <u>Brown v. Board of Education of Topeka</u> decisions, these governmental bodies have primarily concerned themselves with interpreting trend data and funding special programs in their attempts to respond to the mandates of the <u>Adams</u>, <u>Geier</u>, and other court orders that were discussed in great detail in the two preceding chapters. While the role played by government is guided by statutes and court orders and is systematic in carrying the force of law, the motivation for and the role played by private interest groups and the motivation for such involvement in higher education equality is less clear.

There appear to be no discernible patterns to private interest group activities and no stable coalitions among them. Only after several years of government-mandated shifting and busing of elementary and high school students to meet the requirements of the <u>Brown</u> decision did a number of private agencies begin the task of assessing the qualitative consequences for America's primary and secondary schools. The purpose of this chapter is to explore the role being played by various private interest groups in achieving qualitative equality of higher education.

Private interest groups have enjoyed a long history of acceptance and appreciation in the American political process. Interest groups arose out of a need felt by various citizen groups to advocate their special concerns before political officials and policymakers in an attempt to influence the outcome of public policy. These groups represent minority interests in the democratic process before a government that is most frequently concerned with satisfying minority interests. In a diverse population such as in the United States, conflicting interests are commonplace; people typically join together to advance their causes. The role of the private interest groups is to persuade the policymakers to be supportive of their interests in the political process. One higher education

special interest group for example, the American Association
of Community and Junior Colleges (AACJC), came into being
when two-year college officials felt that the special
interests of their institutions were not being represented
by the other higher education associations in which four-
year colleges and universities were the predominant group.
To community college officials, the higher education
associations seemed more attuned to the needs of four-year
colleges and universities while treating two- year colleges
as second-class members.

     Historically, private interest groups have advocated
and persuaded elected policymakers through a variety of
means: enacting legal action, sponsoring research and
policy analysis, publishing important reports, convening
conferences and forums, testifying or otherwise responding
to requests by policymakers, and even conducting public
demonstrations.   Many groups involve themselves
simultaneously in all these activities while some focus on
only some of these strategies.   However, all special
interest groups share the similar motivation of desiring to
effect changes in the behavior of the majority or to effect
changes in the laws and regulations which are perceived to
circumscribe their activities and interests.

     The private interest groups described in this chapter
represent the full range and variety of persuasive
activities.   Moreover, they represent a multiplicity of
methods of organization - membership-based groups,
foundation-funded groups, university "think tanks," and
contracted consultant services, to name a few.

     Private interest groups have been remarkably successful
in democratic societies, particularly in the United States,
in advocating their special causes.   For example, various
environmental groups can rightfully take credit for the
passage of laws that preserve wilderness areas and
endangered species.   On the other hand, special interest
groups have also experienced defeat when the majority
attitude is strongly resistant to their position.   For
example, despite strong opposition from Hispanic and Black
organizations the majority of the Congress is strongly in
favor of laws that place severe limits on immigration into
the United States.   Obviously an issue like higher education
equality is so divisive in America that consensus on
strategies for addressing it have not been developed in the
educational community.   This is reflected in the research
reported in this chapter.

RESEARCH METHOD

     For the purposes of this study, private interest groups
are defined as nongovernmental (federal or state), non-
court-appointed private organizations and associations.
Such groups vary in purpose and operation.   For purposes of
analysis and distinction, private interest groups are
divided into three general clusters.   The first group
consists of organizations not primarily educational in
nature whose overall governing philosophy includes an

interest in educational issues as they affect national policies related to their mission. Examples include the National Urban League, the Joint Center for Policy Studies and the A. Phillip Randolph Institute. The second group is made up of educational organizations that focus upon a special interest or a narrowly prescribed component of education, such as student services, liberal arts, or college libraries. Examples include the Council of University Personnel Administrators, the American Association of University Professors, and the Association of American Law Schools. The third group is composed of the broad-based, national educational organizations of multiple interests, typically headquartered in Washington, D.C. Examples are the American Council on Education, the American Association of Higher Education, the Association of American Universities, and the American Association of State Colleges and Universities. Because of their national stature and broad range of educational interests, one would expect the third group would probably be most involved in higher education equality activities, followed by the second group, with the first cluster of organizations being least active because of their broader focus.

This chapter is based upon a survey of the these private interest group clusters. The survey was conducted in order to ascertain the basis of each organization's interest in the racial equity of higher education, to ascertain the types of activities or services they have initiated, to determine whether their activities or services were self-initiated or requested, to determine the outcome of projects initiated, and to ascertain their plans for future involvement in the higher education equality process.

BASIS FOR PRIVATE INTEREST GROUP INVOLVEMENT IN HIGHER EDUCATION EQUALITY

All these interest groups serveyed have, in their publications or forums, addressed many of the most profound and important philosophical questions facing education in America. As can be expected, they usually address these issues from the perspective of their members or the constituents they represent. Among the many questions addressed by these private interest groups are the following: What is the range of purposes to be served by higher education? What should be the nature and focus of the college curriculum? What is the appropriate role of the federal government in education? What are the appropriate differences in public support provided for private versus public institutions? Should public support be equally distributed for academic and vocational education? And what are the legal and moral rights of students while attending college? Until recently these questions have typically been addressed in the context of the majority population in the United States, with very little regard for minorities. Beginning with the Hayes-Tilden Compromise in 1876 and culminating with its codification into law by the supreme court in 1896 in Plessy v. Ferguson, segregation of the races in most activities, including education, became the law of the land. The years between Plessy (1896) and Brown (1954) yielded few in-depth studies of higher education that gave serious consideration to the condition of Black education except those conducted by Black scholars themselves primarily for Black audiences. Prominent exceptions were Gunnar Myrdal's classic study, An American Dilemma (1939) and D.O.W. Holmes's study, The Evolution of the Negro College (1934). After 1954 (the year of the Brown decision), however, many interest groups (and, of course, many individual scholars) produced numerous studies on "the state of Black education," particularly as it compared to "white education" with which it would ultimately be merged.

Higher education by its nature as an intellectual enterprise has usually been in the forefront of addressing society's critical social and philosophical issues; therefore, higher education and the professional organizations are expected to be in the forefront in addressing the problem of dismantling the historic inequity of education for Blacks and whites in this country. Myrdal's American Dilemma is an example of the higher education community using its collective resources to examine segregation of the races in American society. However, the critical difference in higher education desegregation was that higher education was being asked not only to examine itself, but also to make judgments about who should be educated and who should be hired in its own domain. Self-interest became a decided impediment to objective and scholarly inquiry. Issues such as "quality versus access," and "open versus selective admissions" are issues of intense debates that usually produce more heat than light. Because of the apparent lack of substantial involvement by the private interest groups in clarifying the parameters of equity in higher education and in providing solutions the questions raised in this chapter are important.

The higher education community and its representative interest groups have been somewhat successful in resolving complex problems of major national importance by working cooperatively with federal, state, and local education authorities. It seems unarguable that similar cooperative endeavors could be employed to improve the desegregation planning and implementation in the nineteen states under the Adams mandates, and in other states and institutions that strive for racial equality. However, the data show substantial underutilization and/or underinvolvement of private interest group resources in addressing equality of American higher education.

Twenty percent of the noneducational cluster, 36 percent of the special interest cluster, and 37 percent of the broad-based educational cluster indicated being involved at some time in the past, at present, or intentions for involvement in the future in Black equality activities. Of the total of those indicating some involvement, 20 percent had been previously involved, 60 percent were currently involved, and 20 percent planned some involvement in future equality activities.

Table 9.1 illustrates the interest in equality
expressed by the three types of organizations. The largest
number (24 percent) were involved as a consequence of
collegiate institution requests for various kinds of
service. Secondarily (19 percent), the organizations
responded to individuals at those institutions (or
independent scholars) who requested services or assistance.
A number of organizations (19 percent) voice their concerns
regarding ethnic/racial equity in their own publications
(journal articles, books, newsletters). Very few activities
(4 percent) have been initiated as a consequence of
government sponsored contracts or projects initiated or
recommended by other funding sources. Fifteen percent of
the interest groups have initiated involvement because
member institutions were affected by Adams court decisions.

Table 9.1

Basis of Organizational Interest in Equality Issues

	Non educational	Special interest	National educational	Total	%
1. Adams member institution	2	2	4	8	15
2. Institution requests service	2	4	6	12	24
3. Individual requests service	2	4	4	10	19
4. Government contract			2	2	4
5. Funded projects		2		2	4
6. Publication		4	6	10	19
7. Other		2	6	8	15
Total	6	18	28	52	
Percent	11	35	54		100

Note: Data reported as percentages.

These responses reveal significant underutilization of
private interest group resources. With conspicuous
exceptions, such as the NAACP, these groups were not
motivated to become involved in such controversial and
unpopular problems as racial equality. Moreover, the
peculiar characteristic of the Adams mandate requires state
government educational authorities to submit plans to the
United States Department of Education (DOE). If the DOE

accepts the plan, it is usually approved by the court
(although plaintiffs have the right to challenge the plan).
The theory underlying this process is the assumption that
DOE will "naturally" function in the best interests of the
aggrieved party - previously excluded Blacks. The naiveté
of this assumption lies in its ignorance of the political
reality that the executive branch does not want to offend
powerful state interests by disturbing the status quo in the
distribution of educational resources. As a consequence,
the DOE with relatively limited criticism, has accepted a
number of weak desegregation plans, despite loud outcries
from the Legal Defense Fund and private interest groups
aligned with the plaintiffs. In most instances the courts
have accepted these plans. Most private interest groups
have yet to discover the effective strategies for
influencing state-level planning or court decisions on
equity for Blacks in higher education. Private interest
groups are not usually motivated to draw undue attention to
the situation by mounting highly publicized forums, massive
data collection and publications, or by initiating
conferences intended to persuade drastic changes for
unpopular causes.

Private interest groups, particularly the large
national educational associations, are uniquely qualified to
provide a variety of services to respond to criteria
established by the Department of Education requiring:

■ disestablishing the structure of the dual systems of
higher education;

■ desegregating student enrollments;

■ desegregating faculty, administrative staffs, nonacademic
personnel, and governing boards;

■ establishing an ongoing system of monitoring and
evaluating the process implementing plans. (Haynes,
1978);

Private interest groups are in ideal positions to do the
following:

■ convene conferences of key officials (state and federal
education authorities and institutional presidents) to
determine the ingredients necessary for effective
desegregation and equality plans, and reasonable
timetables for their implementation;

■ provide leadership seminars for deans and academic
department heads in strategies for student and faculty
recruitment or counseling and support for minority
students; and

■ gather data on students, faculty, and administrators and
monitor trend lines over time to determine increasing/
decreasing compliance with desegregation criteria.

Private interest groups are capable of providing various services for their constituency groups under the overall rubric of equity in higher education. For example, student personnel associations can hold workshops to deal with the needs of minority students in residence halls, and in social and cultural activities on college campuses.

The data in Table 9.2 show that private interest groups do in fact provide a variety of services to assist the racial equality process but the services provided are rather infrequent and do not yield substantial nor even measurable results. Most of these services (50 percent) are provided by the national education associations. The most typical kind of service provided is the sponsorship of conferences or workshops (22 percent). Various kinds of research projects are initiated (19 percent) and consultations with affected institutions (19 percent) are held. Less frequent activities of interest groups include collecting data (independent of government data) and providing assistance to colleges and universities in recruiting students and staff to meet racial enrollment and employment goals.

Table 9.2

Desegregation Related Services Provided by Groups

	Non educational	Special interest	National educational	Total	%
1. Research	2	4	8	14	19
2. Consulting	2	6	6	14	19
3. Curriculum			6	6	9
4. Data collection		4	4	8	11
5. Legal briefs			2	2	3
6. Student/Staff recruitment	2		6	8	11
7. Conference/ workshop	2	6	8	16	22
8. Other		2		4	6
Total	8	24	40	72	
Percent	11	33	56		100

Note: Data reported as percentages.

A more detailed analysis of the interest group processes and outcomes indicates both the variety of services as well as the inaction with regard to measuring the impact of those services. For example, conferences and workshops sponsored by private interest groups presumably result in increasing the knowledge of the participants concerning relevant problems and possible solutions. Publications serve the same purpose for a broader audience. Some research reports on historically Black and white universities simply reflect the changing ethnic composition of students and faculty, and the changes in student performance resulting from implementing special programs. Other research reports focus upon the needed changes in institutional characteristics required to meet federal and state guidelines or to improve student performance in integrated colleges and universities. A number of organizations assist universities or state agencies in long-range planning, while others provide technical assistance in curriculum development, establishing new academic programs, and upgrading existing programs. These research efforts and professional services are necessary in order to have a great impact on the racial equality process, in that they point to the causes for problems and determine appropriate strategies and solutions to address those problems.

While some activities are more difficult to quantify, they appear to have a more direct impact on the equality process than some of the more quantifiable services. For example, college recruitment programs that aim to attract a large number of Black students and staff are easily evaluated by measuring the change in student enrollment from year to year. These activities often involve private interest groups as providers of training for admissions officers, affirmative action personnel, and recruiters. On the other hand, the efforts of private interest groups that provide expert legal advice and assistance, or file _amicus curiae_ briefs that significantly affect the court desegregation decisions are sometimes difficult to evaluate because the results of legal opinions are often hard to quantify. For example, the National Association for Equal Opportunity in Higher Education (NAFEO) filed an _amicus_ brief that was accepted by the court. The court, following the position taken by NAFEO, directed that the preponderant burden of desegregation should not be borne by Black colleges. Regardless of how the court order is implemented, its impact will take some time to be realized.

THE IMPACT OF THE FUNDING BASE OF PRIVATE INTEREST GROUPS' INVOLVEMENT IN EQUITY

Funding is an important determinant of the course of action to be taken by private interest groups. Private interests groups are funded from a variety of sources. However, the majority have two major sources of funds that determine their day-to-day operations. First, practically all private interest groups discussed in this chapter are, by definition, membership, or fee organizations, which means

that they represent a constituency of members who pay dues
for services provided.   These funds support the basic
administrative operation and many of the regular services
(journals, membership meetings, workshops) that they provide
for members.   Second, nearly all these associations receive
substantial foundation and corporate grants to underwrite
special projects that are more expensive than what is
covered by the yearly membership fees.   For example, the
American Association of Community and Junior Colleges
"conducts projects dealing with student development with
support from public and private sources (Higher Education
Directory 1982-83)."   Many of these specially funded
projects have their grants routinely renewed for several
years.   Others are funded only for one-time events or
activities.
     For funding higher education equality activities, Table
9.3 indicates that private interest groups rely upon
membership fees for 26 percent of their funding, while 27
percent is from philanthropic foundations and 10 percent
from corporate grants.   This is similar to the funding
source distribution for their general (non-equity-related)
activities.   It is rare (9 percent) for the federal
government to provide support to private associations for
projects dealing with racial equality in higher education.
None of the organizations surveyed indicate receiving
financial assistance from state governments or from any
institutions affected by the federal court orders for higher
education equality projects.

Table 9.3

Primary Funding Base for Private Interest Groups'
Desegregation Efforts

Internal budget	Government grant	State grant	Foundation	Institution	Corporate	Other
26	9	0	27	0	10	28

Note: Data reported in percentages.

     It seems apparent that the minimal involvement of
federal, state, or institutional funding to associations for
desegregation activities reflects, on the one hand, an
unwillingness on the part of government to initiate activist
strategies which may have ameliorated the complex, sometimes
retrogressive process, in implementing desegregation.   On
the other hand, it probably equally reflects the reluctance
of associations to seek out government funds agressively to

initiate such activities on behalf of its members because of the controversial political implications. It must be remembered that the federal government itself (as represented by the Department of Education) has repeatedly been brought into court and forced to take action against states that resisted change in the direction of racial equality. Associations, particularly the national educational groups, also represent collegiate institutions that are also often resistant to change and thus may respond to such activities by withdrawing membership. As a result there is no official advocate for racial equality within the higher education community. Only an "outside" agency, the NAACP Legal Defense Fund, is actively advocating the enforcement of the laws, such as Title VI of the 1964 Civil Rights Act.

Many higher education equality activities, illustrated by responses to the survey discussed in this chapter, could be initiated with association financial and consultative resources that are part of normal association operations. Activities such as research studies and demographic reports, as well as more active interventions, such as training seminars, could be undertaken. However, major interventions such as developing plans for initiating significant new programs and revising curricula would undoubtedly require the infusion of substantial amounts of external funding, either from state or federal governments or from private sources. The dearth of such funding requests by private interest groups and the lack of reliance by states upon private interest groups is testimony to their lack of will or intent to seek out assistance aggressively in solving the many problems of equality in higher education.

The private interest groups, on the other hand, are not under the constraints of court orders or state government reluctance. Moreover, as representatives of the values of the academic community, these groups might be characterized as having the moral obligation to provide leadership in engaging in the movement to achieve higher education equality and assisting higher education institutions and government agencies in delineating the roles and responsibilities of the various actors in this movement.

COORDINATION

Consortial and coordinated arrangements have been a part of higher education throughout its growth and development in this country. A recent example is a major study conducted jointly by the American Association of Collegiate Registrars and Admissions Counselors, American College Testing Program, the College Board, Educational Testing Service, and the National Association of College Admission Counselors to examine the impact of college admissions policies upon the access to college of students from various ethnic and minority groups (AACRAC, ACT, College Board, ETS, NACAC, 1986). The purposes of these types of joint efforts are many: uniformity and efficiency of operation, development of rules and regulations which

apply to all institutions within a consortium, more
efficient use of funds, and pooling of the resources to
solve common problems.

Since many of the private interest groups serve only a
single or narrow range of interests, one would expect a
considerable pooling of resources to address the multiple
problems of educational equality.   Such collaboration of
associations is not uncommon. Moreover, several foundations
also often pool resources to fund projects that would
probably be a strain on the financial capability of any one
of them.   An excellent example of such a coordination of
effort of both associations and foundations is the
Integrated Systems Approach to Improving Management (ISATIM)
Program that provides management improvement consultation to
the forty- two schools of the United Negro College Fund
(UNCF).   The program manual (UNCF, 1981) for the project
states:

> the grant funds made available to UNCF also
> provided that . . . technical assistance . . .
> would be accomplished through contracted
> assistance provided by the American Council on
> Education (ACE), the Association of Governing
> Boards of Universities and Colleges (AGB), and the
> National Association of College and University
> Business Officers (NACUBO), acting cooperatively
> as a group to be known as the "Organizing
> Associations."

In addition to association coordination, the funding for
this project was provided collaboratively by two different
foundations.   One would expect, therefore, considerable
coordination of effort in other higher education arenas
including educational equality.   However, as Table 9.4
illustrates, only 33 percent of the organizations
participating in equality activities reportedly coordinate
their efforts with other organizations. On the other hand,
one organization that reported no coordinated activities was
identified by another organization as assisting it in its
equality project. It is possible that the number of

Table 9.4

Private Interest Groups Involved in Collaborative Activities
Regarding Higher Education Equality (%)

Yes	No	No answer
33	50	17

Note: Numbers reflect percentages of interest groups in the
       survey.

cooperative activities reported is somewhat low because some organizations may see themselves as collaborating only when they are playing a role more active than just supplying data or information to each other. Indeed, most collaborations involve merely sharing data and technical information. Only a small number of cooperative endeavors involve active roles for all parties. The one association directly facilitating state government-university coordination had its funding terminated before its efforts could be concluded. This action, however, seemed related to the organization's management and financial difficulties rather than to any punitive action being taken regarding its advocacy role in implementing educational equality activities.

PROSPECTS FOR FUTURE ROLES

        Private interest groups, as previously indicated, could and should have played a substantial role in implementing educational equality in higher education. They possess the resources and expertise to coordinate and disseminate information effectively as well as the resources to convene and train personnel. The fact that interest groups have participated only minimally is due partly to factors discussed in the previous section, such as the political volatility of the issues. Tables 9.5 and 9.6 illustrate that, while only 40 percent of the organizations responding indicate that their services have facilitated the educational equality process, 63 percent believe that they will play a leading role or a role of some assistance in the future. However, since 40 percent of the reporting organizations did not answer whether their efforts have facilitated or impeded equality, these results must be interpreted with caution. It cannot be determined if the failure to answer might be due to the inability of respondents to assess the effect of their activities. Nineteen percent of the organizations expect to play only a minor role in educational equality in the future. These organizations tended to be more narrowly focused in their endeavors. Eighteen percent of the groups did not respond to this question.
        Possibly more important than an association's capability of assisting educational equality is the presumed moral requirement, as institutional spokespersons for the higher education community, of wanting to assist or even lead this process. Despite limited actual involvement, several associations do offer comments regarding what was not being done and suggest what should be done by private interest groups to assist in the higher education equality process. Strengthening federal desegregation guidelines is a frequent suggestion, with one organization even recommending "intervention with the current administration" to urge stronger advocacy by the government on behalf of compliance with federal court orders. Other recommendations include improving the recruitment of minority students, upgrading programs and curricula at historically Black institutions, studying the impact of promotion and tenure

decisions on Black faculty at predominantly white institutions, and strengthening the enforcement of federal court mandates, which are described by one interest group as currently being "at a low ebb."

Table 9.5

Groups' Perception of Efforts Facilitating/Impeding Equality

Facilitate	Impede	Neutral	No answer
40	0	20	40

Note: Numbers reflect percentages of interest groups in the survey.

Table 9.6

Perception of Future Role in Facilitating Equity

Leading	Some assistance	Moderate	Minimal	No answer
45	18	9	10	18

Note: Numbers reflect percentages of interest groups in the survey.

CONCLUSIONS

     A number of conclusions can be drawn from the survey of private interest groups' participation in higher education equality. It is evident that there is significantly less involvement on the part of these groups in higher education equality than was true of similar private involvement in primary and secondary education in the years following the Brown decision. In a number of cities, monitoring commissions had been appointed by the courts to oversee the Brown desegregation process, often assisted by the consultative expertise of private interest groups. In other cases, special "masters", frequently experts from private interest groups, were appointed by the courts to provide technical assistance in implementing desegregation plans. In many elementary and secondary school desegregation cases, the court did not presume the good intentions or the willingness of boards of education to comply with the law. Indeed, in some instances court masters were given veto power over boards and superintendents if their decisions were believed to be inimical to the desegregation process.

In addition to activist roles, associations have participated in the substantial production of research related to elementary and secondary school desegregation issues. Many believe that the political climate in most of the nation following the Brown decision was very supportive of implementing desegregation "with all deliberate speed." Both government and foundation funds were readily available to organizations assisting desegregation and to individuals conducting research.

Nevertheless, there are important roles for private interest groups to play in achieving higher education equality. Certainly relevant are their traditional roles of consulting with and coordinating affected groups; assisting in curriculum development and staff planning; and developing strategies for student and faculty recruitment. Private interest groups could fill the action vacuum created by the lack of an advocacy group within the higher education community that is committed to the goal of the equitable implementation of equality. Private interest groups could fill the moral vacuum in the higher education community that dissimulates before the question: What must be done? What is missing is imagination and the will to tackle the difficult political issues, accompanied by a membership reluctance to face the need of the academic community to exercise leadership on this most complicated issue.

The issues being confronted in addressing qualitative equality in higher education are considerably more complex than those that confronted associations and researchers regarding elementary and secondary education: college attendance is voluntary while elementary and secondary school attendance is mandatory; students' ability to pay is a factor as is the ability to pass entrance examinations; integration of Black and white faculties and staff is a formidable task; the interests of the plaintiffs, the states, the courts, and the Department of Education may all conflict. The litany of problems could be recited extensively. Yet the question remains: What must be done?

Compounding the problems are the massive political implications of higher education equality and the paradox of results that seem the opposite of similar effects in K-12 desegregation. For example, Haynes (1978, Notes-2) described the former Department of Health, Education and Welfare (now the Department of Education) as accepting state desegregation compliance plans that demonstrably failed to meet the criteria of federal court guidelines. Here, private interest groups, as disinterested parties, could play their mediating and meliorating role in assisting states, in their own long-term interest, to develop equitable desegregation plans that reduce years of court challenges and expensive litigation.

With regard to the paradox of contradictory results, several studies (Blackwell, p. 67; Egerton, p. 3) have found that Black students persisted and had greater success in

segregated Black institutions than in integrated ones.   This
conclusion is the opposite of the result of most elementary
and secondary school desegregation research.   However,
private interest groups in their research may affirm that
(based on the trend of studies thus far) achievement
outcomes for minority students are important independent of
the racial mix of the student bodies; they might suggest
monitoring activities by association experts that focus on
such achievement and outcome measures (retention in program,
grades in courses, progression rates, and graduation) and
they may discover mechanisms to promote such measures in
both historically Black and predominantly white
institutions.   Indeed, such a direction in research might
serve to assess the peculiar qualitative characteristics of
colleges and universities that cause them to retain and
graduate students who by all "objective" criteria - SAT
scores, GPA - are usually inadmissible to and seldom
graduate from predominantly white universities.
     The survey results reported in this chapter indicate
that only a minority of private interest groups play any
role in the higher education equality movement.   And of
those involved, the majority play passive rather than active
roles.   That is, unlike elementary and secondary activities,
higher education activities among private interest groups
are most often initiated by request rather than being self-
initiated.   Earlier in the chapter more active leadership
roles were suggested for private interest groups that could
contribute markedly to a more collaborative and positive
change in achieving higher education equality.   Weinberg
unfortunately observed (1978, p. 328) that "universities
have turned away from federal grants to help implement
equality efforts and when federal grants are received for
such efforts, vague names are used to describe the efforts."
This same characterization may also apply to private
interest groups that are facing the formidable, political,
and conflicting interest barriers in this arena.
     It becomes eminently clear that a number of critical
equity issues need to be engaged by private interest groups.
Indeed, certain issues can only be effectively studied by
such groups, particularly since private interests can be
somewhat objective in addressing such issues and also
benefit from the specialized expertise of their membership.
None of the private interest groups have addressed the
question of how public historically Black colleges, for
example, can achieve desegregation and yet retain an
historical racial identity, nor have the private interest
groups taken a position on whether such a result is even
desirable.   No private association has attempted to address
the philosophical question of what level of commitment is
required of higher education to provide equal quality
education to the portion of the population whose achievement
on standardized tests often falls below the entrance or exit
requirements of colleges and universities.   The answers to
these complex questions have, in the past, been influenced
more within political and governmental organizations than by
persuasion from private interest groups.   Yet, as with other
important societal issues, the research activities conducted

by private interest groups often lead to the best solutions
for public problems.

The respondents to the survey reported in this chapter
have identified some of the critical issues that need to be
addressed by private interest groups for which there are
partial or complete voids. The understanding of the factors
related to the differential persistence of Black students on
traditionally Black and on predominantly white campuses is
critical to improving retention and success under higher
education desegregation (Louis, p. 3). Strategies to
enhance such retention and the study of model programs that
succeed, obviously, are equally worthy of evaluation and
dissemination. Certainly the changes in political climate
and societal tolerance require analysis to determine their
impact on desegregation decisions and court orders in
different historical periods. The contributions of the
qualitative aspects of successful desegregation, the
nondemographic supportive and enhancement factors, are also
critical issues to be considered. The study of the fate of
the public Black colleges and their role in a desegregated
environment cannot be delayed because of the awesome
complexities of that issue.

Private interest groups are best suited to take the
lead in addressing these critical issues and in using their
prestige and influence to persuade publicly elected
officials to develop strategies to address the equality
issues in higher education.

The Washington, D.C., associations are probably best
suited to take the lead in not only lining out the critical
issues to be studied and addressed, but in using their
prestige and influence to get the relevant actor-
institutional, state, and federal representatives - together
to develop the agreements and mount the strategies to attack
the various problems described as confronting desegregation
in higher education. The more narrowly focused associations
and the noneducational groups can both singly and
collectively lend their material resources and human
resources to addressing the problems delineated by the major
associations. Undoubtedly foundations and corporations
would be eager to fund collaborative and rational strategies
designed to assist in solving one of the most complex issues
facing contemporary American society. Such a simplistic
outline as this should not suggest that the problem is
simplistic. Doing the sort of political compromising and
calming of anxieties of various constituencies involved to
arrive at the necessary agreements is recognized to be an
excruciatingly complicated process, requiring the most
skillful negotiation and consuming not just months but
perhaps years. Moreover, given the present political
realities, there is no assurance of success.

Federal appeals court Judge A. Leon Higginbotham (1978,
p. ix) has said, "today, America is finally at the point
where it has the potential to resolve in a positive way so
many problems of the past. If we dare ignore this
opportunity, the alternative will be to drift into further
polarization." Certainly, we can benefit from the
experiences of the past two decades of efforts to achieve

educational equality in higher education. However, it is
crucial that the expertise of private interest groups play a
more active role in this process.

Indeed, a large part of the problem is in the attitude
of the private interest groups themselves. Ballard (1973,
p. 155) has said, "professional associations of scholars,
foundations, educational executives ensconced in the various
agencies should . . . scrutinize their attitudes. The
purpose of such examination, it should be emphasized, is in
their own best interests." In the final analysis, private
interest groups need to undertake the work described in this
study because their commitments to the values of higher
education require it.

REFERENCES

Ballard, A. B. (1973). The education of Black folk: The
    Afro-American struggle for knowledge in white America.
    New York: Harper and Row.

Blackwell, J. E. (1982). Demographics of desegregation. In
    R. Wilson (Ed.), Race and equity in higher education.
    Washington, DC: American Council on Education.

Council for the Advancement and Support of Education (CASE).
    (1982). Higher education directory, 1982-83.
    Washington, DC: Author.

Haynes, L. L. (1978). A critical examination of the Adams
    case: A source book. Washington, DC: Institute for
    Services to Education.

Higginbotham, A. L. (1978). In the matter of color. Race
    and the American legal process: The colonial period.
    New York: Oxford University Press.

Holmes, D.O.W. (1934). The evolution of the Negro college.
    New York: Bureau of Publications, Columbia University
    Teachers College.

Louis, C. (1982, April 22). Persistence and performance: A
    case for the use of the ethnographic approach in the
    investigation of the adjustment of Black students on
    predominantly white campuses. Paper presented at the
    12th annual meeting of the National Conference of Black
    Political Scientists, New Orleans, LA.

Myrdal, G. (1944). An American dilemma: The Negro problem
    and modern democracy. New York: Harper & Row.

United Negro College Fund. (1981). ISATIM program manual.
    New York: Author.

Weinberg, M. (1978). <u>Minority students: A research
    appraisal</u>. National Institute of Education, U.S.
    Department of Health, Education and Welfare.
    Washington, DC: U.S. Government Printing Office.

Wilson, R. (Ed.). (1982). <u>Race and equity in higher
    education</u>. Washington, DC: American Council on
    Education.

10

Conclusion: Strategies for Action

A. ROBERT THOENY

This final chapter is intended to draw summary findings from
the research reported in this volume. It therefore
represents an ending, but also a beginning. If there is a
single conclusion of the work reported here, it is that
American higher education today is at a critical juncture in
the path toward full equality for Blacks and whites. The
preceding chapters document the difficult terrain traversed
and portray, in great detail, the current status of Black
undergraduate students in our colleges and universities. It
is most appropriate to pause in this journey to take stock
of our condition, to confirm our commitment to see the
journey through, and to set a course for the decades ahead.
    Let us begin by observing our progress. In our haste
to press forward, we often forget that we have made
remarkable progress. Now and then we need to herald the
accomplishments of those many Black Americans who have
prepared themselves for college, competed successfully in
the college environment, and moved on to productive and
successful careers. If we are to encourage the next
generation of Black college students to prepare and persist,
we must proclaim the accomplishments of earlier generations
of Black graduates.
    The contributing authors have provided evidence of
substantial progress. In discussing the performance of
students at Black and at white universities, Michael
Nettles, Jomills Braddock and James McPartland, and Willie
Pearson all note the essential role played by Black colleges
in preparing Black leaders during the first part of this
century. Walter Allen reminds us that many Blacks have
succeeded in overcoming the difficulties presented to the
racial minority at white colleges and universities, and the
numerous statistics reported in the chapters written by
Nettles chart the progress of Black students in all types of
institutions.
    But a second look indicates that increases in the
number of Blacks entering and completing college (the
quantitative measure of movement toward equality) has not
been matched by advances in the qualitative dimensions of
the Black college experience. Differences between white and

198   Black Undergraduate Student Equality

Black students extend well beyond race. For a variety of reasons which are explored by the contributions to this volume, the college and university systems of this nation have related to the Black and white citizens in different ways. The results have produced a serious imbalance in the qualitative dimension of postsecondary education experienced by Blacks and whites.

One more aspect of the current condition must be discussed before we can turn our attention to strategies for change. If one word describes the present state of affairs it is "stagnation." Not only is there lack of qualitative progress, but the trend of quantitative gain has halted and shows signs of reversal! What can account for this? Our authors provide some clues, but at this stage of understanding one can only offer informed speculation.

Three factors appear to have contributed to the stagnation. The first is the absence of new tools to leverage the next phase of progress. The old tools which have brought us this far in the journey appear ill suited to the tasks ahead. The principal lever of past progress has been government, particularly its judicial branch. With the national government in the lead, barriers to increased participation by Blacks in higher education (quantitative and qualitative) were removed. This permitted equality in the college experience; it did not assure that equality. Recent government efforts to effect qualitative advancement, described by Cynthia Brown and John Williams, have had only limited success. Perhaps it is time to discard that tool in favor of other implements of change.

A second possible factor contributing to stagnation is, oddly enough, the rapid pace of initial progress itself. It is reasonable to surmise that once legal barriers were removed, the first group of young Blacks to enter white institutions were those best prepared for this experience, both in terms of their academic preparation and family background. In this sense, the first quantitative and qualitative gains were "easy," if not for the individuals involved, then for society. Further progress required attracting and qualifying black youth in the second tier of academic preparation and favorable family circumstances. As a consequence, the pace of change slowed. We may now be at a point where it will be difficult to maintain the pace of progress simply because future gains require enrolling and graduating those least well prepared. In short, the pace of progress towards equality in higher education is likely to slow until the slower rate of change toward better K-12 school preparation and toward more supportive Black family conditions catches up.

Finally, the stagnation is likely to have resulted, in part, from waning public attention to the issue of racial equality in higher education. Rapid gains were made at a time when the achievement of quality was viewed as a high priority social and national goal. That is not longer the case. The public spotlight has shifted from concern for perfecting American society to concern for revitalizing the economic competitiveness of the American people. The recent attention to improving the quality of education for all students and at all levels, the primary motivation for the current accountability and outcomes assessment movement, has, as Williams notes, produced greater concern for raising standards and testing students than it has for enlarging access; such testing may have a chilling effect on increasing enrollment and graduation of Blacks.

If the current lack of progress has its basis in the three factors identified above, what are the prospects for resuming movement toward equality and which strategies offer the greatest promise of bringing this about? It is obvious that higher education can do little to eliminate the three adverse factors. It can only counter the deleterious effects. And higher education cannot do that alone. The assistance of other sectors in society will be required. What are the strategies for action and how should the labor be divided?

The first strategy is to increase attention to the qualitative dimensions of the Black college experience. This can be done in several ways. Pearson points the way with his call for increasing efforts to interest Black youth in science, prepare them in mathematics and secondary school science so that they will choose college majors in scientific fields, obtain bachelor of science degrees, and go on to graduate school or employment in the high paying and prestigious fields of engineering and science. Concentration on this task will produce the added benefit of providing visible role models of success in societal positions long held in high regard by Blacks and whites alike. This should increase the confidence and motivation of the next generation of Black youth as they prepare for college entry.

Beyond focusing on recruitment into the sciences, colleges and universities should take it upon themselves to identify any disparities which exist on their individual campuses between the performance of Black and white students - without regard to their college majors - and identify the cause of any such disparity. Next, colleges and universities should devote attention and resources to remedying the condition. This might include increasing financial support for Black students, reducing their feelings of discrimination, addressing the academic needs of these students in special ways and, in general, attempting to eliminate disparities by any and all of the means suggested by Nettles.

Yet another way to increase attention to the qualitative dimension is to provide and feature scholarship awards for Black students. Black students at all levels should be seen as qualifying for assistance on the basis of their academic achievement and not only on the basis of their financial need. Competition for scholarships held for Blacks only will accomplish this. It is important to stress that scholarship funding of this sort should not be increased at the expense of funds for needy students. This merit-based funding must be in addition to need-based funding, or else qualitative gains will be made at.the expense of quantitative gains.

Increasing the availability of Black scholarship

programs in both the K-12 and postsecondary systems offers an excellent opportunity for participation by national and state government and by private groups. The former can and should provide public monies for this purpose while the latter can be instrumental in raising private funds from individuals and foundations.

A second strategy, which reinforces aspects of the first, is to target energy toward key levers which can accelerate the pace of change. According to the research reported in this book, these include attention to positive role models, the certainty of reward for having successfully completed college, and the self-image and self-confidence of Black youth.

The value of the scientist as role model was pointed out earlier. Another area of targeted attention to role models is the faculty and staff of higher education institutions. Everywhere that Black students are expected to study in increased numbers, Blacks must be seen in important and respected teaching and staff positions.

More attention must be paid to the placement of Black college graduates in prestigious graduate schools and in responsible, well-remunerated employment. The rewards of attending college and persisting to graduation must be highly visible to Black youths and their families. Colleges can help in this regard, but the business community must take leadership in this effort. Here is yet another opportunity for the private groups which Reginald Wilson analyzes to make important contributions by mediating, facilitating, and defining issues.

The self-image and self-confidence of Black youth will be enhanced by additional and more visible role models, by taking note of the benefits which accrue to Black college graduates, and by the availability and use of Black scholarship programs. But here a critical component of the system takes center stage. The Black family and the Black community must take the lead in implementing this strategy. Black youth, in increasing numbers, must value academic achievement and must be imbued with the belief that academic achievement leading to college entry will lead to college graduation and postgraduation success. The rest of society can play a supporting role, but the burden of bringing about this change rests squarely upon the shoulders of the Black community, for in the final analysis a change in cultural or family values must come from within.

To conclude then, all sectors of society must contribute in a coordinated manner to start the engine of progress moving again. Government's contribution should no longer emphasize the tools of adjudication, but its role as a funding agent. Business must make certain that higher education is the avenue to a good life for Blacks, as it is for whites. Black families must take it upon themselves to change the image and confidence levels of their youth, and private groups must help refocus the spotlight on equality issues. Last and most important, colleges and universities must themselves stimulate the pace of progress on their own campuses and beyond the campus in two directions. Colleges and universities must become more involved in the problem of preparing Black youth for college entry, both through supporting the efforts of K-12 educators and by encouraging change within the Black community. In the other direction, colleges and universities must reach out to the postcollege world of their graduates to develop appropriate placements so that the rewards of college completion are in fact realized by all equally.

Let these conclusions become a new beginning.

Book Reviews

Astin, A. W. (1982). <u>Minorities in American higher education</u>. San Francisco: Jossey-Bass, Inc.

This book is an comprehensive study of the past gains, current status, and future prospects for Blacks, Chicanos, Puerto Ricans, and American Indians in American higher education. The book addresses many aspects of minority education, including student demographic characteristics, student choice, student performance, and student attitudes and behaviors. Astin uses data compiled by the Higher Education Research Institute for the Commission on the Higher Education of Minorities, which was convened under a grant from the Ford Foundation. Astin also uses data collected through the Cooperative Institutional Research Program (CIRP) to demonstrate the inferior status of minorities in higher education and the causes for their status.

Blackwell, J. E. (1981). <u>Mainstreaming outsiders: The production of Black professionals</u>. Bay, New York: General Hall.

<u>Mainstreaming Outsiders</u> addresses the problem of the underrepresentation of Blacks in graduate and professional education. It is based on a major study funded by the Southern Education Foundation's Higher Education Program. The primary objective is to assemble data which answers questions regarding equal educational opportunity for Blacks in the areas of access to, extent of institutional change in, political support from, and the existence of role models in support of higher education which leads to the participation of Blacks in doctoral level study and in the professions. Data is assembled and analyzed in terms of these major issues as related to seven professions (dentistry, optometry, pharmacy, veterinary medicine, engineering and architecture, social work, and law; and, higher education at the doctoral level). The thesis of the study is that the development of Blacks in graduate

education and the professions should be viewed in the context of the expansion of the educational opportunity structure. In doing so, the author first reviews the historical development of higher education opportunities for Blacks, then addresses any changes in these developments within the context of remaining and existing structural problems which affect the maximum participation of Blacks in higher education and the professions.

Orfield, G., et al. (1984). The Chicago study of access and choice in higher education. Report to the Illinois Senate, Committee on Higher Education, University of Chicago.

This report assesses the extent to which prospective minority students in metropolitan Chicago have real access to higher education and choice among institutions of higher education. It shows that there are extreme differences in levels of college education between the inner city and the suburbs, and among various population subgroups within and around the Chicago area. Orfield's research shows the flow of students across the metropolitan Chicago area through 229 high schools, and into and out of almost sixty colleges and universities. It describes this overall system of educational mobility and educational failure in the Chicago area, and reports on what happens to Black, white, and Latino students from the city and suburbs. The study shows an interlocking system of educational stratification that treats minority and low-income students differently. The higher education system does not operate to equalize opportunity but has powerful institutional features that tend to perpetuate separation and inequality.

Pruitt, A. S. (1987). In pursuit of equality in higher education. New York: General Hall, Inc.

The focus of this book is upon desegregation in higher education. It presents the findings of research projects with the support of the Southern Education Foundation (SEF) over the past decade. Studies reported on were commissioned in the aftermath of the Adams v. Richardson court order of 1977. Of special interest was the expectation that the results would influence educational policy and practices. The book is divided into seven parts and has seventeen chapters and many distinguished authors.

Thomas, G. (Ed.). (1981). Black students in higher education. Westport, CT: Greenwood Press.

This book addresses three issues: (1) Black access to higher education; (2) the academic, social, and psychological experiences of Blacks in various types of higher educational institutions; and (3) the retention and completion status of Blacks in higher education. Thomas

also reviews the history of Black participation in higher
education and provides a profile of Blacks currently
participating in higher education. He also addresses the
importance of academic admissions criteria and financial aid
for Black student access and persistence at various levels
of higher education.

Thompson, D. C. (1986). A Black elite: A profile of
     graduates of UNCF colleges. New York: Greenwood
     Press.

This volume is the product of a three-year study (1982-1985)
of Blacks graduating from UNCF colleges. It is the first
such study since Charles S. Johnson's The Negro College
Graduate (1938). This profile on Blacks in higher education
includes a description and interpretation of their
socioeconomic origins, racial disadvantages, academic
handicaps and successes, philosophies of human relations,
levels and fields of postbaccalaureate education, career
patterns, social class identities, community services, civil
rights attitudes and activities, political persuasions, and
leadership styles and achievements. The central finding of
this study is that graduates of the forty-two United Negro
College Fund (UNCF) member institutions constitute an
integral, creative element within this nation's college-
educated Black elite which diligently strives for personal
success and racial advancement in American society.

Williams, J. B. (1987). Title VI regulation of higher
     education: Problems and progress. New York: Teachers
     College Press.

Writers of this volume explore the manner in which
compliance with Title VI has been undertaken. Through
formal research and other forms of inquiry, the contributors
describe: (1) the federal-state-local regulatory process,
(2) state and local desegregation remedies, (3) problems
directly and indirectly associated with the implementation
of desegregation remedies, and (4) the effects of Title VI
upon targeted minority populations.

Williams, R. (1982). Race and equity in higher education.
     Washington, DC: American Council on Education.

This is a report on a three-day seminar jointly sponsored by
the American Council on Education and the Aspen Institute
for Humanistic Studies held in the fall of 1981. The
seminar focused on desegregation of higher education and was
attended by a small group of academicians and
administrators, attorneys, government officials, and
association executives. The discussions and debates
centered on a wide range of racial issues affecting higher
education in general and public colleges and universities in
particular. The main conclusion reached in these

discussions was that "desegregation" of higher education means more than "open access" or another means of preserving historic white universities as "white" and historic Black colleges as "Black". The state's duty is to come forward with a plan that realistically promises to integrate the state systems of higher education on a nondiscriminatory basis. This task has yet to be completed.

Index _____

About the Contributors

WALTER R. ALLEN is currently Associate Professor of Sociology at the Center for Afro-American-African Studies, University of Michigan, Ann Arbor. He has held faculty appointments at the University of North Carolina, Howard University, Duke University and the University of Zimbabwe. He also completed a Rockefeller Foundation Postdoctoral Fellowship (1982-1983) and Senior Fulbright Fellowships to the University of Zimbabwe (1984, 1986). Allen's research and teaching interests focus on family systems, child socialization and development, the political economy of race relations and postsecondary education. Since 1983 he has served as Associate Editor for the Journal of Negro Education.

JOMILLS HENRY BRADDOCK, II, is a Principal Research Scientist at the Center for Social Organization of Schools/Center for Research on Elementary and Middle Schools, and Associate Professor of Sociology, the Johns Hopkins University. His broad research interests encompass issues of inequality and social justice including extensive examination of the long-term effects of school desegregation on Black young adults. He has written numerous articles, book chapters, and research monographs on these topics. Among journals where his work is published are the Harvard Educational Review, Journal of Social Issues, Journal of Negro Education, Sociology of Education, Phi Delta Kappa, International Journal of Sociology and Social Policy, Youth and Society, and Review of Research in Education.

CYNTHIA G. BROWN is the Director of the Resource Center on Educational Equity of the Council of Chief State School Officers. She has spent 20 years working in a variety of professional positions on civil rights and educational equity issues. She was the first Assistant Secretary for Civil Rights in the U.S. Department of Education. Prior to that she served as Principal Deputy of HESW's Office for Civil Rights during the Carter Administration. Subsequent

to this government service, she was co-director of The
Equality Center.   She has also worked for the Lawyers'
Committee for Civil Rights Under Law, and the Children's
Defense Fund.

JAMES M. MCPARTLAND is Co-Director of the Center for Social
Organization of Schools/Center for Research on Elementary
and Middle Schools, and Professor of Sociology, the Johns
Hopkins University.   His research interests include
sociology of education, race and ethnic relations, and
research methodology.   His earlier experience included
contributions to the national studies, "Equality of
Education Opportunity" (1966), and "Racial Isolation in the
Public Schools" (1967).   His recent works include "Violence
in the Schools" and "Control and Differentiation in the
Structure of American Education," which appeared in
Sociology of Education (1982).

MICHAEL T. NETTLES is a Senior Research Scientist in the
Education Policy Research and Services Division of the
Educational Testing Service.   Prior to joining Educational
Testing Service, Dr. Nettles was Assistant Director for
Academic Affairs at the Tennessee Higher Education
Commission.   His most recent publications are on college
students' performance and experiences.   His current research
activities include developing prototype outcome assessments
for colleges and universities, developing models for
longitudinal student research for community colleges,
assessing the effects of financial assistance upon graduate
student attendance and performance, and improving the
performance and experiences of minority doctoral students in
U.S. graduate schools.

WILLIE PEARSON, JR., is currently Associate Professor of
Sociology at Wake Forest University in Winston-Salem, North
Carolina.   Dr. Pearson has held research or teaching
appointments at Southern Illinois University at Carbondale,
the University of Central Arkansas, Louisiana Tech
University, and Grambling State University.   He has also
been a postdoctoral fellow at Educational Testing Service,
Princeton, New Jersey.   Dr. Pearson has published
extensively in the sociology of science.   He is the author
of Black Scientists, White Society and Colorless Science
(1985) and coeditor of The Coloring of American Science
(forthcoming).

A. ROBERT THOENY is Executive Director of the State of
Washington Higher Education Coordinating Board.   He has been
a tenured faculty member and administrator at the United
States Air Force Academy and Memphis State University.   Dr.
Thoeny has published in the area of public policy and
administration.   From 1981 until 1986 he was the Associate
Director for Academic Affairs at the Tennessee Higher

Education Commission, an assignment that included responsibility for monitoring the progress of Tennessee's desegregation efforts.

JOHN B. WILLIAMS is a Lecturer on Education and Assistant to the President at Harvard University. He holds overall responsibility for affirmative action and equal employment opportunity programs at Harvard. He also teaches courses and conducts research on the politics of education, government regulation of higher education, public policy implementation, and urban education. Dr. Williams previously taught at Vanderbilt University and has held a variety of positions in state and federal government. For several years he conducted community-based projects aimed at improving urban schools in New Jersey.

REGINALD WILSON is Director of the Office of Minority Concerns of the American Council on Education. Prior to his current position, Dr. Wilson was president of Wayne County Community College in Detroit, Michigan. He has also served as Director of Test Development and Research, Director of Black Studies, and Director of Upward Bound at Wayne County Community College. Dr. Wilson is coauthor of Human Development in the Urban Community and is the editor of Race and Equity in Higher Education.